SELECTED ENGLISH CLASSICS

General Editor : A. H. R. Ball, M.A.

SELECTIONS FROM DE QUINCEY

SELECTIONS FROM
De Quincey

Edited by
A. H. R. BALL, M.A.

Vice-Principal, Manchester Central High School for Boys
Late Senior English Master, Liverpool Collegiate School

GINN AND COMPANY LTD.
QUEEN SQUARE, LONDON, W.C.1

GINN AND COMPANY LTD.

All Rights Reserved

053203

Printed in Great Britain
by Turnbull & Spears, Edinburgh

PREFACE

DE QUINCEY'S position as one of our most important prose-writers is indisputed : he will always be worthy of study for his splendid style, his fervid imagination, and his range of subjects alone. This volume is intended to illustrate in addition his pre-eminent gift of narration and his rare faculty of exposition, through which, Professor Saintsbury said, " probably more boys have been brought to a love of literature proper by De Quincey than by any other writer whatever." In recent years, however, he has been kept from his rightful place in youthful studies, possibly because of the diffuseness and irregularity of his work—the fatal tendency to discursiveness and digression. But these faults, if faults they be, are obviated by careful selection, and the residue is pure gold.

Continuous and representative extracts are here given from the vivid account of his schooldays in Manchester, the opium experiences, the poetic dream-fancies, the allegories, *The English Mail-Coach*, *Joan of Arc*, the *Revolt of the Tartars*, and the literary criticism. The Introduction provides a brief sketch of De Quincey's life and work, an account of the characteristics of his dream-faculty, and, for more advanced students, a full treatment of the main features of his style and language. Detailed textual and critical notes are appended, making the volume complete in itself, and there is a list of questions and essay subjects.

In preparing this volume the editor had the privilege of access to the special De Quincey Collection in the Manchester City Library, and he has to thank the staff of the Reference Library for their ready help. He is also grateful to Mr W. Holdgate of Liverpool, and to Mr G. A. Twentyman, of the Manchester Grammar School, for reading the proofs, and for their criticism and suggestions.

A. H. R. B.

Manchester
1932

CONTENTS

INTRODUCTION :   PAGE
    THOMAS DE QUINCEY ix
    WORKS xvi
    CHARACTERISTICS xxiii
    STYLE xxvii

AUTOBIOGRAPHY :
    DE QUINCEY'S SCHOOLDAYS 1
    THE BORE AT CHESTER 27
    FAREWELL TO WALES 33
    LONDON 39

DREAM-PHANTASIES :
    INTRODUCTION TO OPIUM 50
    THE MALAY 53
    OPIUM-DREAMS 57
    LEVANA AND OUR LADIES OF SORROW . . 71
    SAVANNAH-LA-MAR 80

THE ENGLISH MAIL-COACH :
    THE GLORY OF MOTION 83
    GOING DOWN WITH VICTORY 96
    THE VISION OF SUDDEN DEATH . . . 105
    DREAM-FUGUE 123

BIOGRAPHY :
    JOAN OF ARC 134

HISTORY:
    PAGE

    REVOLT OF THE TARTARS 152

LITERARY CRITICISM:

    THE MEANING OF LITERATURE 196

    ON THE KNOCKING AT THE GATE IN *MACBETH* . 203

NOTES 211

QUESTIONS AND ESSAY SUBJECTS . . . 247

SUGGESTIONS FOR READING 251

INTRODUCTION

THOMAS DE QUINCEY

DE QUINCEY is a writer whose life and personality are closely connected with his work. He tells us much of them himself, at least of his early years; and between the *Confessions*—one of the few satisfactory pieces of self-revelation in literature— and the *Autobiographic Sketches* we have a fairly complete account of the formative influences of his childhood.

Like Byron, he could trace his ancestry back to the Conquest; but in De Quincey's life descent counts for much less than in that of the poet. In the thirteenth century the family was of the nobility: in the late eighteenth their descendants, as plain Quinceys, without the aristocratic *De* which the Opium-Eater resuscitated, were successful merchants. In 1779 we find Thomas's father a wealthy trader in Manchester, with flourishing connections in America and the West Indies. He was, moreover, a man of cultured tastes and some literary ability, and, had he lived, he might have been held to his son by close bonds of sympathy. The mother, a lady of good family, was only a negative factor. "An intellectual woman," her son called her, conscientiously devoted to her children, but austere and unapproachable, lacking the sympathy necessary to understand the exceptional and wayward nature of her child.

Thomas, the Opium-Eater, was the fifth of a family of eight. He was born at Manchester on 15th August, 1785, and for eleven years lived near the city at "Greenhay," a large country house, then still in rustic seclusion. His father, who suffered from consumption and lived much abroad, came home from Madeira in the child's seventh year, only to die. This was but the first of a series of misfortunes which played upon his nervously responsive mind and impressed him with the terrors of human nature. His second sister died before he was two ; Elizabeth, the eldest, to whom he was specially attached, followed four years later ; and he was himself a shy, frail, and ailing child, kept in constant and servile subjection to his robust elder brother, William, " the son of eternal racket," whose " genius for mischief," his victim reports, " amounted to inspiration." Under his despotism Thomas was introduced to " a world of evil and strife," and roused from sickly dreaming to a new estimate of life.

At the death of her husband Mrs De Quincey was left in good circumstances, but the family was large, and careful management was necessary. They stayed on at " Greenhay " until 1796, when the establishment was moved to Bath, and Thomas, who had been educated by a private tutor, was entered at the Grammar School. Here he made excellent progress : at twelve he was a prodigy in Latin and Greek, a student of metaphysics, and a great reader. " That boy," said his master, " could harangue an Athenian mob better than you or I could address an English one." An unfortunate accident caused his removal from the school within three years, and after an extensive tour with an Eton friend and a period at a private school in Wiltshire, he was sent as a boarder to Manchester Grammar School in 1800, to spend three years qualifying for admission to Brasenose College, Oxford. His account of his schooldays is given in the following pages, and the story is well known. The strict régime of the old but kindly headmaster, restriction from all physical exercise, combined with a slightly snobbish attitude towards the poorer day-boys, made him out of sympathy with the atmosphere of the school. He writes to his mother of the life as one which deprives him " of health, of society, of amusement, of liberty, of congeniality of pursuits, and one which, to complete the precious picture, admits of no variety." He received little sympathy, and in July 1802, he decided to run away. He walked to Chester, where his mother was, and faced her wrath ; but the intercession of a genial uncle resulted in a proposal that he should receive the slender allowance of a guinea a week, with leave to do as he pleased. He set out again on foot for North Wales, and plunged into the strangest chapter of his life.

The solitary tramp in Wales lasted for three months, during which De Quincey eked out his guinea by alternating his lodging between inns and cottages and, at times, bivouacking in the open. In November the pleasant experience ended : he took the coach for London, where he had heard one could hire two furnished rooms at a weekly cost of half a guinea. He was now seventeen years old, so that if he could borrow £200 from a moneylender on his expectations under his father's will, it would carry him over the four years of his minority and liberate him from maternal authority. Accordingly he applied to a Jew, named Dell, who entrusted all negotiations to a scandalous attorney called Brunell, whose policy, in turn, was one of continual delay. Brunell, however, was a student of English literature, and De Quincey won his heart, with the result that when the boy's money was nearly exhausted, he was allowed to take shelter at night in the attorney's strange household in Soho. There he spent his nights, sharing the house with a single wretched servant girl, often depending for food on the remains of Brunell's breakfast or the beneficence of his friends—the poor and outcasts of the London streets which he haunted throughout the day. The tragical sufferings and deprivations which followed his failure to raise money are reflected in the *Confessions.* Both body and soul bore the mark of them to the end of his life. " Eccovi ! " Carlyle said of him later,

" look at him : this child has been in Hell." In April, 1803, in the depth of his despair, he was, in some unexplained way, discovered by his friends and returned to the family at Chester. Eventually it was resolved that he should be given a bare subsistence allowance to go to Oxford.

In the autumn of 1803 De Quincey entered Worcester College, Oxford, where for five years he lived a quiet, studious life, practically isolating himself from the social intercourse of the university. Three features only stand out in these years. The first is that he laid the foundation of the wide range of knowledge which is the mark of his literary work. He took up the study of German metaphysics—still regarded as a daring step—, and in addition to Hebrew and the Classics rounded off his extensive knowledge of English literature by a study of the later poets. The second is the beginning of his connection with the Lake poets, some of whom—Wordsworth, Coleridge, and Southey—he met in person. Finally, there is his first experience of opium. He began to take opium in 1804 during an attack of neuralgia, and until 1812 he continued its use, in moderation, to relieve the pains of his hereditary stomach trouble. Suddenly he found that peace of mind and intellectual pleasures took the place of pain : he discovered the faculty of gorgeous dreaming. De Quincey was a wiry man in spite of his ailments, used to walking fifteen miles a day, and he fended off the evil effects of excess for some time. In fact, except for the three years of intensified horror from 1817 to 1819, to which the nightmares belong, and one or two relapses, for most of his life he found and kept to the line of safety between necessity and self-indulgence. In 1808 he left the university without a degree. It was reported that he did brilliant papers, but was too shy to face the oral examination.

On leaving Oxford De Quincey was apparently in good pecuniary circumstances, and the next two years he divided between London and the Lakes. In 1807 he had gone into the West Country, where his mother was residing near Bristol, to seek out Coleridge, then the object of his special admiration. He found the great man at Bridgwater, and the meeting led to his introduction to the whole of Coleridge's circle—Hazlitt, Lamb, Wordsworth, and Southey. Two years later he became himself a lakist. Wordsworth had moved from Dove Cottage, his home at Grasmere, to the larger house Allan Bank, and De Quincey took over the tenancy. Here he resided for the next twenty years, and in this pleasant spot he reached both the heights of happiness and the depths of despair. His friendship with the poets did not last long: after the first burst of enthusiasm the close imaginative contact with Wordsworth was broken, and Southey was always too stern a character for the wayward and sensitive Opium-Eater. Nor was he much more at home with Bishop Watson, the great man of the district. But two friends grappled him by the heart : Charles Lloyd and John Wilson. The former was a Quaker of wealth and good family, a man of winning charm of manner, an idealist of the emotional kind, and withal an acute critic on the moral side of literature. Unfortunately De Quincey's friendship again was to be but one of his descents into calamitous hearts, for, some years later, this fine character lost his reason and retired abroad to die. John Wilson was a man of different calibre, almost of De Quincey's own age, a magnificent specimen of physical manhood, just down from Oxford. This connection had a great effect on De Quincey's fortunes, for it introduced him to the Edinburgh group of literary men. Meanwhile, in 1816, at the age of thirty-one, De Quincey had married, and there followed the " year of brilliant water " [1] described with pathetic beauty in the *Confessions*—pathetic, for the marriage was soon tried by two severe tests, restricted

[1] See page 53.

resources, and an intense addiction to opium. From 1817 to 1819 is the period of never-ceasing opium-dreams. They gave to literature the gorgeous visions ; to the young wife and mother they must have brought untold agonies. From this state he was suddenly roused by Ricardo's newly published work on political economy, and a growing interest in the subject enabled him to shake himself free from the drug. Moreover, in 1812, he had lost the bulk of his fortune, and in 1819 it was necessary to earn money. He began by accepting the office of editor to a new local paper, the *Westmoreland Gazette*, which he rapidly turned into a journal of philosophy and transcendental metaphysics. It was his introduction to journalism, and for the next thirty years he earned his living and did his best work through this medium.

These thirty years were a period of intense literary activity, partly in London, partly in the Lakes, and finally in Edinburgh. *Recollections of the Lake Poets* had already been drafted in 1808, and in September 1821 there came out in the *London Magazine* the first of the articles which formed the original version of *The Confessions of an English Opium-Eater*. The public clamoured for more, but only one more part appeared, to be followed by a series of articles on a curious variety of subjects, though all marked by a solid basis of information. *On the Knocking at the Gate in Macbeth* is the best-known, and an article on *Goethe* contains some interesting strictures on Carlyle, then just rising on the literary horizon. In 1825 he returned to Grasmere, and events soon drew him over the border. John Wilson had lost his fortune, and he had been obliged to go to Edinburgh, where his manly frankness and great generosity of heart made him the successor of Scott in the regard of the city. In 1817 Blackwood's *Edinburgh Magazine* was founded, with Wilson and Lockhart as principal contributors. Up to this time the life and morals of the people had been entrusted to the Whig periodical, the *Edinburgh Review*, and its Tory counterblast, the *Quarterly* in London, and while these papers collected and solidified much disconnected and sporadic public opinion, their faults were equally wide. They were marred by shallowness in spiritual matters, by bitterness in criticism, and by a steadfast refusal to admit creative or original work. Lockhart and Wilson were Tories, and they wanted a Tory organ in Edinburgh which would include the lighter type of imaginative literature. Wilson naturally sought contributions from De Quincey, who, in 1830, gathered his family about him and settled permanently in Edinburgh. He was then forty-five years of age, and he remained in or near the northern city until his death.

For the next ten years De Quincey continued his contributions both to *Blackwood* and to the Whig rival *Tait's Edinburgh Magazine*. In one or the other of these two journals appeared the essay on *Murder considered as one of the Fine Arts* (1827), *Rhetoric* (1828), *The Cæsars* (1832), a novel *Klosterheim* (1832), *Autobiographic Sketches* (1837), *Revolt of the Tartars* (1837), the papers on *Pope* and *Shakespeare* (1838), *Style* (1840), and many others. Not much is known of De Quincey's intimate domestic life, but his daughter's recollections show him in the happiest family relations of his life, watching his children grow up with affectionate care. Eccentric, shy, timid and solitary he was, careless of money, dress or the tongues of men, but he was gentle and lovable as a husband and father. In 1837 his wife died, after one-and-twenty years as the wife of a wayward genius, leaving him in his fifty-second year with six children, the eldest still in her teens. This daughter, Margaret, took command of the situation, and in 1840 they moved to a cottage at Lasswade, about seven miles out of the city, where, with occasional sojournings in Edinburgh, the Opium-Eater lived out the last twenty years of his life.

Though these later years show De Quincey in extreme fragility of body, accentuated by frequent opium-crises, his literary labours show no falling off ; indeed he retained to the end his splendid intellectual power. New articles appeared in *Tait* and *Blackwood* : *Suspiria De Profundis* in 1845, *The Spanish Military Nun* and *Joan of Arc* in 1847, *The English Mail-Coach* and *The Vision of Sudden Death* in 1849. In the 'fifties collected editions of his works were issued both in England and America, and De Quincey himself supervised a volume of Selections in 1853. But by this time he was only a survivor of a former generation, the last representative in Britain of a great era : a " brain-worn veteran," is Prof. Masson's phrase. The well-loved Wilson died in 1854, six years before his feeble-bodied friend, and on 29th October, 1859, at the age of seventy-four, the Opium-Eater sank peacefully to rest, dreaming even in his last hours of childhood days in Manchester seventy years before.

WORKS

De Quincey's best-known contribution to literary criticism is probably the distinction he draws in the Essay on Pope between the " Literature of *Knowledge* " and the " Literature of *Power* " :

> The function of the first is—to *teach* ; the function of the second is—to *move* ; the first is a rudder ; the second an oar or a sail. The first speaks ultimately, it may happen, to the higher understanding or reason, but always *through* affections of pleasure or sympathy. . . . What do you learn from *Paradise Lost* ? Nothing at all. What do you learn from a Cookery Book ? Something new. . . . What you owe to Milton is not any knowledge ; what you owe is *power* —that is, exercise and expansion to your own latent capacity of sympathy with the infinite, where every pulse and each separate influx is a step upwards, a step ascending as upon a Jacob's ladder from earth to mysterious altitudes above the earth.

These two threads are the safest landmarks in De Quincey's own works, and they are the basis of the classification which he attempted in the General Preface to the collected edition. He distributes his writings into three classes : " First into that class which proposes primarily to amuse the reader, but which, in doing so, may or may not happen occasionally to reach a higher station, at which the amusement passes into an impassioned interest." To this class belong the *Autobiographic Sketches*. The second contains " those papers which address themselves purely to the understanding as an insulated faculty ; or do so primarily," such as the biographies and essays on history, theology, politics, and literary criticism. " Finally, as a third class, and, in virtue of their aim, as a far higher class of compositions," he ranks " *The Confessions of an English Opium-Eater*, and also (but more emphatically) the *Suspiria De Profundis*." These, he continues, are " modes of impassioned prose ranging under no precedents that I am aware of in any literature." This classification is useful as a guide to the characteristics of De Quincey's genius, but, as with all clear-cut divisions, it is not entirely safe. In the last chapter of his biography Prof. Masson attempts another method, and adopts the three main divisions : (i) Descriptive, Biographical, and Historical ; (ii) Speculative, Didactic, and Critical Writings ; and (iii) Imaginative Writings and Prose-Poetry ; each with appropriate sub-divisions, and allowing for some overlapping.

(i) DESCRIPTIVE, BIOGRAPHICAL, AND HISTORICAL

First in this class are the self-revelations in the *Autobiographic Sketches* and the *Confessions*, which form the basis of our knowledge of De Quincey's inner life. Though scattered in form, they contain a detailed psychological revelation of his strange childhood and youth, mingled with flashes of curious knowledge, and rising at times into splendid rhapsodies of prose-poetry. Then there are notices of the lives of men of action and letters—Coleridge, Lamb, Wilson, Hazlitt, Shakespeare, Pope, Shelley, and various Germans— and the *Recollections of the Lake Poets*. The last named has been the subject of much heart-burning on account of its strictures on Wordsworth and Coleridge. It is written in the style of a man thinking aloud. The tissue of the book is bare : there is much anecdote and gossip ; but the bulk of it is discriminate portraiture, couched in a compound mood, especially in the case of Wordsworth, where respect struggles with an elvish malice. There is bad taste and bad feeling in the book, but there are passages of beautiful description— the lakeland scenery, walks among the hills by night, the music of the rivers—which are De Quincey's own peculiar additions to the poetry of the Lake District.

Finally in this section there are the historical sketches and descriptions—*The Cæsars* and *The Essenes*, various papers on Greek and Roman History, and two narrative works which, owing to the intermingling of the romantic element, Prof. Masson ranks with the imaginative works : *The Spanish Military Nun* and *Revolt of the Tartars*. The former is founded in the main on authentic documents describing the adventures in Spain and the New World of an escaped nun who adopts the dress of a man, suffers shipwreck and hardships, fights duels, and lives the life of a cavalier. The narrative has been praised for its frolicsome humour and fulness of detail, and some passages have real interest of situation and incident, but as a whole it is apt to become tiring. The *Revolt of the Tartars* is on a higher plane ; it is a first-rate piece of imaginative history. The story describes the escape of a whole nation of Tartars out of Russia into China in 1770 and 1771. The flight is accompanied by every horror of thirst and battle—the hopeless struggle of men, women and children with cold and disease, the relentless pursuit and unceasing attacks by a vast horde of half-civilised tribal enemies who aid the army of Russia, until at last the remnant are received kindly by the Chinese Emperor—and it ends in a curious conflict in which pursuers and pursued plunge into the Lake of Tengis in the double fury of slaughter and the craving to drink. The romantic story, commonly outside the range of the ordinary reader, the multitudes, the vast distances, the tumult and agony, the sublime and traditional names, appealed powerfully to De Quincey's imagination, and the events are described with a minuteness and circumstantiality of detail that produces a remarkable illusion of reality.

(ii) SPECULATIVE, DIDACTIC, AND CRITICAL

From the voluminous writings of this second group, De Quincey's reputation has crystallised out of the essays in literary criticism. Of the papers on philosophy, theology, politics, and political economy, scarcely anything survives for modern readers, but, Prof. Masson asserts,

> If De Quincey surpasses himself anywhere in his didactic papers, it is in those that concern Literary Theory and Criticism. No English writer has left a finer body of disquisition on the science and principles of Literature than will be found in De Quincey's general papers—entitled *Rhetoric, Style,* and *Language,* and his *Letters to a Young Man,* together with his more particular articles entitled *Theory of Greek Tragedy, The Antigone of Sophocles, Milton, Pope,* and *On Wordsworth's Poetry.*

The general mark of these critical writings is a combination of sympathy with poetic power and the scientific attitude. Considering their relatively small bulk they are wonderfully rich in new and illuminating theory. The sense of the confluence of thought and style, the theory of the dependence of literary quality upon social conditions, *e.g.* of the styles of comedy on the security of civil life, point forward to the kind of literary criticism taken up by modern writers like Hippolyte Taine, the French historian of our literature. Passages like the famous one on the Literatures of Thought and Power, and the proper conduct of allegorical figures, remind us of Coleridge in their fertility of discrimination and their instinct for the principles of literary effect. De Quincey, in fact, was largely influenced by Wordsworth and Coleridge. The theory that in the imagination the poet possesses the power to penetrate below the surface ; that this power is one with conscience and the sustaining mind in Nature ; that in this we have the touchstone of poetry : this is first and fundamental in De Quincey too. Furthermore, he saw that poetic genius is hand-in-hand with moral genius, that all kinds of literature revive ideals of hope and truth which, if left to themselves, would languish for want of examples. The whole of the long essay on Pope is a searching examination of his pretensions, first by the imaginative, and secondly by the moral test, as if these two were the same thing in different aspects. All the greatness in Pope, he says, comes from his sub-conscious Christianity, and the unessential and morally poor in his satire, especially on women, become subjects in this paper of ethical disquisitions in which De Quincey's power is seen at its best.

De Quincey was essentially a Romantic, and his critical standpoint in this respect is worth some consideration for its reflection in his works. Apologies for classic ideas at this time were becoming increasingly prominent. The attack on the school of Wordsworth, for instance, was not a trivial one, and in their attempts to rebut his theories by classical examples, Hazlitt, Landor, and Matthew Arnold had found a powerful line of attack. It is summarised in Arnold's Preface to his Poems in 1853. The eternal objects of poetry, he says, are actions : human actions, great actions. And it follows that of all the persons and stories with which the

poet may deal, none have more power over men than the old
fables and figures of Greece. They are more impressive than
any modern personages or problems, for they are more noble,
and their actions are of greater interest. Hence the austere
restraint of Greek tragedy ; the poet has no need to em-
broider the theme with his own feelings. To the Romantics
the images and thoughts in the minds of the characters are
the chief thing ; the Greek regards the whole, and the conduct of the plot is his first consideration. This is the line
that Hazlitt follows in his onslaught on the Lake School,
and Landor takes up the theme in his *Conversation* between
Southey and Porson. Classic and Romantic may meet in
the supreme works of Art, such as *King Lear*, but there are
many in which the difference does remain, and Wordsworth,
as in the lines prefixed to *The White Doe of Rylestone*, deliberately renounces the poetry of action.

What is interesting in De Quincey is the way in which he
joins issue with these critics on the merits of their models.
His case is presented in the essays on *Milton*, and on Keats's
Hyperion. Greek drama, he says, does not fathom all the
depths of the spirit, and so it falls below the Christian conception of life. Only one Greek tragedy rises to sublimity—
the *Prometheus* of Æschylus, and here the story comes down
from a darker mythology in the infancy of the race. These
models do not supply all we want ; for the true sublime we
must go to Milton, or Keats's *Hyperion*. Wordsworth, like
these two, did not fashion his own mythology : he sent down
his plummet into the same depths from which the older stories
rise. And if we want the poetry of action, we must create
such figures as Lear, who certainly is not classical. De
Quincey speaks only of the simplest poems of Wordsworth,
but he makes it clear that the romantic poet has his function :
he startles us into a sense of the mysterious infinity within
ourselves.

(iii) Imaginative Writings and Prose-Poetry

Of De Quincey's writings in this class little need be said; the best of them have taken rank with the great literature of England. They range from humorous extravaganzas like *On Murder considered as one of the Fine Arts*, to novels and romances, prose-phantasies, and lyrical ecstasies, while on the grounds of imaginative power we might include from the earlier class *The Spanish Military Nun*, the *Revolt of the Tartars*, and *Joan of Arc*. *On Murder considered as one of the Fine Arts* is a combination of ghastliness and humour, both more than a little forced. It comprises two papers, a lecture to students of the art, reviewing the different styles of murder in a long historical retrospect, and a report of the club dinner at which, to suitable accompaniments, toasts are drunk to a number of great murderers. It is a good essay in the incongruous—for a few pages, but for more it begins to tire. The novel *Klosterheim* and the shorter romances, largely based on German originals, are of the School of Terror, recalling De Quincey's interest in ghosts, murders, and mysteries. Fiction, however, was not his bent, though his stories are all carefully written. He himself omitted *Klosterheim* from the Collected Edition. It is in the *Confessions* and the prose-fantasies—*The Daughter of Lebanon*, *The English Mail-Coach*, and *Suspiria de Profundis*—that De Quincey reaches his high-water mark. The dream element and the lyrical prose of these works are dealt with in the next two sections of the Introduction, and they are fully represented in the text of this volume. In addition, however, the student should note those parts of the *Suspiria* in which De Quincey gives us not only a marvellous insight into dreams, but brings us face to face with new creations of his own. The common incidents of life are magnified into majestic proportions, and they are used to sustain his sublime imagination. Dim and august shadows rise over the suffering of men. " Levana," " Our Lady of Sighs," " Our Lady of Darkness," are, Professor Masson says, a permanent addition to the mythology of the race.

CHARACTERISTICS

In English literature De Quincey and opium are invariably associated, meaning that he survives for most readers as a writer of fantastic prose, a translator into English of wild and splendid dreams. Actually the influence of opium on the formation of these poetic dream-fancies is much exaggerated ; of equal effect on his imagination and style was his natural dreaminess of manner, intensified by his temperament and habits. His childhood counts for much, and all the characteristics of the dream-faculty can be traced in the incidents related in the *Autobiographic Sketches*.

From his earliest days De Quincey was marked by an unusual sensibility to outward impression. There was a suggestion in the family that the death of his young sister Jane was due in part to the brutal ill-treatment of a servant in whose charge she had been left, and though the boy was but one and a half years old, the feeling which came upon him on seeing the person responsible was one " of shuddering horror, as upon a first glimpse of the truth that I was in a world of evil and strife." Five years later he was acquainted with two unfortunate and weakly girls, the daughters of a neighbouring clergyman, who were obscurely reported to be idiots. They were hated and ill-treated by their mother, and shortly before they fell ill and died the boy witnessed a typical scene of domestic strife. The incidents magnified themselves in his mind, and years after, reading the *Agamemnon* of Æschylus, he recognised his childish emotions. He found himself in Mycenæ retracing the horrors with which he had invested the clergyman's dwelling in Manchester, and he read again the sufferings which had darkened the days of the unfortunate girls. In such incidents is born De Quincey's tragical pity for all the outcasts of mankind, the *pariahs*—all those whom society rejects.

De Quincey early found that he had a strange and wonderfully vivid dream-faculty. There was something abnormal in his psychology which enabled him to see the objects of the inner vision as easily as of the outer. Elizabeth, his favourite sister, died when he was six years old, and he relates how he surreptitiously stole up to her room to see her face once more. Fear fell upon him as a " solemn wind " began to blow through the chamber " like a great *audible* symbol of eternity," and he passed into a strange dream :

> Instantly, when my ear caught this vast Æolian intonation, when my eye filled with the golden fulness of life, the pomps of the heavens above, or the glory of the flowers below, and turning when it settled upon the frost which overspread my sister's face, instantly a trance fell upon me. A vault seemed to open in the zenith of the far blue sky, a shaft which ran up for ever. I, in spirit, rose as if on billows that also ran up the shaft for ever ; and the billows seemed to pursue the throne of God ; but *that* also ran before us and fled away continually. The flight and the pursuit seemed to go on for ever and ever. Frost gathering frost, some Sarsar wind of death, seemed to repel me ; some mighty relation between God and death dimly struggled to evolve itself from the dreadful antagonism between them ; shadowy meanings even yet continue to exercise and torment, in dreams, the deciphering oracle within me. I slept—for how long I cannot say ; slowly I recovered my self-possession ; and, when I woke, found myself standing, as before, close to my sister's bed.

Such impressions of his childhood give the exact stamp of his later imagination : the clearness and intensity of his vision of physical things ; the photographic veracity of his apprehension, particularly of Nature ; the power of painting faces or objects on darkness with distinction. At times he passes into a different key. He recalls the first emotions of this in his seventh year, when his dying father returned home :

> The first notice of the approach was the sudden emerging of horses' heads from the deep gloom of the shady lane ; the next was the mass of white pillows against which the dying patient was reclining. The hearse-like pace at which the carriage moved recalled the overwhelming spectacle of that funeral which had so lately formed part in the most memorable event of my life. But these elements of awe, that might at any rate have struck forcibly upon the mind of a child, were for me, in my condition of morbid nervousness, raised into abiding grandeur by the antecedent experiences of that particular summer night. The listening for hours to the sounds from horses' hoofs upon distant roads, rising and falling, caught and lost, upon the gentle undulation of such fitful airs as might be stirring—the peculiar solemnity of the hours succeeding to sunset—the glory of the dying day—the gorgeousness which, by description, so well I knew of sunset in those West Indian islands from which my father was returning—the knowledge that he returned only to die —the almighty pomp in which this great idea of Death apparelled itself to my young sorrowing heart—the corresponding pomp in which the antagonistic idea, not less mysterious, of life, rose, as if on wings, amidst tropic glories and floral pageantries, that seemed even *more* solemn and pathetic than the vapoury plumes and trophies of mortality —all this chorus of restless images, or of suggestive thoughts, gave to my father's return, which else had been fitted only to interpose one transitory red-letter day in the calendar of a child, the shadowy power of an ineffaceable agency among my dreams.

Here is the artist of the dark sublime, the creator of images strange, appalling, and grotesque, shrouded in obscurity or weird twilight.

The opium-dreams are but a normal development from all this. Their characteristic is a union of the visionary element with a fundamental grain of reality. Imagination is held in check by science and psychology; indeed Prof. Masson's objection is that the visions fail " by too much obtrusion of the self-conscious in their construction,"—there is too much obvious art. De Quincey is able to temper the agony of his passion, to unfold it slowly. He lays it out, not piles it on. There is much of interest to the psychologist—long and precise notations of the effects of opium at its worst— but the outstanding impression is one of gorgeously terrible pictures. Vast architectures rise before him, challenging the stars; mysterious lakes, seas and oceans. Multitudes of swaying faces emerge, now shaping themselves into passionate memories from his childhood, now arranging themselves into armies and processions advancing against the dreamer him-self. He is an alien amidst foreign and monstrous scenery, Oriental or " Nilotic," and to accommodate the splendours that fret his heart there is a terrifying enlargement of space and time. Space swells to infinity, while he lives seventy or a hundred years in a single night. The *Confessions* are full of passages like this, and if we feel at times that the diction is florid, the grandiloquence invariable and indis-criminate, at others, more especially in the *Suspiria* and the *Vision of Sudden Death*, we must admit an art which seems to compass the full scale of musical prose, cadences both terrible and peaceful, " the sobbing of litanies, the thunder-ing of organs, and the mustering of summer clouds."

Most other characteristics of De Quincey's genius have already been touched upon. They were mainly determined by the fact that all his work was written for periodical literature. He was a *polyhistor*, what Prof. Elton calls a " disher-up of curious, sometimes doubtful history and erudition for the cultivated person who insists on having what is readable." [1] The distinction of De Quincey's hundred

[1] *Survey of English Literature, 1780-1830.*

and fifty articles and other compositions, apart from their style, is not the astounding variety of subjects over which they range, but the uniformly high level most of them maintain. He brought to bear on every problem a powerful and original intellect. In analysis, interpretation and penetration, in narration and description, in argument and exposition, in the power to awaken fresh and vivid currents of ideas and emotions, his genius was unequalled in its day, and he imparted to all his works something personal and distinctive. His prose is the mean of the practised thinker, and he never writes of what he does not know. Behind every article is a mind stored with a broad and comprehensive knowledge. Occasionally there is a smell of the lamp, but the pages of the old journals are lit up in his contributions by flashes of striking originality, imaginative narration, fancies of a rich and inventive brain, humour and pathos, introspective biography—interesting details of his life and work, his peculiarities, tastes, misfortunes, pleasures, and recollections—and noble, moving disquisitions in exalted thought and rhythmic phrase which approach the sublime.

STYLE

We learn much about De Quincey's own literary characteristics from his critical writings on the theory of language and style. In the essay on *Style* he takes up as the expression of profound truth a remark of Wordsworth's that in imaginative writing style is not the " *dress* of thoughts," but their " *incarnation.*" Coleridge, too, had recognised the intimacy between manner and matter, and noticed the appropriateness of word-music to thought,[1] but De Quincey worked the proposition out and made it a primary truth for the first time in English criticism. No-one before had started with

[1] See *Biographia Literaria*, xiv, xviii, xxii.

so clear an apprehension of the fact that style and thought can combine into a third thing :

> If language were merely a dress, then you could separate the two ; you could lay the thoughts on the left hand, the language on the right. But generally speaking, you can no more deal thus with poetic thoughts than you can with soul and body. The union is too subtle, the intertexture too ineffable—each co-existing not merely with the other, but each *in* and *through* the other.[1]

The case is more fully developed in the essay on *Language*. We English, De Quincey asserts, always undervalue style ; we regard it as a secondary or even trivial concern, and we read a book almost wholly for what it has to tell. In this we overlook three capital points : that style has an absolute value, and is a pleasant study apart from the subject ; that it makes all the difference in the world to the success of the thoughts since it treats them in the best way to rekindle in the mind a practical sense of their value—it illuminates a matter to the understanding ; and thirdly, that there are cases where the style actually becomes the *incarnation* of the thoughts—it is an element in a fusion, and " a coefficient that, being superadded to something else, absolutely makes the thought as a third and separate existence." If therefore we neglect style, we go near to abolishing a mode of existence.

Two things follow from this : the value of elaboration of style, and the importance of imagery. Every capacious mind when impassioned, De Quincey says, must seek a style which is continuous, elaborate, and sustained—though this does not mean that every mind must write so. In the essay on *Rhetoric* there is a fine appreciation of Burke, and he is praised first for his capaciousness, his large and fine understanding : " His great and peculiar distinction was that he viewed all the objects of the understanding under more

[1] *Style*, Blackwood, 18 0.

relations than other men, and under more complex relations."
Now one cannot hold everything in relation without helping
oneself by the use of concrete images, so the great mind will
think through images, which amplify and dignify the thought.
In practice there is no writer who understands better than
De Quincey how the imagery may spread splendour over the
thought. One of the finest passages in *Recollections of the Lake
Poets* is that which tells of the deaths of George and Sarah
Green in a snowstorm on the hills. They leave six young
children in a snow-bound cottage, and the piece describes in
pathetic detail how the eldest daughter realises that something has happened to her father, and does all she can to
sustain her brothers and sisters. Eventually she goes to the
nearest house, and then as the weeping child tells her tale—
" No tongue can express the fervid sympathy which travelled
through the vale, like fire in an American forest." This is
the short, vivid simile—the flashing instantaneously on the
mind one sharp-glittering phrase, just that vital aspect of a
scene which calls up all the rest. And De Quincey is equally
skilled at beating it out into a long analogy for effect—the
art of painting a word-picture in full detail—as he does with
great power in the description of Charles Lloyd in the same
book.

Again and again De Quincey returns to this theme of the
elaborate style : Lord Bacon lacks the impulse of Burke's
passion, his sentences are " not plants, but seeds ; not oaks
but acorns." [1] Southey, he says, is justly praised for his
" plain, manly, unaffected English," but because of this
manner, when occasion arises for impassioned fervour or
splendid declamation his style betrays its want of that
perfect eloquence which instinctively seeks the periodic
structure. [2] Hazlitt is " not eloquent," because he is " dis-
continuous ; his thoughts are abrupt, insulated, capricious,

---

[1] *Rhetoric*, note on J. Taylor.   [2] *The Lake Poets*.

and non-sequacious." And Lamb similarly—who has an imagination ideally sound and a dramatic intellect and taste in perfection—lacks that constitution of mind which delights in the slow, stately unfolding of a situation. So on occasions requiring a long ascent on untired pinion, " he refuses himself invariably," and, for the same reason, he has no sympathy with the " solemn planetary wheelings of *Paradise Lost*." [1] In all this De Quincey is pleading for a comprehensive style, which includes the short sentence when the matter requires. The simple and the plain are both good, and indispensable, but so is the pomp and splendour. De Quincey often uses the concise style in his own works. The essay on *Casuistry*, which discusses the vexed question of conduct—the justification of killing prisoners of war, suicide, and usury—is a model of argument and erudition : the theme advances by short, decisive moves, and dialogue is skilfully used to vary and change the gist of the style. The same thing is done with great effect in the *Opium-Eater* :

> And what am I doing amongst the mountains ? Taking opium. Yes ; but what else ? Why, reader, in 1812, the year we are now arrived at, as well as for some years previous, I have been chiefly studying German metaphysics, in the writings of Kant, Fichte, Schelling, &c. And how, and in what manner, do I live ? In short, what class or description of men do I belong to ? I am at this period—viz. in 1812— living in a cottage ; and with a single female servant (honi soit qui mal y pense), who, amongst my neighbours, passes by the name of my " housekeeper."

But though De Quincey's style includes the short and concise manner, his famous style is that of the visions. The Periodic Style is of two main kinds—that of Johnson and that of Burke. In Burke, balance and antithesis and parallels hang, as it were, against each other, or branch off

---

[1] Review of Talfourd's *Final Memorials of Charles Lamb.*

from each other; in Johnson they hang dead like scales.
Take any sentence you please from Dr Johnson, De Quincey
says in the essay on *Rhetoric*,

> and it will be found to contain a thought, good or bad, fully
> preconceived. Whereas in Burke, whatever may have been
> the preconception, it receives a new determination or in-
> flexion at every clause of the sentence. Some collateral
> adjunct of the main proposition, some temperament or
> restraint, some oblique glance at its remote affinities, will
> invariably be found to attend the progress of his sentences,
> like the spray from a waterfall, or the scintillations from
> the iron under the blacksmith's hammer. Hence whilst a
> writer of Dr Johnson's class seems only to look back upon
> his thoughts, Burke looks forward, and does in fact advance
> and change his own station concurrently with the advance
> of the sentences.

The vital kind of periodic prose comes down from Jeremy
Taylor and Sir Thomas Browne through Burke to De Quincey,
and thence to Ruskin. De Quincey's style, too, is dynamic,
—circling, yet ever moving on. But he is distinguished from
the others of his class by two features: the unevenness of
his style—the frequent drop from the sublime to the trivial,
the habit of mixing solemnity with the jocular vein—and
his digressiveness, which alloys impassioned eloquence with
an element of fertile rhetoric. Rhetoric and Eloquence are
carefully distinguished by De Quincey:

> By Eloquence, we understand the overflow of powerful
> feelings upon occasions fitted to excite them. But Rhetoric
> is the art of aggrandizing and bringing out into strong relief,
> by means of various and striking thoughts, some aspect of
> truth which of itself is supported by no spontaneous feelings,
> and therefore rests upon artificial aids.[1]

Rhetoric is used to convince the understanding; eloquence
to move the feelings. De Quincey combines both intellect
and passion, and so his style is a slow, stately march which

---

[1] Essay on *Rhetoric*.

resembles that of Jeremy Taylor and Sir Thomas Browne.
And yet he is like neither of these two. Taylor, he says, is
" restless, fervid, aspiring, scattering abroad a prodigality of
life " ; Browne is " deep, tranquil, and majestic." The
energy of De Quincey's passion has a lower pulse than that
of Taylor, and prodigality is not one of his notes ; neither is
he tranquil. The images in his dreams are tumultuous and
streaming, but he always seems to be suffering, not creating
these dreams, to be the spectator of his own imagination as
if it were other than his own. The attitude of the dreamer
is his characteristic attitude, and so there is not in him the
violent clash between intellect and passion, as in Taylor,
simply because the passion is not strong enough. De Quincey
is ever a shy, sensitive, sympathetic spirit, and the intellectual
parts and the passions in him merge and blend. Sometimes
the passion is suspended while the intellect plays on—hence
the digressiveness : the digressions serve to lead up to, or
away from, the passions.

Lastly we have to consider De Quincey as a master of
melodious prose. There are certain qualities in his style
which approximate to the effects of music, to which he was
unusually responsive. The deficiency of Lamb, that he had
no sense of the rhythmical in prose composition, De Quincey
ascribes to the fact that " the sense of music was utterly
obliterated as with a sponge by nature herself from Lamb's
organisation." [1] And in the *Opium-Eater* he tells us of his
visits to the Opera House ; how he thrilled with pleasure to
hear the angelic Grassini :

> Shivering with expectation I sat, when the time drew near
> for her golden epiphany ; shivering I rose from my seat,
> incapable of rest, when that heavenly and harp-like voice
> sang its own victorious welcome. I question whether any
> Turk, of all that ever entered the paradise of opium-eaters,
> can have had half the pleasure I had.

[1] Review of Talfourd's *Final Memorials of Charles Lamb*.

These musical qualities in De Quincey's prose may be summarised as follows :

(i) The law of ebb-and-flow, which is elaborated in the essay on Keats, is always observed. Every great work of art, he says, tends after distress and tumult to end in peace :

> Peace, then, severe tranquillity, the brooding calm, or γαλήνη of the Greeks, is the final key into which all the storms of passion modulate themselves in the hands of great poets. All tumult is for the sake of rest—tempest, but the harbinger of calm—and suffering, good only as the condition of permanent repose.[1]

(ii) The artistic use of the principle of antagonism, or contrast, which De Quincey finds in *Paradise Lost* when images of great architectural grandeur are made to arise in the solitude and remoteness of Paradise, is a common device in his own work. This is the secret of the essay *On the Knocking at the Gate in Macbeth*, his best-known contribution to Shakespearian criticism. He arrives at the conclusion that antagonism is the explanation of the perplexity he has always felt over this point. During the scene the murderers are taken "out of the region of human things, human purposes, human desires. They are transfigured"— we must feel that they are cut off by an immeasurable gulf from the world of ordinary life. And this is conveyed to us when the deed is done by the reaction following the knocking at the gate: we are conscious of "the re-establishment of the goings-on of the world in which we live." A frequent trick of De Quincey's composition is to turn aside from a narrative and deviate into a psychological dissection of his emotion at the time. In the passage referred to above,[2] when the little child steals in awe to the death-chamber of his sister, the dramatic suspense is heightened by a pause of several pages while he considers why death should be more appalling in

---

[1] " Dr Samuel Parr," *Blackwood*, Jan. 1831.   [2] See page xxiv.

summer than in winter. Almost all the ecstasies of lyrical prose are preceded by contrasting passages of simple, incisive language. In the *Opium-Eater* the eastern visions are introduced by a long dialectical disquisition on the causes of his horror of Chinese manners and modes of life and scenery. It is very cunningly done—he leads up to the point of tension, and then at the breathless moment there is a sharp, sudden, assailing note of antagonism, intensifying all that has gone before.

(iii) De Quincey is peculiar among English prose-writers up to his time in the careful and conscious elaboration of his rhythm. "Rhythm," he says, "is not only the cause of impassioned feeling, but the subtle ally of it." It is easy to discover in his work elaborate patterns and chains of words which actually fall into stanzas—strophe and antistrophe ; and with these solemn and intricate paces of rhythm there is always the word-music. De Quincey had a fine sensibility for sound, and he understood the sonorous aspects of our literature. Brougham advised students of the grand style to keep to the Saxon element in English. De Quincey's deliberate choice when he needs the higher harmonies is often an unusually learned combination of Latin, or Greek, or other polysyllabic words. He is not only a master of *pronunciability*, Prof. Masson says, "mere *pronunciability* was not enough for him, and *musical beauty* had to be superadded."

(iv) De Quincey also makes an heroic attempt in his prose at appropriating the power of music in the management of the subject-matter. He goes so far as to call one of the parts of the *Vision of Sudden Death* a "dream-fugue." A fugue is a piece of music in which the melody is repeated by different parts until all have sounded, which is the end of the first variation, when episodes, or passages open to free treatment, are introduced. This continual recurrence of the same subject in different modifications seemed to De Quincey to correspond to the way in which the mind is persecuted by a scene or an idea in a dream. The *Vision of Sudden Death* begins characteristically with a sober dissertation on the fact that death is most painful when it offers, or seems to offer, a chance of escape, and it is still more so when one flinches from the occasion and death descends through our default. This leads to a picture of the midnight coach before the Post Office at Manchester, bound for Glasgow. De Quincey is the only outside passenger, and when the driver has fallen asleep he sees approaching a slightly-built gig, with a woman in it. This is one of the great instances of De Quincey's management of suspense. We are given the whole chain of the argument, his frantic efforts to seize the reins, an exact notation of every movement and gesture of the threatened man, a vivid sense of the torrential speed and the shock of the actual occurrence. Then comes the fugue —all the incidents and images in his memory connected with coaches mingle together in his dreams, continually repeating the central incident. He is in a ship bearing down on a pinnace containing the woman of the gig, or he is lying in a boat anchored by the seashore when over the sands comes running the woman of the accident, and in a panic she sinks into the quicksands. Though the piece is overdone and full of false notes, though it emphasises De Quincey's terrible incapacity for humour, it is an interesting experiment. It is an attempt in the anarchy or mosaic of his dreams to use the utmost effects of music for a colossal form of impassioned horror. We are swept on from movement to movement until all the threads are gathered up, as it were, in a magnificent orchestral climax. It is not word-painting, but word-music: the emotions are thrilled by direct sensuous appeal. And the same effect can be traced in all his most exquisite passages. " They are intended to be musical compositions in which the words have to play the part of notes in music,

They are impassioned, not in the sense of expressing any definite sentiment, but because, from the structure and combination of the sentences, they harmonise with certain phases of emotion." [1] Mrs Browning, speaking of one of De Quincey's articles, said that her eyes did not read it, but that her "heart *trembled* through it from end to end."

(v) The last musical character, particularly in the visions, is the use of indeterminate outlines, the shadowiness of the characters. Presences and faces we cannot see rise out of the vast architectures and mysterious lakes, the chasms and sunless abysses :

> Then suddenly would come a dream of far different char-acter—a tumultuous dream—commencing with a music such as now I often heard in sleep—music of preparation and of awakening suspense. The undulations of fast-gathering tumults were like the opening of the Coronation Anthem ; and, like *that*, gave the feeling of a multitudinous move-ment, of infinite cavalcades filing off, and the tread of innumerable armies. The morning was come of a mighty day—a day of crisis and of ultimate hope for human nature, then suffering mysterious eclipse, and labouring in some dread extremity.

This is the power which gives solemnity to the history of Carlyle, and dignity and splendour to the work of Ruskin, Tennyson, and Browning. There is something in it of the force and appeal found as a rule only in the finest verse. Like that it "steals upon the soul with music, dies off, and leaves it satisfied." It suggests that Infinity which Ruskin describes as a kind of "Typical Beauty"—of all visible things "the least material, the least finite, the farthest with-drawn from the earth prison-house, most typical of the nature of God, the most suggestive of the glory of His dwelling-place." [2]

[1] Leslie Stephen, *Hours in a Library*.
[2] *Modern Painters II*.

SELECTIONS

AUTOBIOGRAPHY

De Quincey's Schooldays

It was in the closing autumn (or rather in the opening winter) of 1800 that my first introduction took place to the Manchester Grammar School. The school-room showed already in its ample proportions some hint of its pretensions as an endowed school, or school of 5 that class which I believe peculiar to England. To this limited extent had the architectural sense of power been timidly and parsimoniously invoked. Beyond that, nothing had been attempted; and the dreary expanse of white-washed walls, that at so small a cost might 10 have been embellished by plaster-of-Paris friezes and large medallions, illustrating to the eye of the youthful student the most memorable glorifications of literature —these were bare as the walls of a poor-house or a lazaretto; buildings whose functions, as thoroughly 15 sad and gloomy, the mind recoils from drawing into relief by sculpture or painting. But this building was dedicated to purposes that were noble. The naked walls clamoured for decoration: and how easily might tablets have been moulded—exhibiting (as a first homage to 20 literature) Athens, with the wisdom of Athens, in the person of Pisistratus, concentrating the general energies upon the revisal and re-casting of the *Iliad*. Or (second) the Athenian captives in Sicily, within the fifth century B.C., as winning noble mercy for themselves by some 25

Repeated air
Of sad Electra's poet.

1

Such, and so sudden, had been the oblivion of earthly
passions wrought by the contemporary poet of Athens
that in a moment the wrath of Sicily, with all its billows,
ran down into a heavenly calm ; and he that could
5 plead for his redemption no closer relation to Euripides
than the accident of recalling some scatterings from
his divine verses suddenly found his chains dropping
to the ground, and himself, that in the morning had
risen a despairing slave in a stone-quarry, translated
10 at once as a favoured brother into a palace of Syracuse.
Or, again, how easy to represent (third) " the great
Emathian conqueror," that in the very opening of his
career, whilst visiting Thebes with vengeance, nevertheless relented at the thought of literature, and

15   Bade spare
        The house of Pindarus, when temple and tower
        Went to the ground.

Alexander might have been represented amongst the
colonnades of some Persian capital — Ecbatana or
20 Babylon, Susa or Persepolis — in the act of receiving
from Greece, as a *nuzzur* more awful than anything
within the gift of the " barbaric East," a jewelled casket
containing the *Iliad* and the *Odyssey*; creations that
already have lived almost as long as the Pyramids.
25   Puritanically bald and odious, therefore, in my eyes,
was the hall up which my guardian and myself paced
solemnly—though not Miltonically " riding up to the
Soldan's chair," yet, in fact, within a more limited
kingdom, advancing to the chair of a more absolute
30 despot. This potentate was the headmaster, or *archididascalus*, of the Manchester Grammar School ; and
that school was variously distinguished. It was
(1) ancient, having in fact been founded by a bishop
of Exeter in an early part of the sixteenth century, so

as to be now, in 1856, more than 330 years old ; (2) it was rich, and was annually growing richer ; and (3) it was dignified by a beneficial relation to the magnificent University of Oxford.

The headmaster at that time was Mr Charles Lawson. In former editions of this work I created him a doctor ; my object being to evade too close an approach to the realities of the case, and consequently to personalities, which (though indifferent to myself) would have been in some cases displeasing to others. A doctor, however, Mr Lawson was not ; nor in the account of law a clergyman. Yet most people, governed unconsciously by the associations surrounding their composite idea of a dignified schoolmaster, invested him with the clerical character. And in reality he *had* taken deacon's orders in the Church of England. But not the less he held himself to be a layman, and was addressed as such by all his correspondents of rank, who might be supposed best to understand the technical rules of English etiquette. Etiquette in such cases cannot entirely detach itself from law. Now, in English law, as was shown in Horne Tooke's case, the rule is, *"Once a clergyman, and always a clergyman."* The sacred character with which ordination clothes a man is indelible. But, on the other hand, who *is* a clergyman ? Not he that has taken simply the initial orders of a deacon,— so at least I have heard,—but he that has taken the second and full orders of a priest. If otherwise, then there was a great mistake current amongst Mr Lawson's friends in addressing him as an esquire.

Squire or not a squire, however, parson or not a parson—whether sacred or profane—Mr Lawson was in some degree interesting by his position and his recluse habits. Life was over with him, for its hopes and for

its trials.　Or at most one trial yet awaited him ; which
was—to fight with a painful malady, and fighting to
die.　He still had his dying to do : he was in arrear
as to *that* : else all was finished.　It struck me (but,
5 with such limited means for judging, I might easily be
wrong) that his understanding was of a narrow order.
His senior *alumni* were always working their way
through some great scenic poet that had shaken the
stage of Athens ; and more than one of his classes,
10 never ending, still beginning, were daily solacing him
with the gaieties of Horace, in his Epistles or in his
Satires.　The Horatian jests indeed to *him* never grew
old.　On coming to the *plagosus Orbilius*, or any other
sally of pleasantry, he still threw himself back in his
15 arm-chair, as he *had* done through fifty years, with what
seemed heart-shaking bursts of sympathetic merriment.
Mr Lawson, indeed, could afford to be sincerely mirthful
over the word *plagosus*.　There are gloomy tyrants,
exulting in the discipline of fear, to whom and to whose
20 pupils this word must call up remembrances too degrading for any but affected mirth.　Allusions that are too
fearfully personal cease to be subjects of playfulness.
Sycophancy only it is that laughs ; and the artificial
merriment is but the language of shrinking and grovel-
25 ling deprecation.　Different, indeed, was the condition
of the Manchester Grammar School.　It was honourable
both to the masters and the upper boys, through whom
only such a result was possible, that in that school,
during my knowledge of it (viz. during the closing year
30 of the eighteenth century and the two opening years
of the nineteenth), all punishments that appealed to
the sense of bodily pain had fallen into disuse ; and
this at a period long before any public agitation had
begun to stir in that direction.　How then was dis-

cipline maintained ? It was maintained through the
self-discipline of the senior boys, and through the
efficacy of their example, combined with their system
of rules. Noble are the impulses of opening manhood
where they are not utterly ignoble : at that period, I 5
mean, when the poetic sense begins to blossom, and
when boys are first made sensible of the paradise that
lurks in female smiles. Had the school been entirely
a day-school, too probable it is that the vulgar brawling
tendencies of boys left to themselves would have pre- 10
vailed. But it happened that the elder section of the
school—those on the brink of manhood, and by incalculable degrees the more scholar-like section, all who
read, meditated, or began to kindle into the love of
literature—were boarders in Mr Lawson's house. The 15
students, therefore, of the house carried an overwhelming influence into the school. They were bound together
by links of brotherhood ; whereas the day-scholars were
disconnected. Over and above this, it happened luckily
that there was no playground, not the smallest, attached 20
to the school ; that is, none was attached to the *upper*
or *grammar* school. But there was also, and resting on
the same liberal endowment, a *lower* school, where the
whole machinery of teaching was applied to the lowest
mechanical accomplishments of reading and writing. 25
The hall in which this servile business was conducted
ran under the upper school ; it was, therefore, I presume, a subterraneous duplicate of the upper hall.
And, since the upper rose only by two or three feet
above the level of the neighbouring streets, the lower 30
school should naturally have been at a great depth
below these streets. In that case it would be a dark
crypt, such as we see under some cathedrals ; and it
would have argued a singular want of thoughtfulness

in the founder to have laid one part of his establishment under an original curse of darkness. As the access to this plebeian school lay downwards through long flights of steps, I never found surplus energy enough for in-5 vestigating the problem. But, as the ground broke away precipitously at that point into lower levels, I presume, upon consideration, that the subterranean crypt will be found open on one side to visitations from sun and moon. So that, for this base mechanic school 10 there may, after all, have been a playground. But for ours in the upper air, I repeat, there was none ; not so much as would have bleached a lady's pocket-hand-kerchief ; and this one defect carried along with it unforeseen advantages.

15 Lord Bacon it is who notices the subtle policy which may lurk in the mere external figure of a table. A square table, having an undeniable head and foot, two polar extremities of what is highest and lowest, a peri-helion and an aphelion, together with equatorial sides, 20 opens at a glance a large career to ambition ; whilst a circular table sternly represses all such aspiring dreams, and so does a triangular table. Yet, if the triangle should be right-angled, then the Lucifer seated at the right angle might argue that he *subtended* all the tenants 25 of the hypothenuse ; being, therefore, as much nobler than they as Atlas was nobler than the globe which he carried. It was, by the way, some arrangement of this nature which constituted the original feature of dis-tinction in John o' Groat's house, and not at all (as 30 most people suppose) the high northern latitude of this house. John, it seems, finished the feuds for preced-ency, not by legislating this way or that, but by cutting away the possibility of such feuds through the assist-ance of a round table. The same principle must have

guided King Arthur amongst his knights, Charlemagne amongst his paladins, and sailors in their effectual distribution of the peril attached to a mutinous remonstrance by the admirable device of a " round-robin." Even two little girls, as Harrington remarks in his *Oceana*, have oftentimes hit upon an expedient, through pure mother-wit, more effectual than all the schools of philosophy could have suggested, for insuring the impartial division of an orange ; which expedient is that either of the two shall divide, but then that the other shall have the right of choice. You divide, and I choose. Such is the formula ; and an angel could not devise a more absolute guarantee for the equity of the division than by thus forcing the divider to become the inheritor of any possible disadvantages that he may have succeeded in creating by his own act of division. In all these cases one seemingly trivial precaution opens, in the next stage, into a world of irresistible consequences. And, in our case, an effect not less disproportionate followed out of that one accident, apparently so slight, that we had no playground. We of the seniority, who, by thoughtfulness, and the conscious dignity of dealing largely with literature, were already indisposed to boyish sports, found, through the defect of a playground, that our choice and our pride were also our necessity. Even the proudest of us benefited by that coercion ; for many would else have sold their privilege of pride for an hour's amusement, and have become, at least, occasional conformists. A day more than usually fine, a trial of skill more than usually irritating to the sense of special superiority, would have seduced most of us in the end into the surrender of our exclusiveness. Indiscriminate familiarity would have followed as an uncontrollable result ;

since to mingle with others in common acts of business may leave the sense of reserve undisturbed : but all reserve gives way before a common intercourse in pleasure. As it was, what with our confederation through house-membership, what with our reciprocal sympathies in the problems suggested by books, we had become a club of boys (amongst whom might be four or five that were even young men, counting eighteen or nineteen years) altogether as thoughtful and as self-respecting as can often exist even amongst adults. Even the subterraneous school contributed something to our self-esteem. It formed a subordinate section of our own establishment, that kept before our eyes, by force of contrast, the dignity inherent in our own constitution. Its object was to master humble accomplishments that were within the reach of *mechanic* efforts : everything mechanic is limited ; whereas we felt that *our* object, even if our name of *grammar* school presented that object in what seemed too limited a shape, was substantially noble, and tended towards the infinite. But in no long time I came to see that, as to the *name*, we were all of us under a mistake. Being asked what a *grammar* school indicates, what it professes to teach, there is scarcely any man who would not reply, " Teach ? why, it teaches grammar : what else ? " But this is a mistake : as I have elsewhere explained, *grammatica* in this combination does not mean grammar (though grammar also obeys the movements of a most subtle philosophy), but *literature*. Look into Suetonius. Those " *grammatici* " whom he memorialises as an order of men flocking to Rome in the days of the Flavian family, were not *grammarians* at all, but what the French by a comprehensive name style *litterateurs*— that is, they were men who (1) studied literature, (2) who

taught literature, (3) who practically produced literature. And, upon the whole, *grammatica* is perhaps
the least objectionable Latin equivalent for our word
literature.

Two or three days after my inaugural examination
—viz. on the Sunday following—I transferred myself
to headquarters at Mr Lawson's house. About nine
o'clock in the evening, I was conducted by a servant
up a short flight of stairs, through a series of gloomy and
unfurnished little rooms, having small windows but no
doors, to the common room (as in Oxford it would
technically be called) of the senior boys. Everything
had combined to depress me. To leave the society of
accomplished women—*that* was already a signal privation. The season besides was rainy, which in itself
is a sure source of depression ; and the forlorn aspect
of the rooms completed my dejection. But the scene
changed as the door was thrown open : faces kindling
with animation became visible ; and from a company
of boys, numbering sixteen or eighteen, scattered about
the room, two or three, whose age entitled them to the
rank of leaders, came forward to receive me with a
courtesy which I had not looked for. The grave kindness and the absolute sincerity of their manner impressed
me most favourably. I had lived familiarly with boys
gathered from all quarters of the island at the Bath
Grammar School : and for some time (when visiting
Lord Altamont at Eton) with boys of the highest
aristocratic pretensions. At Bath and at Eton, though
not equally, there prevailed a tone of higher polish ;
and in the air, speech, deportment of the majority
could be traced at once a premature knowledge of the
world. They had indeed the advantage over my new

friends in graceful self-possession ; but, on the other hand, the best of them suffered by comparison with these Manchester boys in the qualities of visible self-restraint and of self-respect. At Eton high rank was distributed pretty liberally ; but in the Manchester school the parents of many boys were artisans, or of that rank ; some even had sisters that were menial servants ; and those who stood higher by pretensions of birth and gentle blood were, at the most, the sons of rural gentry or of clergymen. And I believe that, with the exception of three or four brothers, belonging to a clergyman's family at York, all were, like myself, natives of Lancashire. At that time my experience was too limited to warrant me in expressing any opinion, one way or the other, upon the relative pretensions—moral and intellectual—of the several provinces in our island. But since then I have seen reason to agree with the late Dr Cooke Taylor in awarding the pre-eminence, as regards energy, power to face suffering, and other high qualities, to the natives of Lancashire. Even a century back, they were distinguished for the culture of refined tastes. In musical skill and sensibility, no part of Europe, with the exception of a few places in Germany, could pretend to rival them : and, accordingly, even in Handel's days, but for the chorus-singers from Lancashire, his oratorios must have remained a treasure, if not absolutely sealed, at any rate most imperfectly revealed.

In after years, when an undergraduate at Oxford, I had an opportunity of reading as it were in a mirror the characteristic pretensions and the average success of many celebrated schools. Such a mirror I found in the ordinary conversation and in the favourite reading of young gownsmen belonging to the many different

colleges of Oxford. Generally speaking, each college
had a filial connection (strict or not strict) with some
one or more of our great public schools. These,
fortunately for England, are diffused through all her
counties : and, as the main appointments to the capital
offices in such *public* schools are often vested by law in
Oxford or Cambridge, this arrangement guarantees a
sound system of teaching ; so that any failures in the
result must presumably be due to the individual student.
Failures, on the whole, I do not suppose that there
were. Classical attainments that might be styled even
splendid were not then, nor are now, uncommon. And
yet in one great feature many of those schools, even
the very best, when thus tried by their fruits, left a painful memento of failure ; or rather not of failure as in
relation to any purpose that they steadily recognised,
but of *wilful* and *intentional* disregard, as towards a
purpose alien from any duty of theirs, or any task which
they had ever undertaken—a failure, namely, in relation to *modern* literature—a neglect to unroll its mighty
charts : and amongst this modern literature a special
neglect (such as seems almost brutal) of our own English
literature, though pleading its patent of precedency in a
voice so trumpet-tongued. To myself, whose homage
ascended night and day towards the great altars of
English Poetry or Eloquence, it was shocking and
revolting to find in high-minded young countrymen,
burning with sensibility that sought vainly for a corresponding object, deep unconsciousness of an all-suffi-
cient object—namely, in that great inheritance of our
literature which sometimes kindled enthusiasm in our
public enemies. How painful to see or to know that
vast revelations of grandeur and beauty are wasting
themselves for ever—forests teeming with gorgeous life,

floral wildernesses hidden inaccessibly ; whilst, at the
same time, in contra-position to that evil, behold a
corresponding evil—viz. that with equal prodigality
the great capacities of enjoyment are running also to
5 waste, and are everywhere burning out unexercised—
waste, in short, in the world of things *enjoyable*, balanced
by an equal waste in the organs and the machineries of
enjoyment ! This picture—would it not fret the heart
of an Englishman ? Some years (say twenty) after the
10 era of my own entrance at that Oxford which then
furnished me with records so painful of slight regard
to our national literature, behold at the court of
London a French ambassador, a man of genius blazing
(as some people thought) with nationality, but, in fact,
15 with something inexpressibly nobler and deeper—viz.
patriotism. For true and unaffected patriotism will
show its love in a noble form by sincerity and truth.
But nationality, as I have always found, is mean ; is
dishonest ; is ungenerous ; is incapable of candour ;
20 and, being continually besieged with temptations to
falsehood, too often ends by becoming habitually
mendacious. This Frenchman above all things valued
literature : his own trophies of distinction were all won
upon that field : and yet, when called upon to review
25 the literature of Europe, he found himself conscientiously coerced into making his work a mere monument
to the glory of one man, and that man the son of a
hostile land. The name of Milton, in *his* estimate,
swallowed up all others. This Frenchman was Chateau-
30 briand. The personal splendour which surrounded
him gave a corresponding splendour to his act. And,
because he, as an ambassador, was a representative
man, this act might be interpreted as a representative
act. The tutelary genius of France in this instance

might be regarded as bending before that of England.
But homage so free, homage so noble, must be interpreted and received in a corresponding spirit of generosity. It was not, like the testimony of Balaam on
behalf of Israel, an unwilling submission to a hateful
truth : it was a concession, in the spirit of saintly
magnanimity, to an interest of human nature that, *as*
such, transcended by many degrees all considerations
merely national.

Now, then, with this unlimited devotion to one great
luminary of our literary system emblazoned so con-
spicuously in the testimony of a Frenchman—that is,
of one trained, and privileged to be a public enemy—
contrast the humiliating spectacle of young Englishmen
suffered (so far as their training is concerned) to ignore
the very existence of this mighty poet. Do I mean,
then, that it would have been advisable to place the
Paradise Lost, and the *Paradise Regained*, and the
Samson, in the library of schoolboys ? By no means.
That mode of sensibility which deals with the Miltonic
sublimity is rarely developed in boyhood. And these
divine works should in prudence be reserved to the
period of mature manhood. But then it should be
made known that they *are* so reserved, and upon what
principle of reverential regard for the poet himself.
In the meantime, selections from Milton, from Dryden,
from Pope, and many other writers, though not everywhere appreciable by those who have but small experience of life, would not generally transcend the intellect
or sensibility of a boy sixteen or seventeen years old.

The reproach fell heavily, as my own limited experience inclined me to fear, upon most of our great public
schools, otherwise so admirably conducted. But from
the Manchester Grammar School any such reproach

altogether rebounded. My very first conversation with
the boys had arisen naturally upon a casual topic, and
had shown them to be tolerably familiar with the outline of the Christian polemics in the warfare with Jew,
5 Mahometan, Infidel, and Sceptic. But this was an exceptional case ; and naturally it happened that most
of us sought for the ordinary subjects of our conversational discussions in literature—viz. in our own native
literature. Here it was that I learned to feel a deep
10 respect for my new school-fellows : deep it was, then ;
and a larger experience has made it deeper. I have
since known many literary men ; men whose profession
was literature ; who were understood to have dedicated
themselves to literature ; and who sometimes had with
15 some one special section or little nook of literature an
acquaintance critically minute. But amongst such men
I have found but three or four who had a knowledge
which came as near to what I should consider a comprehensive knowledge as really existed amongst those boys
20 collectively. What one boy had not, another had ; and
thus, by continual intercourse, the fragmentary contribution of one being integrated by the fragmentary
contributions of others, gradually the attainments of
each separate individual became, in some degree, the
25 collective attainments of the whole senior common
room. It is true, undoubtedly, that some parts of
literature were inaccessible, simply because the books
were inaccessible to boys at school—for instance,
Froissart in the old translation by Lord Berners, now
30 more than three centuries old ; and some parts were,
to the young, essentially repulsive. But, measuring the
general qualifications by that standard which I have
since found to prevail amongst professional *litterateurs,*
I felt more respectfully towards the majority of my

senior school-fellows than ever I had fancied it possible
that I should find occasion to feel towards any boys
whatever. My intercourse with those amongst them
who had any conversational talents greatly stimulated
my intellect.

But now, at last, came over me, from the mere excess
of bodily suffering and mental disappointments, a frantic
and rapturous re-agency. In the United States the
case is well known, and many times has been described
by travellers, of that furious instinct which, under a
secret call for saline variations of diet, drives all the
tribes of buffaloes for thousands of miles to the common
centre of the " Salt-licks." Under such a compulsion
does the locust, under such a compulsion does the leem-
ing, traverse its mysterious path. They are deaf to
danger, deaf to the cry of battle, deaf to the trumpets
of death. Let the sea cross their path, let armies with
artillery bar the road, even these terrific powers can
arrest only by destroying ; and the most frightful
abysses, up to the very last menace of engulfment, up
to the very instant of absorption, have no power to
alter or retard the line of their inexorable advance.

Such an instinct it was, such a rapturous command
—even so potent, and alas ! even so blind—that, under
the whirl of tumultuous indignation and of new-born
hope, suddenly transfigured my whole being. In the
twinkling of an eye, I came to an adamantine resolution
—not as if issuing from any act or any choice of my
own, but as if passively received from some dark
oracular legislation external to myself. That I would
elope from Manchester—this was the resolution.
Abscond would have been the word, if I had meditated
anything criminal. But whence came the indignation,

and the hope ?   The indignation arose naturally against
my three tormentors (guardian, Archididascalus, and
the professor of tigrology) ; for those who *do* substantially co-operate to one result, however little designing
5 it, unavoidably the mind unifies as a hostile confederacy.
But the hope—how shall I explain *that* ?   Was it the
first-born of the resolution, or was the resolution the
first-born of the hope ?   Indivisibly they went together,
like thunder and lightning ; or each interchangeably ran
10 before and after the other.   Under that transcendent
rapture which the prospect of sudden liberation let
loose, all that natural anxiety which should otherwise
have interlinked itself with my anticipations was actually drowned in the blaze of joy, as the light of the
15 planet Mercury is lost and confounded on sinking too
far within the blaze of the solar beams.   Practically I
felt no care at all stretching beyond two or three weeks.
Not as being heedless and improvident ; my tendencies
lay generally in the other direction.   No ; the cause
20 lurked in what Wordsworth, when describing the festal
state of France during the happy morning-tide of her
First Revolution (1788-90), calls " *the senselessness of
joy* " : this it was, joy—headlong—frantic—irreflective
—and (as Wordsworth truly calls it), for that very
25 reason, *sublime*—which swallowed up all capacities of
rankling care or heart-corroding doubt.   I was, I had
been long, a captive : I was in a house of bondage :
one fulminating word—*Let there be freedom*—spoken
from some hidden recess in my own will, had as by
30 an earthquake rent asunder my prison gates.   At any
minute I could walk out.   Already I trod by anticipation
the sweet pastoral hills, already I breathed gales of the
everlasting mountains, that to my feelings blew from the
garden of Paradise ; and in that vestibule of an earthly

heaven it was no more possible for me to see vividly
or in any lingering detail the thorny cares which might
hereafter multiply around me than amongst the roses
of June, and on the loveliest of June mornings, I could
gather depression from the glooms of the last December. 5

To go was settled. But *when* and *whither ?* *When*
could have but one answer ; for on more reasons than
one I needed summer weather, and as much of it as
possible. Besides that, when August came, it would
bring along with it my own birthday : now, one codicil 10
in my general vow of freedom had been that my seven-
teenth birthday should not find me at school. Still I
needed some trifle of preparation. Especially I needed
a little money. I wrote, therefore, to the only con-
fidential friend that I had—viz. Lady Carbery. Origin- 15
ally, as early friends of my mother's, both she and Lord
Carbery had distinguished me at Bath and elsewhere,
for some years, by flattering attentions ; and, for the
last three years in particular, Lady Carbery, a young
woman some ten years older than myself, and who 20
was as remarkable for her intellectual pretensions as she
was for her beauty and her benevolence, had maintained a correspondence with me upon questions of
literature. She thought too highly of my powers and
attainments, and everywhere spoke of me with an 25
enthusiasm that, if I had been five or six years older,
and had possessed any personal advantages, might have
raised smiles at her expense. To her I now wrote,
requesting the loan of five guineas. A whole week
passed without any answer. This perplexed and made 30
me uneasy : for her ladyship was rich by a vast fortune
removed entirely from her husband's control ; and, as
I felt assured, would have cheerfully sent me twenty
times the sum asked, unless her sagacity had suggested

some suspicion (which seemed impossible) of the real purposes which I contemplated in the employment of the five guineas. Could I incautiously have said anything in my own letter tending that way ? Certainly not ; then why—— But at that moment my speculations were cut short by a letter bearing a coroneted seal. It was from Lady Carbery, of course, and enclosed ten guineas instead of five. Slow in those days were the mails ; besides which, Lady Carbery happened to be down at the seaside, whither my letter had been sent after her. Now, then, including my own pocket-money, I possessed a dozen guineas ; which seemed sufficient for my immediate purpose ; and all ulterior emergencies, as the reader understands, I trampled under foot. This sum, however, spent at inns on the most economic footing, could not have held out for much above a calendar month ; and, as to the plan of selecting secondary inns, these are not always cheaper ; but the main objection is that in the solitary stations amongst the mountains (Cambrian no less than Cumbrian) there is often no choice to be found : the high-priced inn is the only one. Even this dozen of guineas it became necessary to diminish by three. The age of " vails " and perquisites to three or four servants at any gentleman's house where you dined—this age, it is true, had passed away by thirty years perhaps. But that flagrant abuse had no connection at all with the English custom of distributing money amongst that part of the domestics whose daily labours may have been increased by a visitor's residence in the family for some considerable space of time. This custom (almost peculiar, I believe, to the English gentry) is honourable and just. I personally had been trained by my mother, who detested sordid habits, to look upon it as ignominious

in a gentleman to leave a household without acknowledging the obliging services of those who cannot openly
remind him of their claims. On this occasion, mere
necessity compelled me to overlook the housekeeper :
for to her I could not have offered less than two or three 5
guineas ; and, as she was a fixture, I reflected that I
might send it at some future period. To three inferior
servants I found that I ought not to give less than one
guinea each : so much, therefore, I left in the hands of
G——, the most honourable and upright of boys ; since 10
to have given it myself would have been prematurely
to publish my purpose. These three guineas deducted,
I still had nine, or thereabouts. And now all things
were settled, except one : the *when* was settled, and the
how ; but not the *whither*. That was still *sub judice*. 15

My plan originally had been to travel northwards—
viz. to the region of the English Lakes. That little
mountainous district, lying stretched like a pavilion
between four well-known points,—viz. the small towns
of Ulverstone and Penrith as its two poles, south and 20
north ; between Kendal, again, on the east, and Egre-
mont on the west—measuring on the one diameter
about forty miles, and on the other perhaps thirty-five
—had for me a secret fascination, subtle, sweet, fantastic, and even from my seventh or eighth year spiritu- 25
ally strong. The southern section of that district, about
eighteen or twenty miles long, which bears the name
of Furness, figures in the eccentric geography of English
law as a section of Lancashire, though separated from
that county by the estuary of Morecambe Bay : and 30
therefore, as Lancashire happened to be my own native
county, I had from childhood, on the strength of this
mere legal fiction, cherished as a mystic privilege,
slender as a filament of air, some fraction of denizenship

in the fairy little domain of the English Lakes. The
major part of these lakes lies in Westmoreland and
Cumberland : but the sweet reposing little water of
Esthwaite, with its few emerald fields, and the grander
one of Coniston, with the sublime cluster of mountain
groups, and the little network of quiet dells lurking
about its head all the way back to Grasmere, lie in or
near the upper chamber of Furness ; and all these,
together with the ruins of the once glorious abbey, had
been brought out not many years before into sunny
splendour by the great enchantress of that generation
—Anne Radcliffe.   But more even than Anne Radcliffe
had the landscape painters, so many and so various,
contributed to the glorification of the English lake
district ; drawing out and impressing upon the heart
the sanctity of repose in its shy recesses—its alpine
grandeurs in such passes as those of Wastdale-head,
Langdale-head, Borrowdale, Kirkstone, Hawsdale, etc.,
together with the monastic peace which seems to brood
over its peculiar form of pastoral life, so much nobler
(as Wordsworth notices) in its stern simplicity and continual conflict with danger hidden in the vast draperies
of mist overshadowing the hills, and amongst the armies
of snow and hail arrayed by fierce northern winters,
than the effeminate shepherd's life in the classical
Arcadia, or in the flowery pastures of Sicily.

Amongst these attractions that drew me so strongly
to the Lakes, there had also by that time arisen in this
lovely region the deep deep magnet (as to me *only* in
all this world it then was) of William Wordsworth.
Inevitably this close connection of the poetry which
most of all had moved me with the particular region and
scenery that most of all had fastened upon my affections, and led captive my imagination, was calculated,

under ordinary circumstances, to impress upon my
fluctuating deliberations a summary and decisive bias.
But the very depth of the impressions which had been
made upon me, either as regarded the poetry or the
scenery, was too solemn and (unaffectedly I may say it) 5
too spiritual, to clothe itself in any hasty or chance
movement as at all adequately expressing its strength,
or reflecting its hallowed character. If you, reader,
were a devout Mahometan, throwing gazes of mystical
awe daily towards Mecca, or were a Christian devotee 10
looking with the same rapt adoration to St Peter's at
Rome, or to El Kodah, the Holy City of Jerusalem (so
called even amongst the Arabs, who hate both Christian and Jew)—how painfully would it jar upon your
sensibilities if some friend, sweeping past you upon a 15
high road, with a train (according to the circumstances)
of dromedaries or of wheel carriages, should suddenly
pull up, and say, " Come, old fellow, jump up alongside
of me ; I'm off for the Red Sea, and here's a spare
dromedary," or " Off for Rome, and here's a well- 20
cushioned barouche." Seasonable and convenient it
might happen that the invitation were ; but still it
would shock you that a journey which, with or without your consent, could not *but* assume the character
eventually of a saintly pilgrimage, should arise and take 25
its initial movement upon a casual summons, or upon
a vulgar opening of momentary convenience. In the
present case, under no circumstances should I have
dreamed of presenting myself to Wordsworth. The
principle of " veneration " (to speak phrenologically) 30
was by many degrees too strong in me for any such
overture on my part. Hardly could I have found the
courage to meet and to answer such an overture coming
from *him*. I could not even tolerate the prospect (as

a bare possibility) of Wordsworth's hearing my name first of all associated with some case of pecuniary embarrassment. And, apart from all *that*, it vulgarised the whole "interest" (no other term can I find to express the case collectively)—the whole "interest" of poetry and the enchanted land—equally it vulgarised person and thing, the vineyard and the vintage, the gardens and the ladies, of the Hesperides, together with all their golden fruitage, if I should rush upon them in a hurried and thoughtless state of excitement. I remembered the fine caution on this subject involved in a tradition preserved by Pausanias. Those (he tells us) who visited by night the great field of Marathon (where at certain times phantom cavalry careered, flying and pursuing) in a temper of vulgar sight-seeking, and under no higher impulse than the degrading one of curiosity, were met and punished severely in the dark, by the same sort of people, I presume, as those who handled Falstaff so roughly in the venerable shades of Windsor : whilst loyal visitors, who came bringing a true and filial sympathy with the grand deeds of their Athenian ancestors, who came as children of the same hearth, met with the most gracious acceptance, and fulfilled all the purposes of a pilgrimage or sacred mission. Under my present circumstances, I saw that the very motives of love and honour, which would have inclined the scale so powerfully in favour of the northern lakes, were exactly those which drew most heavily in the other direction—the circumstances being what they were as to hurry and perplexity. And just at that moment suddenly unveiled itself another powerful motive against taking the northern direction—viz. consideration for my mother—which made my heart recoil from giving her too great a shock ; and in what other way

could it be mitigated than by my personal presence in a
case of emergency ? For such a purpose North Wales
would be the best haven to make for, since the road
thither from my present home lay through Chester—
where at that time my mother had fixed her residence. 5

If I had hesitated (and hesitate I did very sincerely)
about such a mode of expressing the consideration due
to my mother, it was not from any want of decision in
my feeling, but really because I feared to be taunted
with this act of tenderness, as arguing an exaggerated 10
estimate of my own importance in my mother's eyes.
To be capable of causing any alarming shock, must I
not suppose myself an object of special interest ? No :
I did not agree to that inference. But no matter.
Better to stand ten thousand sneers than one abiding 15
pang, such as time could not abolish, of bitter self-
reproach. So I resolved to face this taunt without
flinching, and to steer a course for St John's Priory—
my mother's residence near Chester.

At length all was ready. Midsummer, like an army 20
with banners, was moving through the heavens ; already
the longest day had passed ; those arrangements, few
and imperfect, through which I attempted some partial
evasion of disagreeable contingencies likely to arise, had
been finished : what more remained for me to do of 25
things that I was able to do ? None ; and yet, though
now at last free to move off, I lingered ; lingered as
under some sense of dim perplexity, or even of relenting
love for the very captivity itself which I was making so
violent an effort to abjure, but more intelligibly for all 30
the external objects, living or inanimate, by which that
captivity had been surrounded and gladdened. What I
was hastening to desert, nevertheless I grieved to desert ;
and, but for the foreign letter, I might have long

continued to loiter and procrastinate. That, however,
through various and urgent motives which it suggested,
quickened my movements ; and the same hour which
brought this letter into my hands witnessed my resolu-
5 tion (uttered *audibly* to myself in my study) that early
on the next day I would take my departure. A day,
therefore, had at length arrived, had somewhat suddenly arrived, which would be the last, the very last,
on which I should make my appearance in the school.

10　　It is a just and a feeling remark of Dr Johnson's that
we never do anything consciously for the last time (of
things, that is to say, which we have been long in the
habit of doing) without sadness of heart. The secret
sense of a farewell or testamentary act I carried along
15 with me into every word or deed of this memorable day.
Agent or patient, singly or one of a crowd, I heard for
ever some sullen echo of valediction in every change,
casual or periodic, that varied the revolving hours from
morning to night. Most of all I felt this valedictory
20 sound as a pathetic appeal when the closing hour of
five P.M. brought with it the solemn evening service of
the English Church—read by Mr Lawson ; read now,
as always, under a reverential stillness of the entire
school. Already in itself, without the solemnity of
25 prayers, the decaying light of the dying day suggests a
mood of pensive and sympathetic sadness. And, if the
changes in the light are less impressively made known
so early as five o'clock in the depth of summer-tide, not
the less we are sensible of being as near to the hours of
30 repose, and to the secret dangers of the night, as if
the season were midwinter. With deepest sympathy I
accompanied the prayer against the perils of darkness—
perils that I seemed to see, in the ambush of midnight
solitude, brooding around the beds of sleeping nations ;

perils from even worse forms of darkness shrouded within the recesses of blind human hearts; perils from temptations weaving unseen snares for our footing; perils from the limitations of our own misleading knowledge. 5

Prayers had finished. The school had dissolved itself. Six o'clock came, seven, eight. By three hours nearer stood the dying day to its departure. By three hours nearer, therefore, stood we to that darkness which our English liturgy calls into such symbolic grandeur, 10 as hiding beneath its shadowy mantle all perils that besiege our human infirmity. But in summer, in the immediate suburbs of midsummer, the vast scale of the heavenly movements is read in their slowness. Time becomes the expounder of Space. And now, though 15 eight o'clock had struck, the sun was still lingering above the horizon: the light, broad and gaudy, having still two hours of travel to face before it would assume that tender fading hue prelusive to the twilight. Now came the last official ceremony of the day: the students 20 were all mustered; and the names of all were challenged according to the order of precedence. My name, as usual, came first. Stepping forward, I passed Mr Lawson, and bowed to him, looking earnestly in his face, and saying to myself, "He is old and infirm, and 25 in this world I shall not see him again." I was right; I never *did* see him again, nor ever shall. He looked at me complacently; smiled placidly; returned my salutation (not knowing it to be my valediction); and we parted for ever. Intellectually, I might not have 30 seen cause to reverence him in any emphatic sense. But very sincerely I respected him as a conscientious man, faithful to his duties, and as, even in his latter ineffectual struggle with these duties, inflicting more

suffering upon himself than upon others ; finally, I
respected him as a sound and accurate (though not
brilliant) scholar.   Personally I owed him much gratitude ; for he had been uniformly kind to me, and had
5 allowed me such indulgences as lay in his power ; and
I grieved at the thought of the mortification I should
inflict upon him.

The morning came which was to launch me into the
world ; that morning from which, and from its con-
10 sequences, my whole succeeding life has, in many
important points, taken its colouring.   At half after
three I rose, and gazed with deep emotion at the ancient
collegiate church, " dressed in earliest light," and
beginning to crimson with the deep lustre of a cloudless
15 July morning.   I was firm and immovable in my purpose, but yet agitated by anticipation of uncertain
danger and troubles.   To this agitation the deep peace
of the morning presented an affecting contrast, and in
some degree a medicine.   The silence was more pro-
20 found than that of midnight : and to me the silence of
a summer morning is more touching than all other
silence, because, the light being broad and strong as
that of noonday at other seasons of the year, it seems
to differ from perfect day chiefly because man is not
25 yet abroad, and thus the peace of nature, and of the
innocent creatures of God, seems to be secure and deep
only so long as the presence of man, and his unquiet
spirit, are not there to trouble its sanctity.   I dressed
myself, took my hat and gloves, and lingered a little
30 in the room.   For nearly a year and a half this room
had been my " pensive citadel " : here I had read and
studied through all the hours of night ; and, though
true it was that, for the latter part of this time, I had
lost my gaiety and peace of mind during the strife and

fever of contention with my guardian, yet, on the other hand, as a boy passionately fond of books, and dedicated to intellectual pursuits, I could not fail to have enjoyed many happy hours in the midst of general dejection.

I shed tears as I looked round on the chair, hearth, writing-table, and other familiar objects, knowing too certainly that I looked upon them for the last time. Whilst I write this, it is nineteen [1] years ago ; and yet, at this moment, I see, as if it were but yesterday, the lineaments and expressions of the object on which I fixed my parting gaze. It was the picture of a lovely lady, which hung over the mantelpiece ; the eyes and mouth of which were so beautiful, and the whole countenance so radiant with divine tranquillity, that I had a thousand times laid down my pen, or my book, to gather consolation from it, as a devotee from his patron saint. Whilst I was yet gazing upon it, the deep tones of the old church clock proclaimed that it was six o'clock. I went up to the picture, kissed it, then gently walked out, and closed the door for ever.

THE BORE AT CHESTER

In the infancy of its course amongst the Denbighshire mountains, the river Dee (famous in our pre-Norman history for the earliest parade of English monarchy) is wild and picturesque ; and even below my mother's Priory it wears a character of interest. But, a mile or so nearer to its mouth, when leaving Chester for Parkgate, it becomes miserably tame ; and the several reaches of the river take the appearance of formal canals. On the right bank of the river runs an artificial mound,

[1] Written in the August of 1821. (D. Q.).

called the Cop. It was, I believe, originally a Danish work ; and certainly its name is Danish (*i.e.* Icelandic, or old Danish), and the same from which is derived our architectural word *coping*. Upon this bank I was walking, and throwing my gaze along the formal vista presented by the river. Some trifle of anxiety might mingle with this gaze at the first, lest perhaps Philistines might be abroad ; for it was just possible that I had been watched. But I have generally found that, if you are in quest of some certain escape from Philistines of whatsoever class—sheriff-officers, bores, no matter what—the surest refuge is to be found amongst hedgerows and fields, amongst cows and sheep : in fact, cows are amongst the gentlest of breathing creatures ; none show more passionate tenderness to their young when deprived of them ; and, in short, I am not ashamed to profess a deep love for these quiet creatures. On the present occasion there were many cows grazing in the fields below the Cop : but all along the Cop itself I could descry no person whatever answering to the idea of a Philistine : in fact, there was nobody at all, except one woman, apparently middle-aged (meaning by *that* from thirty-five to forty-five), neatly dressed, though perhaps in rustic fashion, and by no possibility belonging to any class of my enemies ; for already I was near enough to see so much. This woman might be a quarter of a mile distant, and was steadily advancing towards me—face to face. Soon, therefore, I was beginning to read the character of her features pretty distinctly ; and her countenance naturally served as a mirror to echo and reverberate my own feelings, consequently my own horror (horror without exaggeration it was), at a sudden uproar of tumultuous sounds rising clamorously ahead. *Ahead* I mean in relation to my-

self, but to *her* the sound was from the rear. Our
situation was briefly this. Nearly half a mile behind
the station of the woman, that reach of the river along
which we two were moving came to an abrupt close ;
so that the next reach, making nearly a right-angled 5
turn, lay entirely out of view. From this unseen reach
it was that the angry clamour, so passionate and so
mysterious, arose : and I, for *my* part, having never
heard such a fierce battling outcry, nor even heard *of*
such a cry, either in books or on the stage, in prose or 10
verse, could not so much as whisper a guess to myself
upon its probable cause. Only this I felt, that blind,
unorganised nature it must be—and nothing in human
or in brutal wrath—that could utter itself by such
an anarchy of sea-like uproars. What was it ? Where 15
was it ? Whence was it ? Earthquake was it ? convulsion of the steadfast earth ? or was it the breaking
loose from ancient chains of some deep morass like that
of Solway ? More probable it seemed that the ἄνω
ποτάμων of Euripides (the flowing backwards of rivers 20
to their fountains) now, at last, after ages of expectation, had been suddenly realised. Not long I needed to
speculate ; for within half a minute, perhaps, from the
first arrest of our attention, the proximate cause of this
mystery declared itself to our eyes, although the remote 25
cause (the hidden cause of that visible cause) was still
as dark as before. Round that right-angled turn which
I have mentioned as wheeling into the next succeeding
reach of the river, suddenly as with the trampling of
cavalry—but all dressing accurately—and the water at 30
the outer angle sweeping so much faster than that at the
inner angle as to keep the front of advance rigorously
in line, violently careered round into our own placid
watery vista a huge charging block of waters, filling the

whole channel of the river, and coming down upon us
at the rate of forty miles an hour. Well was it for
us, myself and that respectable rustic woman, us the
Deucalion and Pyrrha of this perilous moment, sole
survivors apparently of the deluge (since by accident
there was at that particular moment on that particular
Cop nothing else to survive), that by means of this Cop,
and of ancient Danish hands (possibly not yet paid for
their work), we *could* survive. In fact, this watery
breastwork, a perpendicular wall of water carrying
itself as true as if controlled by a mason's plumb-line,
rode forward at such a pace that obviously the fleetest
horse or dromedary would have had no chance of
escape. Many a decent railway even, among railways
since born its rivals, would not have had above the
third of a chance. Naturally, I had too short a time
for observing much or accurately ; and universally I am
a poor hand at observing ; else I should say that this
riding block of crystal waters did not gallop, but went
at a long trot ; yes, long trot—that most frightful of
paces in a tiger, in a buffalo, or in a rebellion of waters.
Even a ghost, I feel convinced, would appal me more
if coming up at a long diabolical trot than at a canter
or gallop. The first impulse to both of us was derived
from cowardice ; cowardice the most abject and selfish.
Such is man, though a Deucalion elect ; such is woman,
though a decent Pyrrha. Both of us ran like hares ;
neither did I, Deucalion, think of poor Pyrrha at all
for the first sixty seconds. Yet, on the other hand,
why *should* I ? It struck me seriously that St George's
Channel (and, if so, beyond a doubt, the Atlantic
Ocean) had broke loose, and was, doubtless, playing the
same insufferable gambols upon all rivers along a sea-
board of six to seven thousand miles ; in which case,

as all the race of woman must be doomed, how romantic
a speculation it was for me, sole relic of literature, to
think specially of one poor Pyrrha, probably very
illiterate, whom I had never yet spoken to ! That idea
pulled me up. *Not spoken to her ?* Then I *would* speak
to her ; and the more so because the sound of the
pursuing river told me that flight was useless. And,
besides, if any reporter or sub-editor of some Chester
chronicle should, at this moment, with his glass be
sweeping the Cop, and discover me flying under these
unchivalrous circumstances, he might gibbet me to all
eternity. Halting, therefore (and really I had not run
above eighty or a hundred steps), I waited for my
solitary co-tenant of the Cop. She was a little blown
by running, and could not easily speak ; besides which,
at the very moment of her coming up, the preternatural
column of waters, running in the very opposite direction
to the natural current of the river, came up with us,
ran by with the ferocious uproar of a hurricane, sent
up the sides of the Cop a salute of waters, as if hypo-
critically pretending to kiss our feet, but secretly understood by all parties as a vain treachery for pulling us
down into the flying deluge ; whilst all along both
banks the mighty refluent wash was heard as it rode
along, leaving memorials, by sight and by sound, of
its victorious power. But my female associate in this
terrific drama, what said she, on coming up with me ?
Or what said I ? For, by accident, I it was that spoke
first ; notwithstanding the fact, notorious and undeniable, that *I had never been introduced to her*. Here,
however, be it understood, as a case now solemnly
adjudicated and set at rest, that, in the midst of any
great natural convulsion—earthquake, suppose, water-
spout, tornado, or eruption of Vesuvius—it shall and

may be lawful in all time coming (any usage or tradition to the contrary notwithstanding) for two English people to communicate with each other, although, by affidavit made before two justices of the peace, it shall have been proved that no previous introduction had been possible : in all other cases the old statute of non-intercourse holds good.   Meantime, the present case, in default of more circumstantial evidence, might be regarded, if not as an earthquake, yet as ranking amongst the first-fruits or blossoms of an earthquake.   So I spoke without scruple.   All my freezing English reserve gave way under this boiling sense of having been so recently running for life : and then, again, suppose the water column should come back—riding *along with* the current, and no longer riding *against* it—in that case, we and all the County Palatine might soon have to run for our lives.   Under such threatenings of common peril, surely the παῤῥησία, or unlimited license of speech, ought spontaneously to proclaim itself without waiting for sanction.

So I asked her the meaning of this horrible tumult in the waters : how did she read the mystery ?   Her answer was, that, though she had never before seen such a thing, yet from her grandmother she had often heard of it ; and, if she had run before it, *that* was because *I* ran ; and a little, perhaps, because the noise frightened her.   What was it, then ? I asked.   " It was," she said, " *The Bore* ; and it was an affection to which only some few rivers here and there were liable ; and the Dee was one of these."   So ignorant was I that, until that moment, I had never heard of such a nervous affection in rivers.   Subsequently I found that, amongst English rivers, the neighbouring river Severn, a far more important stream, suffered at spring-tides the same kind of hysterics, and perhaps some few other rivers in this British Island ; but amongst Indian rivers only the Ganges.

FAREWELL TO WALES

The day on which I left Oswestry (convoyed for nearly five miles by my warmhearted friend) was a day of golden sunshine amongst the closing days of November. As truly as Jessica's moonlight (*Merchant of Venice*), this golden sunshine might be said to *sleep* upon the woods and the fields ; so awful was the universal silence, so profound the death-like stillness. It was a day belonging to a brief and pathetic season of farewell summer resurrection, which, under one name or other, is known almost everywhere. In North America it is called the " Indian Summer." In North Germany and Midland Germany it is called the " Old Wives' Summer," and more rarely the " Girls' Summer." It is that last brief resurrection of summer in its most brilliant memorials, a resurrection that has no root in the past nor steady hold upon the future, like the lambent and fitful gleams from an expiring lamp, mimicking what is called the " lightning before death " in sick patients, when close upon their end. There is the feeling of a conflict that has been going on between the lingering powers of summer and the strengthening powers of winter, not unlike that which moves by antagonist forces in some deadly inflammation hurrying forwards through fierce struggles into the final repose of mortification. For a time the equilibrium has been maintained between the hostile forces ; but at last the antagonism is overthrown ; the victory is accomplished for the powers that fight on the side of death ; simultaneously with the conflict, the pain of conflict has departed : and thenceforward the gentle process of collapsing life, no longer fretted by counter movements, slips away with holy peace into the noiseless deeps of the Infinite. So sweet, so ghostly, in its soft, golden smiles, silent as a dream, and quiet as the dying trance of a saint, faded through all its stages this departing day, along the whole length of which I bade farewell for many a year to Wales, and farewell to summer. In the very aspect and the sepulchral stillness of the motionless day, as solemnly it wore away through morning, noontide, afternoon, to meet the darkness that was hurrying to swallow up its beauty, I had a fantastic feeling as though I read the very language of resignation when bending before some irresistible agency. And at intervals I heard—in how different' a key !—the raving, the ever-lasting uproar, of that dreadful metropolis which at every step was coming nearer, and beckoning (as it seemed) to myself for purposes as dim, for issues as incalculable, as the path of cannon-shots fired at random and in darkness.

It was not late, but it was at least two hours after nightfall, when I reached Shrewsbury. Was I not liable to the suspicion of pedestrianism ? Certainly I was : but, even if my criminality had been more un-equivocally attested than it could be under the circum-stances, still there is a *locus penitentiæ* in such a case. Surely a man may repent of *any* crime ; and therefore of pedestrianism. I might have erred ; and a court of *piê poudré* (dusty foot) might have found the evi-dences of my crime on my shoes. Yet secretly I might be forming good resolutions to do so no more. Cer-tainly it looked like this, when I announced myself as a passenger " booked " for that night's mail. This

character at once installed me as rightfully a guest
of the inn, however profligate a life I might have previously led as a pedestrian. Accordingly I was received
with special courtesy; and it so happened that I was
received with something even like pomp. Four wax-
lights carried before me by obedient mutes, these were
but ordinary honours, meant (as old experience had
instructed me) for the first engineering step towards
effecting a lodgment upon the stranger's purse. In
fact the wax-lights are used by innkeepers, both abroad
and at home, to " try the range of their guns." If
the stranger submits quietly, as a good anti-pedestrian
ought surely to do, and fires no counter gun by way
of protest, then he is recognised at once as passively
within range, and amenable to orders. I have always
looked upon this fine of five or seven shillings (for wax
that you do not absolutely need) as a sort of inaugural
honorarium, entrance-money—what in jails used to be
known as *smart*-money—proclaiming me to be a man
comme il faut; and no toll in this world of tolls do I
pay so cheerfully. This, meantime, as I have said,
was too customary a form to confer much distinction.
The wax-lights, to use the magnificent Grecian phrase
ἐπομπεύε, moved pompously before me, as the holy,
holy fire, the inextinguishable fire and its golden hearth,
moved before Cæsar *semper* Augustus, when he made
his official or ceremonial *avatars*. Yet still this moved
along the ordinary channels of glorification : it rolled
along ancient grooves : I might say, indeed, like one
of the twelve Cæsars when dying, *Ut puto, Deus fio*
(It's my private opinion that at this very moment I am
turning into a god) : but still the metamorphosis was
not complete. *That* was accomplished when I stepped
into the sumptuous room allotted to me. It was a

ball-room of noble proportions—lighted, if I choose to
issue orders, by three gorgeous chandeliers, not basely
wrapped up in paper, but sparkling through all their
thickets of crystal branches, and flashing back the soft
5 rays of my tall waxen lights. There were, moreover,
two orchestras, which money would have filled within
thirty minutes. And, upon the whole, one thing only
was wanting—viz. a throne—for the completion of my
apotheosis.

10 It might be seven P.M. when I first entered upon my
kingdom. About three hours later I rose from my chair,
and with considerable interest looked out into the night.
For nearly two hours I had heard fierce winds arising ;
and the whole atmosphere had, by this time, become
15 one vast laboratory of hostile movements in all directions. Such a chaos, such a distracting wilderness of
dim sights, and of those awful " sounds that live in
darkness " (Wordsworth's *Excursion*), never had I
consciously witnessed. Rightly, and by a true instinct,
20 had I made my farewell adieus to summer. All through
the day, Wales and her grand mountain ranges—Pen-
maenmawr, Snowdon, Cader Idris—had divided my
thoughts with London. But now rose London—sole,
dark, infinite—brooding over the whole capacities of
25 my heart. Other object, other thought, I could not
admit. Long before midnight the whole household
(with the exception of a solitary waiter) had retired
to rest. Two hours, at least, were left to me, after
twelve o'clock had struck, for heartshaking reflections.
30 More than ever I stood upon the brink of a precipice ;
and the local circumstances around me deepened
and intensified these reflections, impressed upon them
solemnity and terror, sometimes even horror. It is
all but inconceivable to men of unyielding and callous

sensibilities how profoundly others find their reveries modified and overruled by the external characters of the immediate scene around them. Many a suicide that hung dubiously in the balances has been ratified, and carried into summary effect, through the forlorn, soul-revolting aspect of a crazy, dilapidated home. Oftentimes, without extravagance, the whole difference between a mind that spurns life and the same mind reconciled to life turns upon the outside features of that particular domestic scenery which hourly besieges the eyes. I, in this Shrewsbury hotel, naturally contemplated a group of objects tending to far different results. And yet in some respects they agreed.

The unusual dimensions of the rooms, especially their towering height, brought up continually and obstinately, through natural links of associated feelings or images, the mighty vision of London waiting for me afar off. An altitude of nineteen or twenty feet showed itself unavoidably upon an exaggerated scale in some of the smaller side-rooms, meant probably for cards or for refreshments. This single feature of the rooms—their unusual altitude, and the echoing hollowness which had become the exponent of that altitude—this one terrific feature (for terrific it was in the effect), together with the crowding and evanescent images of the flying feet that so often had spread gladness through these halls on the wings of youth and hope at seasons when every room rang with music : all this, rising in tumultuous vision, whilst the dead hours of night were stealing along—all around me, household and town, sleeping— and whilst against the windows more and more the storm outside was raving, and to all appearance endlessly growing—threw me into the deadliest condition of nervous emotion under contradictory forces, high over which predominated horror recoiling from that unfathomed abyss in London into which I was now so wilfully precipitating myself. Often I looked out and examined the night. Wild it was beyond all description, and dark as " the inside of a wolf's throat." But at intervals, when the wind, shifting continually, swept in such a direction as to clear away the vast curtain of vapour, the stars shone out, though with a light unusually dim and distant. Still, as I turned inwards to the echoing chambers, or outwards to the wild, wild night, I saw London expanding her visionary gates to receive me, like some dreadful mouth of Acheron (*Acherontis avari*). Thou also, Whispering Gallery! once again in those moments of conscious and wilful desolation didst to my ear utter monitorial sighs. For once again I was preparing to utter an irrevocable word, to enter upon one of those fatally tortuous paths of which the windings can never be unlinked.

Such thoughts, and visions without number corresponding to them, were moving across the *camera obscura* of my fermenting fancy, when suddenly I heard a sound of wheels; which, however, soon died off into some remote quarter. I guessed at the truth— viz. that it was the Holyhead Mail wheeling off on its primary duty of delivering its bags at the post-office. In a few minutes it was announced as having changed horses ; and off I was to London.

All the mails in the kingdom, with one solitary exception (that of Liverpool), in those days, were so arranged as to reach London early in the morning. Between the hours of four and six A.M., one after the other, according to their station upon the roll, all the mails from the N[orth], the E[ast], the W[est], the S[outh]—whence, according to some curious etymologists, comes the magical word *NEWS*—drove up successively to the post-office, and rendered up their heart-shaking budgets; none earlier than four o'clock, none later than six. I am speaking of days when all things moved slowly. The condition of the roads was then such that, in order to face it, a corresponding build of coaches hyperbolically massive was rendered necessary : the mails were upon principle made so strong as to be the heaviest of all carriages known to the wit or the experience of man ; and, from these joint evils of ponderous coaches and roads that were quagmires, it was impossible for even the picked breed of English coach-horses, all bone and blood, to carry forward their huge tonnage at a greater rate than six and a half miles an hour. Consequently, it cost eight-and-twenty massy hours for us, leaving Shrews-bury at two o'clock in the dead of night, to reach the General Post-office, and faithfully to deposit upon the threshing-floors of Lombard Street all that weight of love and hatred which Ireland had found herself able to muster through twenty-four hours in the great depôt of Dublin, by way of donation to England.

LONDON

On reflection, I have done myself some injustice. Not altogether without a plan had I been from the first ; and in coming along I had matured it. My success in such a plan would turn upon my chance of borrowing on personal security. £200, without counting any interest upon it, would sub-divide into four sums of £50. Now, what interval was it that divided me from my majority ? Simply an interval of four years. London, I knew or believed, was the dearest of all

cities for three items of expenditure : (1) servants'
wages ; (2) lodgings ; (3) dairy produce. In other
things, London was often cheaper than most towns.
Now, in a London street, having no pretensions beyond
5 those of decent respectability, it has always been
possible for the last half-century to obtain two furnished
rooms at a weekly cost of half a guinea. This sum
(or say £25) deducted would leave me annually about
the same sum for my other expenses. Too certainly
10 I knew that this would suffice. If, therefore, I could
obtain the £200, my plan was to withdraw from the
knowledge of all my connections until I should become
mei juris by course of law. In such a case, it is true
that I must have waived all the advantages, fancied
15 or real, small or great, from residence at a university.
But, as in fact I never drew the slightest advantage
or emolument from any university, my scheme when
realised would have landed me in the same point
which finally I attained by its failure. The plan was
20 simple enough, but it rested on the assumption that I
could melt the obduracy of money-lenders. On this
point I had both hopes and fears. But more irritating
than either was the *delay* which eventually I came to
recognise as an essential element in the policy of all
25 money-lenders : in that way only can they raise up
such claims on behalf of their law-agents as may be
fitted for sustaining their zeal.

.   .   .   .   .   .

I lost no time in opening the business which had
brought me to London. By ten A.M., an hour when
30 all men of business are presumed to be at their posts,
personally or by proxy, I presented myself at the
money-lender's office. My name was already known
there : for I had, by letters from Wales, containing very

plain and very accurate statements of my position in life and my pecuniary expectations (some of which statements it afterwards appeared that he had personally investigated and verified), endeavoured to win his favourable attention. 5

The money-lender, as it turned out, had one fixed rule of action. He never granted a personal interview to any man ; no, not to the most beloved of his clients. One and all—myself, therefore, among the crowd—he referred for information, and for the means of prose- 10 cuting any kind of negotiation, to an attorney, who called himself, on most days of the week, by the name of Brunell, but occasionally (might it perhaps be on *red-letter* days ?) by the more common name of Brown. Mr Brunell-Brown, or Brown-Brunell, had 15 located his hearth (if ever he had possessed one), and his household gods (when they were not in the custody of the sheriff), in Greek Street, Soho. The house was not in itself, supposing that its face had been washed now and then, at all disrespectable. But it wore an 20 unhappy countenance of gloom and unsocial fretfulness, due in reality to the long neglect of painting, cleansing, and in some instances of repairing. There were, however, no fractured panes of glass in the windows ; and the deep silence which invested the house, not only 25 from the absence of all visitors, but also of those common household functionaries, bakers, butchers, beer-carriers, sufficiently accounted for the desolation, by suggesting an excuse not strictly true—viz. that it might be tenantless. The house already had tenants 30 through the day, though of a noiseless order, and was destined soon to increase them.

Mr Brown-Brunell, after reconnoitring me through a narrow side-window (such as is often attached to front-

doors in London), admitted me cheerfully, and conducted me, as an honoured guest, to his private *officina
diplomatum* at the back of the house. From the expression of his face, but much more from the contra-
5 dictory and self-counteracting play of his features, you
gathered in a moment that he was a man who had
much to conceal, and much, perhaps, that he would
gladly forget. His eye expressed wariness against
surprise, and passed in a moment into irrepressible
10 glances of suspicion and alarm. No smile that ever
his face naturally assumed but was pulled short up by
some freezing counteraction, or was chased by some
close-following expression of sadness. One feature
there was of relenting goodness and nobleness in Mr
15 Brunell's character, to which it was that subsequently
I myself was most profoundly indebted for an asylum
that saved my life. He had the deepest, the most
liberal, and unaffected love of knowledge, but, above
all, of that specific knowledge which we call literature.
20 His own stormy (and no doubt oftentimes disgraceful)
career in life, that had entangled him in perpetual
feuds with his fellow-men, he ascribed, with bitter
imprecations, to the sudden interruption of his studies
consequent upon his father's violent death, and to the
25 necessity which threw him, at a boyish age, upon a
professional life in the lower branches of law—threw
him, therefore, upon daily temptations, by surrounding
him with opportunities for taking advantages not
strictly honourable, before he had formed any fixed
30 principles at all. From the very first, Mr Brunell had
entered zealously into such conversation with myself
as either gave openings for reviving his own delight-
ful remembrances of classic authors, or brought up
sometimes doubts for solution, sometimes perplexities

and cases of intricate construction for illustration and disentanglement.

I continued for seven or eight weeks to live most parsimoniously in lodgings. These lodgings, though barely decent in my eyes, ran away with at the least two-thirds of my remaining guineas. At length, whilst it was yet possible to reserve a solitary half-guinea towards the more urgent interest of finding daily food, I gave up my rooms, and, stating exactly the circumstances in which I stood, requested permission of Mr Brunell to make use of his large house as a nightly asylum from the open air. Parliament had not then made it a crime, next door to a felony, for a man to sleep out-of-doors (as some twenty years later was done by our benign legislators) ; as yet *that* was no crime. By the law I came to know sin, and looking back to the Cambrian hills from distant years, discovered to my surprise what a parliamentary wretch I had been in elder days, when I slept amongst cows on the open hill-sides. Lawful as yet this was ; but not, therefore, less full of misery. Naturally, then, I was delighted when Mr Brunell not only most readily assented to my request, but begged of me to come that very night, and turn the house to account as fully as I possibly could. The cheerfulness of such a concession brought with it one drawback. I now regretted that I had not, at a much earlier period, applied for this liberty ; since I might thus have saved a considerable fund of guineas, applicable, of course, to all urgent necessities, but at this particular moment to one of clamorous urgency—viz. the purchase of blankets. O ancient women, daughters of toil and suffering, amongst all the hardships and bitter inheritances of flesh that ye are called upon to face, not one—not even hunger—seems in my eyes comparable to that of nightly cold. To seek a refuge from cold in bed, and then, from the thin, gauzy texture of the miserable, worn-out blankets, "not to sleep a wink," as Wordsworth records of poor old women in Dorsetshire, where coals, from local causes, were at the very dearest—what a terrific enemy was *that* for poor old grandmothers to face in fight ! How feelingly I learned at this time, as heretofore I had learned on the wild hill-sides in Wales, what an unspeakable blessing is that of warmth ! A more killing curse there does not exist for man or woman than that bitter combat between the weariness that prompts sleep and the keen, searching cold that forces you from the first access of sleep to start up horror-stricken, and to seek warmth vainly in renewed exercise, though long since fainting under fatigue. However, even without blankets, it was a fine thing to have an asylum from the open air, and to be assured of this asylum as long as I was likely to want it.

Towards nightfall I went down to Greek Street, and found, on taking possession of my new quarters, that the house already contained one single inmate—a poor, friendless child, apparently ten years old ; but she seemed hunger-bitten ; and sufferings of that sort often make children look older than they are. From this forlorn child I learned that she had slept and lived there alone for some time before I came ; and great joy the poor creature expressed when she found that I was in future to be her companion through the hours of darkness. The house could hardly be called large— that is, it was not large on each separate storey ; but, having four storeys in all, it was large enough to impress vividly the sense of its echoing loneliness ; and, from the want of furniture, the noise of the rats made a prodigious uproar on the staircase and hall ; so that, amidst the real fleshly ills of cold and hunger, the forsaken child had found leisure to suffer still more from the self-created one of ghosts. Against these enemies I could promise her protection ; human companionship was in itself protection ; but of other and more needful aid I had, alas ! little to offer. We lay upon the floor, with a bundle of law-papers for a pillow, but with no other covering than a large horseman's cloak ; afterwards, however, we discovered in a garret an old sofa-cover, a small piece of rug, and some fragments of other articles, which added a little to our comfort. The poor child crept close to me for warmth, and for security against her ghostly enemies. When I was not more than usually ill, I took her into my arms, so that, in general, she was tolerably warm, and often slept when I could not ; for, during the last two months of my sufferings, I slept much in the daytime, and was apt to fall into transient dozings at all hours. But my sleep distressed me more than my watching ; for, besides the tumultuousness of my dreams (which were only not so awful as those which I shall have hereafter to describe as produced by opium), my sleep was never more than what is called *dog-sleep* ; so that I could hear myself moaning ; and very often I was awakened suddenly by my own voice. About this time, a hideous sensation began to haunt me as soon as I fell into a slumber, which has since returned upon me, at different periods of my life—viz. a sort of twitching (I knew not where, but apparently about the region of the stomach), which compelled me violently to throw out my feet for the sake of relieving it. This sensation coming on as soon as I began to sleep, and the effort to relieve it constantly awaking me, at length I slept only from exhaustion; and, through increasing weakness (as I said before), I was constantly falling asleep and constantly awaking. Too generally the very attainment of any deep repose seemed as if mechanically linked to some fatal necessity of self-interruption. It was as though a cup were gradually filled by the sleepy overflow of some natural fountain, the fulness of the cup expressing symbolically the completeness of the rest: but then, in the next stage of the process, it seemed as though the rush and torrent-like babbling of the redundant waters, when running over from every part of the cup, interrupted the slumber which in their earlier stage of silent gathering they had so naturally produced. Such and so regular in its swell and its collapse—in its tardy growth and its violent dispersion—did this endless alternation of stealthy sleep and stormy awaking travel through stages as natural as the increments of twilight, or the kindlings of the dawn: no rest that was not a prologue to terror; no sweet tremulous pulses of restoration that did not suddenly explode through rolling clamours of fiery disruption.

Meantime, the master of the house sometimes came in upon us suddenly, and very early; sometimes not till ten o'clock; sometimes not at all. He was in constant fear of arrest. Improving on the plan of Cromwell, every night he slept in a different quarter of London; and I observed that he never failed to examine, through a private window, the appearance of those who knocked at the door, before he would allow it to be opened. He breakfasted alone; indeed, his tea equipage would hardly have admitted of his hazarding an invitation to a second person, any more than the quantity of esculent *material*, which, for the most part, was little more than a roll, or a few biscuits, purchased on his road from the place where he had slept. Or, if he *had* asked a party, as I once learnedly observed to him, the several members of it must have *stood* in the relation to each other (not *sat* in any relation whatever) of succession, and not of co-existence ; in the relation of parts of time, and not of the parts of space. During his breakfast, I generally contrived a reason for loung-ing in ; and, with an air of as much indifference as I could assume, took up such fragments as might chance to remain ; sometimes, indeed, none at all remained. In doing this, I committed no robbery, except upon Mr Brunell himself, who was thus obliged, now and then, to send out at noon for an extra biscuit ; but he, through channels subsequently explained, was repaid a thousand-fold ; and, as to the poor child, *she* was never admitted into his study (if I may give that name to his chief depository of parchments, law-writings, etc.) ; that room was to her the Bluebeard room of the house, being regularly locked on his departure to dinner, about six o'clock, which usually was his final departure for the day. Whether this child were an illegitimate daughter of Mr Brunell, or only a servant, I could not ascertain ; she did not herself know ; but certainly she was treated altogether as a menial servant. No sooner did Mr Brunell make his appearance than she went below-stairs, brushed his shoes, coat, etc. ; and, except when she was summoned to run upon some errand, she never emerged from the dismal Tartarus of the kitchens to the upper air, until my welcome knock towards nightfall called up her little trembling footsteps to the front-door. Of her life during the daytime, how-ever, I knew little but what I gathered from her own account at night ; for, as soon as the hours of business commenced, I saw that my absence would be acceptable ; and, in general, therefore, I went off and sat in the parks or elsewhere until the approach of twilight.

But who, and what, meantime, was the master of the house himself ? Reader, he was one of those anomalous practitioners in lower departments of the law who, on prudential reasons, or from necessity, deny themselves all indulgence in the luxury of too delicate a conscience. In many walks of life a conscience is a more expensive encumbrance than a wife or a carriage ; and, as people talk of " laying down " their carriages, so I suppose my friend Mr Brunell had " laid down " his conscience for a time ; meaning, doubtless, to resume it as soon as he could afford it. He was an advertising attorney, who continually notified to the public, through the morning papers, that he undertook to raise loans for approved parties in what would generally be regarded as desperate cases—viz. where there was nothing better than *personal* security to offer. But, as he took good care to ascertain that there were ample funds in reversion to be counted on, or near connections that would not suffer the family name to be dishonoured, and as he insured the borrower's life over a sufficient period, the risk was not great ; and even of this the whole rested upon the actual money-lender, who stood aloof in the background, and never revealed himself to clients in his proper person, transacting all affairs through his proxies learned in the law—Mr Brunell or others. The inner economy of such a man's daily life would present a monstrous picture. Even with my limited opportunities for observing what went on, I saw scenes of intrigue and complex chicanery at which I sometimes smile to this day, and at which I smiled then in spite of my misery. My situation, however, at that time, gave me little experience, in my own person, of any qualities in Mr Brunell's character but such as did him honour ; and of his whole strange composition I ought to forget everything, but that towards me he was obliging, and, to the extent of his power, generous.

That power was not, indeed, very extensive. However, in common with the rats, I sat rent free ; and, as Dr Johnson has recorded that he never but once in his life had as much wall-fruit as he wished, so let me be grateful that, on that single occasion, I had as large a choice of rooms, or even of apartments, in a London mansion—viz., as I am now at liberty to add, at the north-west corner of Greek Street, being the house on that side the street nearest to Soho Square —as I could possibly desire. Except the Bluebeard room, which the poor child believed to be permanently haunted, and which, besides, was locked, all others, from the attics to the cellars, were at our service. " The world was all before us," and we pitched our tent for the night in any spot we might fancy.

DREAM-PHANTASIES

Introduction to Opium

IT is very long since I first took opium ; *so* long that, if it had been a trifling incident in my life, I might have forgotten its date : but cardinal events are not to be forgotten ; and, from circumstances connected with it,
5 I remember that this inauguration into the use of opium must be referred to the spring or to the autumn of 1804 ; during which seasons I was in London, having come thither for the first time since my entrance at Oxford. And this event arose in the following way :
10 From an early age I had been accustomed to wash my head in cold water at least once a day. Being suddenly seized with toothache, I attributed it to some relaxation caused by a casual intermission of that practice, jumped out of bed, plunged my head into a basin of
15 cold water, and with hair thus wetted went to sleep. The next morning, as I need hardly say, I awoke with excruciating rheumatic pains of the head and face, from which I had hardly any respite for about twenty days. On the twenty-first day I think it was, and on a Sunday,
20 that I went out into the streets ; rather to run away, if possible, from my torments, than with any distinct purpose of relief. By accident, I met a college acquaintance, who recommended opium. Opium ! dread agent of unimaginable pleasure and pain ! I had heard of it
25 as I had heard of manna or of ambrosia, but no further. How unmeaning a sound was opium at that time ! what solemn chords does it now strike upon my heart !

what heart-quaking vibrations of sad and happy remembrances! Reverting for a moment to these, I feel a mystic importance attached to the minutest circumstances connected with the place, and the time, and the man (if man he was), that first laid open to me 5 the paradise of opium-eaters. It was a Sunday afternoon, wet and cheerless; and a duller spectacle this earth of ours has not to show than a rainy Sunday in London. My road homewards lay through Oxford Street; and near "the *stately* Pantheon" (as Mr 10 Wordsworth has obligingly called it) I saw a druggist's shop. The druggist (unconscious minister of celestial pleasures!), as if in sympathy with the rainy Sunday, looked dull and stupid, just as any mortal druggist might be expected to look on a rainy London Sunday; 15 and, when I asked for the tincture of opium, he gave it to me as any other man might do; and, furthermore, out of my shilling returned to me what seemed to be real copper halfpence, taken out of a real wooden drawer. Nevertheless, and notwithstanding all such 20 indications of humanity, he has ever since figured in my mind as a beatific vision of an immortal druggist, sent down to earth on a special mission to myself. And it confirms me in this way of considering him that, when I next came up to London, I sought him near 25 the stately Pantheon, and found him not; and thus to me, who knew not his name (if, indeed, he had one), he seemed rather to have vanished from Oxford Street than to have flitted into any other locality, or (which some abominable man suggested) to have absconded 30 from the rent. The reader may choose to think of him as, possibly, no more than a sublunary druggist; it may be so, but my faith is better. I believe him to have evanesced. So unwillingly would I connect any mortal remembrances with that hour, and place, and creature that first brought me acquainted with the celestial drug.

Arrived at my lodgings, it may be supposed that I lost not a moment in taking the quantity prescribed. I was necessarily ignorant of the whole art and mystery of opium-taking ; and what I took I took under every disadvantage. But I took it ; and in an hour, O heavens ! what a revulsion ! what a resurrection, from its lowest depths, of the inner spirit ! what an apocalypse of the world within me ! That my pains had vanished was now a trifle in my eyes ; this negative effect was swallowed up in the immensity of those positive effects which had opened before me, in the abyss of divine enjoyment thus suddenly revealed. Here was a panacea, a φάρμακον νηπενθές for all human woes ; here was the secret of happiness, about which philosophers had disputed for so many ages, at once discovered ; happiness might now be bought for a penny, and carried in the waistcoat-pocket ; portable ecstasies might be had corked up in a pint-bottle ; and peace of mind could be sent down by the mail.

O just, subtle, and all-conquering opium ! that, to the hearts of rich and poor alike, for the wounds that will never heal, and for the pangs of grief that " tempt the spirit to rebel," bringest an assuaging balm ;— eloquent opium ! that with thy potent rhetoric stealest away the purposes of wrath, pleadest effectually for relenting pity, and through one night's heavenly sleep callest back to the guilty man the visions of his infancy, and hands washed pure from blood ;—O just and righteous opium ! that to the chancery of dreams summonest, for the triumphs of despairing innocence, false witnesses ; and confoundest perjury, and dost reverse the sentences of unrighteous judges;—thou buildest upon the bosom of darkness, out of the fantastic imagery of the brain, cities and temples, beyond the art of Phidias and Praxiteles, beyond the splendours of Babylon and Hekatómpylos; and, "from the anarchy 5 of dreaming sleep," callest into sunny light the faces of long-buried beauties, and the blessed household countenances, cleansed from the "dishonours of the grave." Thou only givest these gifts to man; and thou hast the keys of Paradise, O just, subtle, and mighty opium! 10

THE MALAY

If any man, poor or rich, were to say that he would tell us what had been the happiest day in his life, and the why and the wherefore, I suppose that we should all cry out, Hear him! hear him! As to the happiest day, that must be very difficult for any wise man to 15 assign; because any event that could occupy so distinguished a place in a man's retrospect of life, or be entitled to have shed a special, separate, and supreme felicity on any one day, ought to be of such an enduring character as that (accidents apart) it should have 20 continued to shed the same felicity, or one not distinguishably less, on very many years together. To the happiest *lustrum*, however, or even to the happiest *year*, a man may perhaps allowably point without discountenance from wisdom. This year, in *my* case, reader, 25 was the one which we have now reached; though it stood, I confess, as a parenthesis between years of a gloomier character. It was a year of brilliant water (to speak after the manner of jewellers), set, as it were, and insulated, in the gloomy umbrage of opium. 30 Strange as it may sound, I had a little before this time

descended suddenly, and without any considerable effort, from three hundred and twenty grains of opium (that is, eight thousand drops of laudanum) per day, to forty grains, or one-eighth part. Instantaneously, and
5 as if by magic, the cloud of profoundest melancholy which rested upon my brain, like some black vapours that I have seen roll away from the summit of a mountain, drew off in one week ; passed away with its murky banners as simultaneously as a ship that has been
10 stranded, and is floated off by a spring-tide,

That moveth altogether, if it move at all.

Now, then, I was again happy : I now took only one thousand drops of laudanum per day—and what was that ? A latter spring had come to close up the season
15 of youth. My brain performed its functions as healthily as ever before. I read Kant again ; and again I understood him, or fancied that I did. Again my feelings of pleasure expanded themselves to all around me ; and, if any man from Oxford or Cambridge, or from neither,
20 had been announced to me in my unpretending cottage, I should have welcomed him with as sumptuous a reception as so poor a man could offer. Whatever else might be wanting to a wise man's happiness, of laudanum I would have given him as much as he
25 wished, and in a silver-gilt, if not golden, cup. And, by the way, now that I speak of giving laudanum away, I remember about this time a little incident, which I mention because, trifling as it was, the reader will soon meet it again in my dreams, which it influenced more
30 fearfully than could be imagined. One day a Malay knocked at my door. What business a Malay could have to transact amongst the recesses of English mountains is not my business to conjecture ; but possibly he

was on his road to a seaport—viz., Whitehaven, Work-
ington, etc.—about forty miles distant.

The servant who opened the door to him was a young
girl, born and bred amongst the mountains, who had
never seen an Asiatic dress of any sort : his turban, 5
therefore, confounded her not a little ; and, as it turned
out that *his* knowledge of English was exactly commensurate with *hers* of Malay, there seemed to be an
impassable gulf fixed between all communication of
ideas, if either party had happened to possess any. In 10
this dilemma, the girl, recollecting the reputed learning
of her master (and, doubtless, giving me credit for a
knowledge of all the languages of the earth, besides,
perhaps, a few of the lunar ones), came and gave me to
understand that there was a sort of demon below, whom 15
she clearly imagined that my art could exorcise from
the house. The group which presented itself, arranged
as it was by accident, though not very elaborate, took
hold of my fancy and my eye more powerfully than
any of the statuesque attitudes or groups exhibited 20
in the ballets at the opera-house, though so osten-
tatiously complex. In a cottage kitchen, but not looking so much like *that* as a rustic hall of entrance, being
pannelled on the wall with dark wood, that from age
and rubbing resembled oak, stood the Malay, his turban 25
and loose trousers of dingy white relieved upon the
dark pannelling ; he had placed himself nearer to the
girl than she seemed to relish, though her native spirit
of mountain intrepidity contended with the feeling of
simple awe which her countenance expressed as she 30
gazed upon the tiger-cat before her. A more striking
picture there could not be imagined than the beautiful
English face of the girl, and its exquisite bloom, together
with her erect and independent attitude, contrasted

with the sallow and bilious skin of the Malay, veneered
with mahogany tints by climate and marine air, his
small, fierce, restless eyes, thin lips, slavish gestures
and adorations. Half-hidden by the ferocious-looking
5 Malay, was a little child from a neighbouring cottage,
who had crept in after him, and was now in the act of
reverting its head and gazing upwards at the turban
and the fiery eyes beneath it, whilst with one hand he
caught at the dress of the lovely girl for protection.

10 My knowledge of the oriental tongues is not remarkably extensive, being, indeed, confined to two words—
the Arabic word for barley, and the Turkish for opium
(*madjoon*), which I have learned from *Anastasius*. And,
as I had neither a Malay dictionary, nor even Adelung's
15 *Mithridates*, which might have helped me to a few
words, I addressed him in some lines from the *Iliad* ;
considering that, of such languages as I possessed,
the Greek, in point of longitude, came geographically
nearest to an oriental one. He worshipped me in a
20 devout manner, and replied in what I suppose to have
been Malay. In this way I saved my reputation as a
linguist with my neighbours ; for the Malay had no
means of betraying the secret. He lay down upon
the floor for about an hour, and then pursued his
25 journey. On his departure, I presented him, *inter
alia*, with a piece of opium. To him, as a native of
the East, I could have no doubt that opium was not
less familiar than his daily bread ; and the expression
of his face convinced me that it was. Nevertheless, I
30 was struck with some little consternation when I saw
him suddenly raise his hand to his mouth, and bolt
the whole, divided into three pieces, at one mouth-
ful. The quantity was enough to kill some half-dozen
dragoons, together with their horses, supposing neither

bipeds nor quadrupeds to be regularly trained opium-eaters. I felt some alarm for the poor creature ; but what could be done ? I had given him the opium in pure compassion for his solitary life, since, if he had travelled on foot from London, it must be nearly three 5 weeks since he could have exchanged a thought with any human being. Ought I to have violated the laws of hospitality by having him seized and drenched with an emetic, thus frightening him into a notion that we were going to sacrifice him to some English idol ? No : there 10 was clearly no help for it. The mischief, if any, was done. He took his leave, and for some days I felt anxious ; but, as I never heard of any Malay, or of any man in a turban, being found dead on any part of the very slenderly peopled road between Grasmere and White- 15 haven, I became satisfied that he was familiar with opium, and that I must doubtless have done him the service I designed, by giving him one night of respite from the pains of wandering.

Opium-Dreams

The first notice I had of any important change going 20 on in my physical economy was from the re-awaking of a state of eye oftentimes incident to childhood. I know not whether my reader is aware that many children have a power of painting, as it were, upon the darkness all sorts of phantoms : in some that power is 25 simply a mechanic affection of the eye ; others have a voluntary or semi-voluntary power to dismiss or summon such phantoms ; or, as a child once said to me, when I questioned him on this matter, " I can tell them to go, and they go ; but sometimes they come 30 when I don't tell them to come." He had by one-half as unlimited a command over apparitions as a Roman centurion over his soldiers. In the middle of 1817 this faculty became increasingly distressing to me: at night, when I lay awake in bed, vast processions moved along continually in mournful pomp; friezes of never-ending stories, that to my feelings were as sad and solemn as stories drawn from times before Œdipus or Priam, before Tyre, before Memphis. And, concurrently with this, a corresponding change took place in my dreams; a theatre seemed suddenly opened and lighted up within my brain, which presented nightly spectacles of more than earthly splendour. And the four following facts may be mentioned, as noticeable at this time :—

1. That, as the creative state of the eye increased, a sympathy seemed to arise between the waking and the dreaming states of the brain in one point—that whatsoever I happened to call up and to trace by a voluntary act upon the darkness was very apt to transfer itself to my dreams; and at length I feared to exercise this faculty; for, as Midas turned all things to gold that yet baffled his hopes and defrauded his human desires, so whatsoever things capable of being visually represented I did but think of in the darkness, immediately shaped themselves into phantoms for the eye ; and, by a process apparently no less inevitable, when thus once traced in faint and visionary colours, like writings in sympathetic ink, they were drawn out, by the fierce chemistry of my dreams, into insufferable splendour that fretted my heart.

2. This and all other changes in my dreams were accompanied by deep-seated anxiety and funereal melancholy, such as are wholly incommunicable by words. I seemed every night to descend—not meta-

phorically, but literally to descend—into chasms and
sunless abysses, depths below depths, from which it
seemed hopeless that I could ever re-ascend. Nor did
I, by waking, feel that I *had* re-ascended. Why should
I dwell upon this ? For indeed the state of gloom which
attended those gorgeous spectacles, amounting at last
to utter darkness, as of some suicidal despondency,
cannot be approached by words.

3. The sense of space, and in the end the sense of
time, were both powerfully affected. Buildings, land-
scapes, etc., were exhibited in proportions so vast as the
bodily eye is not fitted to receive. Space swelled, and
was amplified to an extent of unutterable and self-
repeating infinity. This disturbed me very much less
than the vast expansion of time. Sometimes I seemed
to have lived for seventy or a hundred years in one
night ; nay, sometimes had feelings representative of
a duration far beyond the limits of any human experience.

4. The minutest incidents of childhood, or forgotten
scenes of later years, were often revived. I could not
be said to recollect them ; for, if I had been told of
them when waking, I should not have been able to
acknowledge them as parts of my past experience.
But, placed as they were before me in dreams like
intuitions, and clothed in all their evanescent circumstances and accompanying feelings, I *recognised* them
instantaneously. I was once told by a near relative of
mine that, having in her childhood fallen into a river,
and being on the very verge of death but for the
assistance which reached her at the last critical moment,
she saw in a moment her whole life, clothed in its forgotten incidents, arrayed before her as in a mirror,
not successively, but simultaneously ; and she had a

faculty developed as suddenly for comprehending the
whole and every part. This, from some opium experiences, I can believe ; I have, indeed, seen the same thing
asserted twice in modern books, and accompanied by
5 a remark which probably is true—viz. that the dread
book of account which the Scriptures speak of is, in
fact, the mind itself of each individual. Of this, at
least, I feel assured, that there is no such thing as
ultimate *forgetting* ; traces once impressed upon the
10 memory are indestructible ; a thousand accidents
may and will interpose a veil between our present
consciousness and the secret inscriptions on the mind.
Accidents of the same sort will also rend away this
veil. But alike, whether veiled or unveiled, the in-
15 scription remains for ever ; just as the stars seem to
withdraw before the common light of day, whereas,
in fact, we all know that it is the light which is drawn
over them as a veil, and that they are waiting to be
revealed whenever the obscuring daylight itself shall
20 have withdrawn.

Having noticed these four facts as memorably dis-
tinguishing my dreams from those of health, I shall
now cite a few illustrative cases ; and shall then cite
such others as I remember, in any order that may give
25 them most effect as pictures to the reader.

I had been in youth, and ever since, for occasional
amusement, a great reader of Livy, whom I confess
that I prefer, both for style and matter, to any other
of the Roman historians ; and I had often felt as
30 solemn and appalling sounds, emphatically representative of Roman majesty, the two words so often
occurring in Livy, *Consul Romanus* ; especially when
the consul is introduced in his military character.
I mean to say that the words *king, sultan, regent*, etc.,

or any other titles of those who embody in their own persons the collective majesty of a great people, had less power over my reverential feelings. I had also, though no great reader of History, made myself critically familiar with one period of English history 5 —viz. the period of the Parliamentary War—having been attracted by the moral grandeur of some who figured in that day, and by the interesting memoirs which survive those unquiet times. Both these parts of my lighter reading, having furnished me 10 often with matter of reflection, now furnished me with matter for my dreams. Often I used to see, after painting upon the blank darkness a sort of re-hearsal whilst waking, a crowd of ladies, and perhaps a festival and dances. And I heard it said, or I said to 15 myself, "These are English ladies from the unhappy times of Charles I. These are the wives and daughters of those who met in peace, and sat at the same tables, and were allied by marriage or by blood; and yet, after a certain day in August 1642, never smiled upon 20 each other again, nor met but in the field of battle; and at Marston Moor, at Newbury, or at Naseby, cut asunder all ties of love by the cruel sabre, and washed away in blood the memory of ancient friendship." The ladies danced, and looked as lovely as at the court of 25 George IV. Yet even in my dream I knew that they had been in the grave for nearly two centuries. The pageant would suddenly dissolve; and, at a clapping of hands, would be heard the heart-shaking sound of *Consul Romanus*; and immediately came "sweeping 30 by," in gorgeous paludaments, Paullus or Marius, girt around by a company of centurions, with the crimson tunic hoisted on a spear, and followed by the *alalagmos* of the Roman legions.

Many years ago, when I was looking over Piranesi's *Antiquities of Rome*, Coleridge, then standing by, described to me a set of plates from that artist, called his " Dreams," and which record the scenery of his own
5 visions during the delirium of a fever. Some of these (I describe only from memory of Coleridge's account) represented vast Gothic halls ; on the floor of which stood mighty engines and machinery, wheels, cables, catapults, etc., expressive of enormous power put forth,
10 or resistance overcome. Creeping along the sides of the walls, you perceived a staircase ; and upon this, groping his way upwards, was Piranesi himself. Follow the stairs a little farther, and you perceive them reaching an abrupt termination, without any balustrade, and
15 allowing no step onwards to him who should reach the extremity, except into the depths below. Whatever is to become of poor Piranesi, at least you suppose that his labours must now in some way terminate. But raise your eyes, and behold a second flight of stairs
20 still higher, on which again Piranesi is perceived, by this time standing on the very brink of the abyss. Once again elevate your eye, and a still more aerial flight of stairs is descried ; and there, again, is the delirious Piranesi, busy on his aspiring labours : and so on, until
25 the unfinished stairs and the hopeless Piranesi both are lost in the upper gloom of the hall. With the same power of endless growth and self-reproduction did my architecture proceed in dreams. In the early stage of the malady, the splendours of my dreams were
30 indeed chiefly architectural ; and I beheld such pomp of cities and palaces as never yet was beheld by the waking eye, unless in the clouds. From a great modern poet I cite the part of a passage which describes, as an appearance actually beheld in the

clouds, what in many of its circumstances I saw frequently in sleep :—

> The appearance, instantaneously disclosed,
> Was of a mighty city—boldly say
> A wilderness of building, sinking far   5
> And self-withdrawn into a wondrous depth,
> Far sinking into splendour without end !
> Fabric it seemed of diamond and of gold,
> With alabaster domes and silver spires,
> And blazing terrace upon terrace, high   10
> Uplifted ; here, serene pavilions bright,
> In avenues disposed ; there, towers begirt
> With battlements that on their restless fronts
> Bore stars—illumination of all gems !
> By earthly nature had the effect been wrought   15
> Upon the dark materials of the storm
> Now pacified ; on them, and on the coves,
> And mountain-steeps and summits, whereunto
> The vapours had receded, taking there
> Their station under a cerulean sky.   20

The sublime circumstance—" that on their *restless* fronts bore stars"—might have been copied from my own architectural dreams, so often did it occur.

To my architecture succeeded dreams of lakes and silvery expanses of water : these haunted me so much that I feared lest some dropsical state or tendency of the brain might thus be making itself (to use a metaphysical word) *objective*, and that the sentient organ might be projecting itself as its own object. For two months I suffered greatly in my head—a part of my bodily structure which had hitherto been so clear from all touch or taint of weakness (physically, I mean) that I used to say of it, as the last Lord Orford said of his stomach, that it seemed likely to survive the rest of my person. Till now I had never felt a headache even, or any the slightest pain, except rheumatic pains caused by my own folly.

The waters gradually changed their character—from translucent lakes, shining like mirrors, they became seas and oceans. And now came a tremendous change, which, unfolding itself slowly like a scroll, through many months, promised an abiding torment ; and, in fact, it never left me, though recurring more or less inter-mittingly. Hitherto the human face had often mixed in my dreams, but not despotically, nor with any special power of tormenting. But now that affection which I have called the tyranny of the human face began to unfold itself. Perhaps some part of my London life might be answerable for this. Be that as it may, now it was that upon the rocking waters of the ocean the human face began to reveal itself ; the sea appeared paved with innumerable faces, upturned to the heavens ; faces, imploring, wrathful, despairing ; faces that surged upwards by thousands, by myriads, by generations : infinite was my agitation ; my mind tossed, as it seemed, upon the billowy ocean, and weltered upon the weltering waves.

May 1818.—The Malay has been a fearful enemy for months. Every night, through his means, I have been transported into Asiatic scenery. I know not whether others share in my feelings on this point ; but I have often thought that, if I were compelled to forego England, and to live in China, among Chinese manners and modes of life and scenery, I should go mad. The causes of my horror lie deep, and some of them must be common to others. Southern Asia, in general, is the seat of awful images and associations. As the cradle of the human race, if on no other ground, it would have a dim, reverential feeling connected with it. But there are other reasons. No man can pretend that the wild, barbarous, and capricious superstitions of Africa, or of savage tribes elsewhere, affect him in the way that he is affected by the ancient, monumental, cruel, and elaborate religions of Hindostan. The mere antiquity of Asiatic things, of their institutions, histories—above all, of their mythologies, etc.—is so impressive that to me the vast age of the race and name overpowers the sense of youth in the individual. A young Chinese seems to me an antediluvian man renewed. Even Englishmen, though not bred in any knowledge of such institutions, cannot but shudder at the mystic sublimity of *castes* that have flowed apart, and refused to mix, through such immemorial tracts of time ; nor can any man fail to be awed by the sanctity of the Ganges, or by the very name of the Euphrates. It contributes much to these feelings that South-eastern Asia is, and has been for thousands of years, the part of the earth most swarming with human life, the great *officina gentium*. Man is a weed in those regions. The vast empires, also, into which the enormous population of Asia has always been cast, give a further sublimity to the feelings associated with all oriental names or images. In China, over and above what it has in common with the rest of Southern Asia, I am terrified by the modes of life, by the manners, by the barrier of utter abhorrence placed between myself and *them*, by counter-sympathies deeper than I can analyse. I could sooner live with lunatics, with vermin, with crocodiles or snakes. All this, and much more than I can say, the reader must enter into before he can comprehend the unimaginable horror which these dreams of oriental imagery and mythological tortures impressed upon me. Under the connecting feeling of tropical heat and vertical sun-

lights, I brought together all creatures, birds, beasts, reptiles, all trees and plants, usages and appearances, that are found in all tropical regions, and assembled them together in China or Hindostan. From kindred
5 feelings, I soon brought Egypt and her gods under the same law. I was stared at, hooted at, grinned at, chattered at, by monkeys, by paroquets, by cockatoos. I ran into pagodas, and was fixed for centuries at the summit, or in secret rooms ; I was the idol ; I was the
10 priest ; I was worshipped ; I was sacrificed. I fled from the wrath of Brahma through all the forests of Asia ; Vishnu hated me ; Seeva lay in wait for me. I came suddenly upon Isis and Osiris : I had done a deed, they said, which the ibis and the crocodile trembled at. Thousands
15 of years I lived and was buried in stone coffins, with mummies and sphinxes, in narrow chambers at the heart of eternal pyramids. I was kissed, with cancerous kisses, by crocodiles, and was laid, confounded with all unutterable abortions, amongst reeds and Nilotic mud.
20 Some slight abstraction I thus attempt of my oriental dreams, which filled me always with such amazement at the monstrous scenery that horror seemed absorbed for a while in sheer astonishment. Sooner or later came a reflux of feeling that swallowed up the astonishment,
25 and left me, not so much in terror, as in hatred and abomination of what I saw. Over every form, and threat, and punishment, and dim sightless incarceration, brooded a killing sense of eternity and infinity. Into these dreams only it was, with one or two slight excep-
30 tions, that any circumstances of physical horror entered. All before had been moral and spiritual terrors. But here the main agents were ugly birds, or snakes, or crocodiles, especially the last. The cursed crocodile became to me the object of more horror than all the

rest. I was compelled to live with him ; and (as was always the case in my dreams) for centuries. Sometimes I escaped, and found myself in Chinese houses. All the feet of the tables, sofas, etc., soon became instinct with life : the abominable head of the crocodile, and his leering eyes, looked out at me, multiplied into ten thousand repetitions ; and I stood loathing and fascinated. So often did this hideous reptile haunt my dreams that many times the very same dream was broken up in the very same way : I heard gentle voices speaking to me (I hear everything when I am sleeping), and instantly I awoke ; it was broad noon, and my children were standing, hand in hand, at my bedside, come to show me their coloured shoes, or new frocks, or to let me see them dressed for going out. No experience was so awful to me, and at the same time so pathetic, as this abrupt translation from the darkness of the infinite to the gaudy summer air of highest noon, and from the unutterable abortions of miscreated gigantic vermin to the sight of infancy and innocent *human* natures.

June 1819.—I have had occasion to remark, at various periods of my life, that the deaths of those whom we love, and, indeed, the contemplation of death generally, is (*cæteris paribus*) more affecting in summer than in any other season of the year. And the reasons are these three, I think : first, that the visible heavens in summer appear far higher, more distant, and (if such a solecism may be excused) more infinite ; the clouds by which chiefly the eye expounds the distance of the blue pavilion stretched over our heads are in summer more voluminous, more massed, and are accumulated in far grander and more towering piles ; secondly, the light and the appearances of the declining

and the setting sun are much more fitted to be types
and characters of the infinite ; and, thirdly (which is
the main reason), the exuberant and riotous prodigality of life naturally forces the mind more power-
5 fully upon the antagonist thought of death, and the
wintry sterility of the grave. For it may be observed
generally that, wherever two thoughts stand related
to each other by a law of antagonism, and exist, as
it were, by mutual repulsion, they are apt to suggest
10 each other. On these accounts it is that I find it impossible to banish the thought of death when I am walking
alone in the endless days of summer ; and any particular death, if not actually more affecting, at least
haunts my mind more obstinately and besiegingly, in
15 that season. Perhaps this cause, and a slight incident
which I omit, might have been the immediate occasions
of the following dream, to which, however, a predisposi-
tion must always have existed in my mind ; but,
having been once roused, it never left me, and split
20 into a thousand fantastic variations, which often
suddenly re-combined, locked back into startling unity,
and restored the original dream.

I thought that it was a Sunday morning in May ;
that it was Easter Sunday, and as yet very early in the
25 morning. I was standing, as it seemed to me, at the
door of my own cottage. Right before me lay the very
scene which could really be commanded from that
situation, but exalted, as was usual, and solemnised by
the power of dreams. There were the same mountains,
30 and the same lovely valley at their feet ; but the mountains were raised to more than Alpine height, and there
was interspace far larger between them of savannahs
and forest lawns ; the hedges were rich with white
roses ; and no living creature was to be seen, excepting

that in the green churchyard there were cattle tranquilly reposing upon the verdant graves, and particularly round about the grave of a child whom I had once tenderly loved, just as I had really beheld them, a little before sunrise, in the same summer when that child died. I gazed upon the well-known scene, and I said to myself, " It yet wants much of sunrise ; and it is Easter Sunday ; and that is the day on which they celebrate the first-fruits of Resurrection. I will walk abroad ; old griefs shall be forgotten to-day : for the air is cool and still, and the hills are high, and stretch away to heaven ; and the churchyard is as verdant as the forest lawns, and the forest lawns are as quiet as the churchyard ; and with the dew I can wash the fever from my forehead ; and then I shall be unhappy no longer." I turned, as if to open my garden gate, and immediately I saw upon the left a scene far different ; but which yet the power of dreams had reconciled into harmony. The scene was an oriental one ; and there also it was Easter Sunday, and very early in the morning. And at a vast distance were visible, as a stain upon the horizon, the domes and cupolas of a great city—an image or faint abstraction, caught perhaps in childhood from some picture of Jerusalem. And not a bow-shot from me, upon a stone, shaded by Judean palms, there sat a woman ; and I looked, and it was— Ann ! She fixed her eyes upon me earnestly ; and I said to her at length, " So, then, I have found you at last." I waited ; but she answered me not a word. Her face was the same as when I saw it last ; the same, and yet, again, how different ! Seventeen years ago, when the lamplight of mighty London fell upon her face, as for the last time I kissed her lips (lips, Ann, that to me were not polluted!), her eyes were streaming with

tears. The tears were now no longer seen. Sometimes
she seemed altered ; yet again sometimes *not* altered ;
and hardly older. Her looks were tranquil, but with
unusual solemnity of expression, and I now gazed upon
5 her with some awe. Suddenly her countenance grew
dim ; and, turning to the mountains, I perceived
vapours rolling between us ; in a moment all had
vanished ; thick darkness came on ; and in the twinkling of an eye I was far away from mountains; and by
10 lamplight in London, walking again with Ann—just
as we had walked, when both children, eighteen years
before, along the endless terraces of Oxford Street.

Then suddenly would come a dream of far different
character—a tumultuous dream—commencing with a
15 music such as now I often heard in sleep—music of
preparation and of awakening suspense. The undula-
tions of fast-gathering tumults were like the opening of
the Coronation Anthem ; and, like *that*, gave the feeling
of a multitudinous movement, of infinite cavalcades
20 filing off, and the tread of innumerable armies. The
morning was come of a mighty day—a day of crisis
and of ultimate hope for human nature, then suffering mysterious eclipse, and labouring in some dread
extremity. Somewhere, but I knew not where—some-
25 how, but I knew not how—by some beings, but I knew
not by whom—a battle, a strife, an agony, was travelling through all its stages—was evolving itself, like the
catastrophe of some mighty drama, with which my
sympathy was the more insupportable from deepening
30 confusion as to its local scene, its cause, its nature, and
its undecipherable issue. I (as is usual in dreams where,
of necessity, we make ourselves central to every movement) had the power, and yet had not the power, to
decide it. I had the power, if I could raise myself

to will it ; and yet again had not the power, for
the weight of twenty Atlantics was upon me, or the
oppression of inexpiable guilt. "Deeper than ever
plummet sounded," I lay inactive. Then, like a chorus,
the passion deepened. Some greater interest was at 5
stake, some mightier cause, than ever yet the sword
had pleaded, or trumpet had proclaimed. Then came
sudden alarms ; hurryings to and fro ; trepidations of
innumerable fugitives, I knew not whether from the
good cause or the bad ; darkness and lights ; tempest 10
and human faces ; and at last, with the sense that all
was lost, female forms, and the features that were worth
all the world to me ; and but a moment allowed—and
clasped hands, with heart-breaking partings, and then
—everlasting farewells ! and, with a sigh such as the 15
caves of hell sighed when the incestuous mother uttered
the abhorred name of Death, the sound was reverberated—everlasting farewells ! and again, and yet again
reverberated—everlasting farewells !

And I awoke in struggles, and cried aloud, " I will 20
sleep no more ! "

LEVANA AND OUR LADIES OF SORROW

OFTENTIMES at Oxford I saw Levana in my dreams. I
knew her by her Roman symbols. Who is Levana ?
Reader, that do not pretend to have leisure for very
much scholarship, you will not be angry with me for 25
telling you. Levana was the Roman goddess that
performed for the new-born infant the earliest office
of ennobling kindness—typical, by its mode, of that
grandeur which belongs to man everywhere, and of that
benignity in powers invisible, which even in Pagan 30
worlds sometimes descends to sustain it. At the very

moment of birth, just as the infant tasted for the first
time the atmosphere of our troubled planet, it was laid
on the ground. *That* might bear different interpreta-
tions. But immediately, lest so grand a creature should
5 grovel there for more than one instant, either the
paternal hand, as proxy for the goddess Levana, or
some near kinsman, as proxy for the father, raised it
upright, bade it look erect as the king of all this world,
and presented its forehead to the stars, saying, perhaps,
10 in his heart—" Behold what is greater than yourselves ! "
This symbolic act represented the function of Levana.
And that mysterious lady, who never revealed her face
(except to me in dreams), but always acted by delega-
tion, had her name from the Latin verb (as still it is
15 the Italian verb) *levare*, to raise aloft.

This is the explanation of Levana. And hence it
has arisen that some people have understood by Levana
the tutelary power that controls the education of the
nursery. She, that would not suffer at his birth even a
20 prefigurative or mimic degradation for her awful ward,
far less could be supposed to suffer the real degradation
attaching to the non-development of his powers. She
therefore watches over human education. Now, the
word *edŭco*, with the penultimate short, was derived (by
25 a process often exemplified in the crystallisation of
languages) from the word *edūco*, with the penultimate
long. Whatsoever *educes* or develops—*educates*. By
the education of Levana, therefore, is meant—not the
poor machinery that moves by spelling-books and
30 grammars, but that mighty system of central forces
hidden in the deep bosom of human life, which by
passion, by strife, by temptation, by the energies of
resistance, works for ever upon children—resting not
day or night, any more than the mighty wheel of day

and night themselves, whose moments, like restless spokes, are glimmering for ever as they revolve.

If, then, these are the ministries by which Levana works, how profoundly must she reverence the agencies of grief ! But you, reader, think—that children gener- ally are not liable to grief such as mine. There are two senses in the word *generally*—the sense of Euclid where it means *universally* (or in the whole extent of the *genus*), and a foolish sense of this world where it means *usually*. Now I am far from saying that children universally are capable of grief like mine. But there are more than you ever heard of, who die of grief in this island of ours. I will tell you a common case. The rules of Eton require that a boy on the *Foundation* should be there twelve years : he is superannuated at eighteen, consequently he must come at six. Children torn away from mothers and sisters at that age not unfrequently die. I speak of what I know. The complaint is not entered by the registrar as grief; but *that* it is. Grief of that sort, and at that age, has killed more than ever have been counted amongst its martyrs.

Therefore it is that Levana often communes with the powers that shake man's heart : therefore it is that she dotes upon grief. " These ladies," said I softly to myself, on seeing the ministers with whom Levana was conversing, " these are the Sorrows ; and they are three in number, as the *Graces* are three, who dress man's life with beauty ; the *Parcae* are three, who weave the dark arras of man's life in their mysterious loom always with colours sad in part, sometimes angry with tragic crimson and black ; the *Furies* are three, who visit with retributions called from the other side of the grave offences that walk upon this ; and once even the *Muses* were but three, who fit the harp, the

trumpet, or the lute, to the great burdens of man's
impassioned creations. These are the Sorrows, all
three of whom I know." The last words I say *now* ;
but in Oxford I said—" one of whom I know, and the
5 others too surely I *shall* know." For already, in my
fervent youth, I saw (dimly relieved upon the dark
background of my dreams) the imperfect lineaments of
the awful sisters. These sisters—by what name shall
we call them ?

10   If I say simply—" The Sorrows," there will be a
chance of mistaking the term ; it might be understood of
individual sorrow—separate cases of sorrow—whereas
I want a term expressing the mighty abstractions that
incarnate themselves in all individual sufferings of
15 man's heart ; and I wish to have these abstractions
presented as impersonations, that is, as clothed with
human attributes of life, and with functions pointing
to flesh. Let us call them, therefore, *Our Ladies of
Sorrow*. I know them thoroughly, and have walked
20 in all their kingdoms. Three sisters they are, of
one mysterious household ; and their paths are wide
apart ; but of their dominion there is no end. Them I
saw often conversing with Levana, and sometimes
about myself. Do they talk, then ? Oh, no ! Mighty
25 phantoms like these disdain the infirmities of language.
They may utter voices through the organs of man when
they dwell in human hearts, but amongst themselves
is no voice nor sound—eternal silence reigns in *their*
kingdoms. *They* spoke not as they talked with Levana.
30 *They* whispered not. *They* sang not. Though oftentimes methought they *might* have sung ; for I upon
earth had heard their mysteries oftentimes deciphered
by harp and timbrel, by dulcimer and organ. Like
God, whose servants they are, they utter their pleasure,

not by sounds that perish, or by words that go astray, but by signs in heaven—by changes on earth—by pulses in secret rivers—heraldries painted on darkness —and hieroglyphics written on the tablets of the brain. *They* wheeled in mazes ; *I* spelled the steps. *They* telegraphed from afar ; *I* read the signals. *They* conspired together ; and on the mirrors of darkness *my* eye traced the plots. *Theirs* were the symbols; *mine* are the words.

What is it the sisters are ? What is it that they do ? Let me describe their form, and their presence ; if form it were that still fluctuated in its outline ; or presence it were that for ever advanced to the front, or for ever receded amongst shades.

The eldest of the three is named *Mater Lachrymarum*, Our Lady of Tears. She it is that night and day raves and moans, calling for vanished faces. She stood in Rama, when a voice was heard of lamentation —Rachel weeping for her children, and refusing to be comforted. She it was that stood in Bethlehem on the night when Herod's sword swept its nurseries of Innocents, and the little feet were stiffened for ever, which, heard at times as they tottered along floors overhead, woke pulses of love in household hearts that were not unmarked in heaven.

Her eyes are sweet and subtle, wild and sleepy by turns ; oftentimes rising to the clouds ; oftentimes challenging the heavens. She wears a diadem round her head. And I knew by childish memories that she could go abroad upon the winds, when she heard the sobbing of litanies or the thundering of organs, and when she beheld the mustering of summer clouds. This sister, the elder, it is that carries keys more than papal at her girdle, which open every cottage and every palace. She, to my knowledge, sate all last summer by the bedside of the blind beggar, him that so often and so gladly I talked with, whose pious daughter, eight years old, with the sunny countenance, resisted 5 the temptations of play and village mirth to travel all day long on dusty roads with her afflicted father. For this did God send her a great reward. In the spring-time of the year, and whilst yet her own spring was budding, He recalled her to himself. But her blind 10 father mourns for ever over *her* ; still he dreams at midnight that the little guiding hand is locked within his own ; and still he wakens to a darkness that is *now* within a second and a deeper darkness. This *Mater Lachrymarum* also has been sitting all this winter of 15 1844-45 within the bedchamber of the Czar, bringing before his eyes a daughter (not less pious) that vanished to God not less suddenly, and left behind her a darkness not less profound. By the power of her keys it is that Our Lady of Tears glides a ghostly intruder into the 20 chambers of sleepless men, sleepless women, sleep-less children, from Ganges to the Nile, from Nile to Mississippi. And her, because she is the first-born of her house, and has the widest empire, let us honour with the title of " Madonna."

25 The second sister is called *Mater Suspiriorum*, Our Lady of Sighs. She never scales the clouds, nor walks abroad upon the winds. She wears no diadem. And her eyes, if they were ever seen, would be neither sweet nor subtle ; no man could read their story ; they would 30 be found filled with perishing dreams, and with wrecks of forgotten delirium. But she raises not her eyes ; her head, on which sits a dilapidated turban, droops for ever ; for ever fastens on the dust. She weeps not. She groans not. But she sighs inaudibly at intervals.

Her sister, Madonna, is oftentimes stormy and frantic ;
raging in the highest against heaven ; and demand-
ing back her darlings. But Our Lady of Sighs never
clamours, never defies, dreams not of rebellious aspirations. She is humble to abjectness. Hers is the meek- 5
ness that belongs to the hopeless. Murmur she may,
but it is in her sleep. Whisper she may, but it is to
herself in the twilight. Mutter she does at times, but
it is in solitary places that are desolate as she is desolate,
in ruined cities, and when the sun has gone down to his 10
rest. This sister is the visitor of the Pariah, of the Jew,
of the bondsman to the oar in Mediterranean galleys, of
the English criminal in Norfolk Island, blotted out from
the books of remembrance in sweet far-off England, of
the baffled penitent reverting his eye for ever upon a 15
solitary grave, which to him seems the altar overthrown
of some past and bloody sacrifice, on which altar no
oblations can now be availing, whether towards pardon
that he might implore, or towards reparation that he
might attempt. Every slave that at noonday looks up 20
to the tropical sun with timid reproach, as he points
with one hand to the earth, our general mother, but for
him a stepmother, as he points with the other hand to
the Bible, our general teacher, but against *him* sealed
and sequestered ;—every woman sitting in darkness, 25
without love to shelter her head, or hope to illumine her
solitude, because the heaven-born instincts kindling in
her nature germs of holy affections, which God im-
planted in her womanly bosom, having been stifled by
social necessities, now burn sullenly to waste, like 30
sepulchral lamps amongst the ancients ;—every nun
defrauded of her unreturning May-time by wicked
kinsmen, whom God will judge ;—every captive in
every dungeon ;—all that are betrayed, and all that are

rejected; outcasts by traditionary law, and children
of *hereditary* disgrace—all these walk with Our Lady of
Sighs. She also carries a key; but she needs it little.
For her kingdom is chiefly amongst the tents of Shem,
and the houseless vagrant of every clime. Yet in the
very highest ranks of man she finds chapels of her own;
and even in glorious England there are some that, to
the world, carry their heads as proudly as the reindeer,
who yet secretly have received her mark upon their
foreheads.

But the third sister, who is also the youngest——
Hush! whisper, whilst we talk of *her*! Her kingdom
is not large, or else no flesh should live; but within
that kingdom all power is hers. Her head, turreted
like that of Cybele, rises almost beyond the reach of
sight. She droops not; and her eyes rising so high,
might be hidden by distance. But, being what they
are, they cannot be hidden; through the treble veil of
crape which she wears, the fierce light of a blazing
misery, that rests not for matins or for vespers—for
noon of day or noon of night—for ebbing or for flowing tide—may be read from the very ground. She
is the defier of God. She also is the mother of lunacies,
and the suggestress of suicides. Deep lie the roots of
her power; but narrow is the nation that she rules.
For she can approach only those in whom a profound
nature has been upheaved by central convulsions;
in whom the heart trembles and the brain rocks under
conspiracies of tempest from without and tempest
from within. Madonna moves with uncertain steps,
fast or slow, but still with tragic grace. Our Lady of
Sighs creeps timidly and stealthily. But this youngest
sister moves with incalculable motions, bounding, and
with a tiger's leaps. She carries no key; for, though

coming rarely amongst men, she storms all doors at which she is permitted to enter at all. And *her* name is *Mater Tenebrarum*—Our Lady of Darkness.

These were the *Semnai Theai*, or Sublime Goddesses —these were the *Eumenides*, or Gracious Ladies (so called by antiquity in shuddering propitiation)—of my Oxford dreams. Madonna spoke. She spoke by her mysterious hand. Touching my head, she beckoned to Our Lady of Sighs ; and *what* she spoke, translated out of the signs which (except in dreams) no man reads, was this :—

" Lo ! here is he, whom in childhood I dedicated to my altars. This is he that once I made my darling. Him I led astray, him I beguiled, and from heaven I stole away his young heart to mine. Through me did he become idolatrous ; and through me it was, by languishing desires, that he worshipped the worm, and prayed to the wormy grave. Holy was the grave to him ; lovely was its darkness ; saintly its corruption. Him, this young idolater, I have seasoned for thee, dear gentle Sister of Sighs ! Do thou take him now to *thy* heart, and season him for our dreadful sister. And thou "—turning to the *Mater Tenebrarum*, she said—" wicked sister, that temptest and hatest, do thou take him from *her*. See that thy sceptre lie heavy on his head. Suffer not woman and her tenderness to sit near him in his darkness. Banish the frailties of hope—wither the relentings of love—scorch the fountains of tears : curse him as only thou canst curse. So shall he be accomplished in the furnace—so shall he see the things that ought *not* to be seen—sights that are abominable, and secrets that are unutterable. So shall he read elder truths, sad truths, grand truths, fearful truths. So shall he rise again *before* he dies. And so shall our commission be accomplished which from God we had—to plague his heart until we had unfolded the capacities of his spirit."

SAVANNAH-LA-MAR

GOD smote Savannah-la-mar, and in one night, by earthquake, removed her, with all her towers standing and population sleeping, from the steadfast foundations of the shore to the coral floors of ocean. And God said—" Pompeii did I bury and conceal from men through seventeen centuries : this city I will bury, but not conceal. She shall be a monument to men of my mysterious anger, set in azure light through generations to come ; for I will enshrine her in a crystal dome of my tropic seas." This city, therefore, like a mighty galleon with all her apparel mounted, streamers flying, and tackling perfect, seems floating along the noiseless depths of ocean ; and oftentimes in glassy calms, through the translucid atmosphere of water that now stretches like an air-woven awning above the silent encampment, mariners from every clime look down into her courts and terraces, count her gates, and number the spires of her churches. She is one ample cemetery, and *has* been for many a year ; but, in the mighty calms that brood for weeks over tropic latitudes, she fascinates the eye with a *Fata-Morgana* revelation, as of human life still subsisting in submarine asylums sacred from the storms that torment our upper air.

Thither, lured by the loveliness of cerulean depths, by the peace of human dwellings privileged from molestation, by the gleam of marble altars sleeping in everlasting sanctity, oftentimes in dreams did I and the Dark Interpreter cleave the watery veil that divided

us from her streets. We looked into the belfries,
where the pendulous bells were waiting in vain for the
summons which should awaken their marriage peals;
together we touched the mighty organ-keys, that
sang no *jubilates* for the ear of heaven, that sang no 5
requiems for the ear of human sorrow; together we
searched the silent nurseries, where the children were
all asleep, and *had* been asleep through five generations.
" They are waiting for the heavenly dawn," whispered
the Interpreter to himself: " and, when *that* comes, 10
the bells and organs will utter a *jubilate* repeated by
the echoes of Paradise." Then, turning to me, he
said—" This is sad, this is piteous; but less would not
have sufficed for the purpose of God. Look here. Put
into a Roman clepsydra one hundred drops of water; 15
let these run out as the sands in an hour-glass, every
drop measuring the hundredth part of a second, so
that each shall represent but the three-hundred-and-
sixty-thousandth part of an hour. Now, count the
drops as they race along; and, when the fiftieth of the 20
hundred is passing, behold! forty-nine are not, because
already they have perished, and fifty are not, because
they are yet to come. You see, therefore, how narrow,
how incalculably narrow, is the true and actual present.
Of that time which we call the present, hardly a 25
hundredth part but belongs either to a past which has
fled, or to a future which is still on the wing. It has
perished, or it is not born. It was, or it is not. Yet
even this approximation to the truth is *infinitely* false.
For again subdivide that solitary drop, which only 30
was found to represent the present, into a lower series
of similar fractions, and the actual present which you
arrest measures now but the thirty-sixth millionth of
an hour; and so by infinite declensions the true and

very present, in which only we live and enjoy, will vanish into a mote of a mote, distinguishable only by a heavenly vision. Therefore the present, which only man possesses, offers less capacity for his footing than 5 the slenderest film that ever spider twisted from her womb. Therefore, also, even this incalculable shadow from the narrowest pencil of moonlight is more transitory than geometry can measure, or thought of angel can overtake. The time which *is* contracts into a 10 mathematic point ; and even that point perishes a thousand times before we can utter its birth. All is finite in the present ; and even that finite is infinite in its velocity of flight towards death. But in God there is nothing finite ; but in God there is nothing transitory ; 15 but in God there *can* be nothing that tends to death. Therefore it follows that for God there can be no present. The future is the present of God, and to the future it is that he sacrifices the human present. Therefore it is that he works by earthquake. There- 20 fore it is that he works by grief. O, deep is the plough- ing of earthquake ! O, deep "—(and his voice swelled like a *sanctus* rising from a choir of a cathedral)—" O, deep is the ploughing of grief ! But oftentimes less would not suffice for the agriculture of God. Upon a 25 night of earthquake he builds a thousand years of pleasant habitations for man. Upon the sorrow of an infant he raises oftentimes from human intellects glorious vintages that could not else have been. Less than these fierce ploughshares would not have stirred 30 the stubborn soil. The one is needed for Earth, our planet—for Earth itself as the dwelling-place of man ; but the other is needed yet oftener for God's mightiest instrument—yes " (and he looked solemnly at myself), " is needed for the mysterious children of the Earth ! "

THE ENGLISH MAIL-COACH

SECTION I—THE GLORY OF MOTION

SOME twenty or more years before I matriculated at Oxford, Mr Palmer, at that time M.P. for Bath, had accomplished two things, very hard to do on our little planet, the Earth, however cheap they may be held by eccentric people in comets : he had invented mail-coaches, and he had married the daughter of a duke. He was, therefore, just twice as great a man as Galileo, who did certainly invent (or, which is the same thing, discover) the satellites of Jupiter, those very next things extant to mail-coaches in the two capital pretensions of speed and keeping time, but, on the other hand, who did *not* marry the daughter of a duke.

These mail-coaches, as organised by Mr Palmer, are entitled to a circumstantial notice from myself, having had so large a share in developing the anarchies of my subsequent dreams : an agency which they accomplished, first, through velocity, at that time unprecedented—for they first revealed the glory of motion ; secondly, through grand effects for the eye between lamplight and the darkness upon solitary roads ; thirdly, through animal beauty and power so often displayed in the class of horses selected for this mail service ; fourthly, through the conscious presence of a central intellect, that, in the midst of vast distances—of storms, of darkness, of danger—overruled all obstacles into one steady co-operation to a national result. For my own feeling, this post-office service spoke as by some mighty

orchestra, where a thousand instruments, all disregard-
ing each other, and so far in danger of discord, yet all
obedient as slaves to the supreme *baton* of some great
leader, terminate in a perfection of harmony like that of
5 heart, brain, and lungs in a healthy animal organisation.   But, finally, that particular element in this whole
combination which most impressed myself, and through
which it is that to this hour Mr Palmer's mail-coach
system tyrannises over my dreams by terror and terrific
10 beauty, lay in the awful *political* mission which at that
time it fulfilled.   The mail-coach it was that distributed
over the face of the land, like the opening of apocalyptic
vials, the heart-shaking news of Trafalgar, of Salamanca,
of Vittoria, of Waterloo.   These were the harvests that,
15 in the grandeur of their reaping, redeemed the tears and
blood in which they had been sown.   Neither was the
meanest peasant so much below the grandeur and the
sorrow of the times as to confound battles such as these,
which were gradually moulding the destinies of Christen-
20 dom, with the vulgar conflicts of ordinary warfare, so
often no more than gladiatorial trials of national prowess.
The victories of England in this stupendous contest
rose of themselves as natural *Te Deums* to heaven ;
and it was felt by the thoughtful that such victories,
25 at such a crisis of general prostration, were not more
beneficial to ourselves than finally to France, our
enemy, and to the nations of all western or central
Europe, through whose pusillanimity it was that the
French domination had prospered.
30   The mail-coach, as the national organ for publishing
these mighty events, thus diffusively influential, became
itself a spiritualised and glorified object to an impassioned heart ; and naturally, in the Oxford of that
day, *all* hearts were impassioned, as being all (or nearly

all) in *early* manhood. In most universities there is
one single college ; in Oxford there were five-and-
twenty, all of which were peopled by young men, the
élite of their own generation ; not boys, but men :
none under eighteen. In some of these many colleges 5
the custom permitted the student to keep what are
called " short terms " ; that is, the four terms of
Michaelmas, Lent, Easter, and Act, were kept by a
residence, in the aggregate, of ninety-one days, or
thirteen weeks. Under this interrupted residence, it 10
was possible that a student might have a reason for
going down to his home four times in the year. This
made eight journeys to and fro. But, as these homes
lay dispersed through all the shires of the island, and
most of us disdained all coaches except his Majesty's 15
mail, no city out of London could pretend to so extensive a connection with Mr Palmer's establishment
as Oxford. Three mails, at the least, I remember
as passing every day through Oxford, and benefiting
by my personal patronage—viz., the Worcester, the 20
Gloucester, and the Holyhead mail. Naturally, therefore, it became a point of some interest with us, whose
journeys revolved every six weeks on an average, to
look a little into the executive details of the system.
With some of these Mr Palmer had no concern ; they 25
rested upon bye-laws enacted by posting-houses for
their own benefit, and upon other bye-laws, equally
stern, enacted by the inside passengers for the illustration of their own haughty exclusiveness. These last
were of a nature to rouse our scorn ; from which the 30
transition was not very long to systematic mutiny.
Up to this time, say 1804, or 1805 (the year of Trafalgar),
it had been the fixed assumption of the four inside
people (as an old tradition of all public carriages derived

from the reign of Charles II) that they, the illustrious quaternion, constituted a porcelain variety of the human race, whose dignity would have been compromised by exchanging one word of civility with the three miserable delf-ware outsides. Even to have kicked an outsider might have been held to attaint the foot concerned in that operation, so that, perhaps, it would have required an Act of Parliament to restore its purity of blood. What words, then, could express the horror, and the sense of treason, in that case, which *had* happened, where all three outsides (the trinity of Pariahs) made a vain attempt to sit down at the same breakfast-table or dinner-table with the consecrated four? I myself witnessed such an attempt; and on that occasion a benevolent old gentleman endeavoured to soothe his three holy associates, by suggesting that, if the outsides were indicted for this criminal attempt at the next assizes, the court would regard it as a case of lunacy or *delirium tremens* rather than of treason. England owes much of her grandeur to the depth of the aristocratic element in her social composition, when pulling against her strong democracy. I am not the man to laugh at it. But sometimes, undoubtedly, it expressed itself in comic shapes. The course taken with the infatuated outsiders, in the particular attempt which I have noticed, was that the waiter, beckoning them away from the privileged *salle-à-manger*, sang out, " This way, my good men," and then enticed these good men away to the kitchen. But that plan had not always answered. Sometimes, though rarely, cases occurred where the intruders, being stronger than usual, or more vicious than usual, resolutely refused to budge, and so far carried their point as to have a separate table arranged for themselves in a corner of the general room.

Yet, if an Indian screen could be found ample enough
to plant them out from the very eyes of the high table, or
dais, it then became possible to assume as a fiction of law
that the three delf fellows, after all, were not present.
They could be ignored by the porcelain men, under the   5
maxim that objects not appearing and objects not
existing are governed by the same logical construction.

Such being, at that time, the usage of mail-coaches,
what was to be done by us of young Oxford ? We, the
most aristocratic of people, who were addicted to the   10
practice of looking down superciliously even upon the
insides themselves as often very questionable characters
—were we, by voluntarily going outside, to court
indignities ? If our dress and bearing sheltered us
generally from the suspicion of being " raff " (the name   15
at that period for " snobs "), we really *were* such constructively by the place we assumed. If we did not
submit to the deep shadow of eclipse, we entered at
least the skirts of its penumbra. And the analogy of
theatres was valid against us—where no man can com-   20
plain of the annoyances incident to the pit or gallery,
having his instant remedy in paying the higher price of
the boxes. But the soundness of this analogy we disputed. In the case of the theatre, it cannot be pretended that the inferior situations have any separate   25
attractions, unless the pit may be supposed to have an
advantage for the purposes of the critic or the dramatic
reporter. But the critic or reporter is a rarity. For
most people, the sole benefit is in the price. Now,
on the contrary, the outside of the mail had its   30
own incommunicable advantages. These we could not
forego. The higher price we would willingly have paid,
but not the price connected with the condition of riding
inside ; which condition we pronounced insufferable.

The air, the freedom of prospect, the proximity to the horses, the elevation of seat : these were what we required ; but, above all, the certain anticipation of purchasing occasional opportunities of driving.

5   Such was the difficulty which pressed us ; and under the coercion of this difficulty we instituted a searching inquiry into the true quality and valuation of the different apartments about the mail. We conducted this inquiry on metaphysical principles ; and it was
10 ascertained satisfactorily that the roof of the coach, which by some weak men had been called the attics, and by some the garrets, was in reality the drawing-room ; in which drawing-room the box was the chief ottoman or sofa ; whilst it appeared that the *inside*,
15 which had been traditionally regarded as the only room tenantable by gentlemen, was, in fact, the coal-cellar in disguise.

Great wits jump. The very same idea had not long before struck the celestial intellect of China. Amongst
20 the presents carried out by our first embassy to that country was a state-coach. It had been specially selected as a personal gift by George III ; but the exact mode of using it was an intense mystery to Pekin. The ambassador, indeed (Lord Macartney), had made
25 some imperfect explanations upon this point ; but, as His Excellency communicated these in a diplomatic whisper at the very moment of his departure, the celestial intellect was very feebly illuminated, and it became necessary to call a cabinet council on the grand
30 state question, " Where was the Emperor to sit ? " The hammer-cloth happened to be unusually gorgeous ; and, partly on that consideration, but partly also because the box offered the most elevated seat, was nearest to the moon, and undeniably went foremost,

it was resolved by acclamation that the box was the imperial throne, and, for the scoundrel who drove— he might sit where he could find a perch. The horses, therefore, being harnessed, solemnly his imperial majesty ascended his new English throne under a flourish of trumpets, having the first lord of the treasury on his right hand, and the chief jester on his left. Pekin gloried in the spectacle ; and in the whole flowery people, constructively present by representa- tion, there was but one discontented person, and *that* was the coachman. This mutinous individual audaci- ously shouted, " Where am *I* to sit ? " But the privy council, incensed by his disloyalty, unanimously opened the door, and kicked him into the inside. He had all the inside places to himself ; but such is the rapacity of ambition that he was still dissatisfied. " I say," he cried out in an extempore petition addressed to the Emperor through the window—" I say, how am I to catch hold of the reins ? "—" Anyhow," was the imperial answer ; " don't trouble *me*, man, in my glory. How catch the reins ? Why, through the windows, through the keyholes—*any*how." Finally this con- tumacious coachman lengthened the check-strings into a sort of jury-reins communicating with the horses ; with these he drove as steadily as Pekin had any right to expect. The Emperor returned after the briefest of circuits ; he descended in great pomp from his throne, with the severest resolution never to remount it. A public thanksgiving was ordered for his majesty's happy escape from the disease of a broken neck ; and the state-coach was dedicated thenceforward as a votive offering to the god Fo Fo—whom the learned more accurately called Fi Fi.

No dignity is perfect which does not at some point

ally itself with the mysterious. The connection of the
mail with the state and the executive government—a
connection obvious, but yet not strictly defined—gave
to the whole mail establishment an official grandeur
5 which did us service on the roads, and invested us with
seasonable terrors. Not the less impressive were those
terrors because their legal limits were imperfectly ascertained. Look at those turnpike gates: with what
deferential hurry, with what an obedient start, they fly
10 open at our approach ! Look at that long line of carts
and carters ahead, audaciously usurping the very crest
of the road. Ah ! traitors, they do not hear us as yet ;
but, as soon as the dreadful blast of our horn reaches
them with proclamation of our approach, see with what
15 frenzy of trepidation they fly to their horses' heads, and
deprecate our wrath by the precipitation of their crane-
neck quarterings. Treason they feel to be their crime ;
each individual carter feels himself under the ban of
confiscation and attainder ; his blood is attainted
20 through six generations ; and nothing is wanting but
the headsman and his axe, the block and the sawdust,
to close up the vista of his horrors. What ! shall it
be within benefit of clergy to delay the king's message
on the high road ?—to interrupt the great respirations,
25 ebb and flood, *systole* and *diastole*, of the national intercourse ?—to endanger the safety of tidings running
day and night between all nations and languages ? Or
can it be fancied, amongst the weakest of men, that the
bodies of the criminals will be given up to their widows
30 for Christian burial ? Now, the doubts which were
raised as to our powers did more to wrap them in terror,
by wrapping them in uncertainty, than could have been
effected by the sharpest definitions of the law from the
Quarter Sessions. We, on our parts (we, the collective

mail, I mean), did our utmost to exalt the idea of our
privileges by the insolence with which we wielded them.
Whether this insolence rested upon law that gave it a
sanction, or upon conscious power that haughtily dis-
pensed with that sanction, equally it spoke from a 5
potential station ; and the agent, in each particular
insolence of the moment, was viewed reverentially, as
one having authority.

Sometimes after breakfast his Majesty's mail would
become frisky ; and, in its difficult wheelings amongst 10
the intricacies of early markets, it would upset an
apple-cart, a cart loaded with eggs, etc. Huge was the
affliction and dismay, awful was the smash. I, as far
as possible, endeavoured in such a case to represent the
conscience and moral sensibilities of the mail ; and, 15
when wildernesses of eggs were lying poached under
horses' hoofs, then would I stretch forth my hands in
sorrow, saying (in words too celebrated at that time,
from the false echoes of Marengo), " Ah ! wherefore
have we not time to weep over you ? "—which was 20
evidently impossible, since, in fact, we had not time to
laugh over them. Tied to post-office allowance in some
cases of fifty minutes for eleven miles, could the royal
mail pretend to undertake the offices of sympathy and
condolence ? Could it be expected to provide tears 25
for the accidents of the road ? If even it seemed to
trample on humanity, it did so, I felt, in discharge of its
own more peremptory duties.

Upholding the morality of the mail, *a fortiori* I
upheld its rights ; as a matter of duty, I stretched to 30
the uttermost its privilege of imperial precedency, and
astonished weak minds by the feudal powers which I
hinted to be lurking constructively in the charters of
this proud establishment. Once I remember being on

the box of the Holyhead mail, between Shrewsbury
and Oswestry, when a tawdry thing from Birmingham,
some "Tallyho" or "Highflyer," all flaunting with
green and gold, came up alongside of us. What a
5 contrast to our royal simplicity of form and colour in
this plebeian wretch! The single ornament on our
dark ground of chocolate colour was the mighty shield
of the imperial arms, but emblazoned in proportions
as modest as a signet-ring bears to a seal of office.
10 Even this was displayed only on a single panel, whispering, rather than proclaiming, our relations to the
mighty state; whilst the beast from Birmingham, our
green-and-gold friend from false, fleeting, perjured
Brummagem, had as much writing and painting on
15 its sprawling flanks as would have puzzled a decipherer
from the tombs of Luxor. For some time this Birmingham machine ran along by our side—a piece of familiarity that already of itself seemed to me sufficiently
jacobinical. But all at once a movement of the horses
20 announced a desperate intention of leaving us behind.
"Do you see *that*?" I said to the coachman.—"I
see," was his short answer. He was wide awake—yet
he waited longer than seemed prudent; for the horses
of our audacious opponent had a disagreeable air of
25 freshness and power. But his motive was loyal; his
wish was that the Birmingham conceit should be
full-blown before he froze it. When *that* seemed
right, he unloosed, or, to speak by a stronger word, he
sprang, his known resources: he slipped our royal
30 horses like cheetahs, or hunting-leopards, after the
affrighted game. How they could retain such a
reserve of fiery power after the work they had accomplished seemed hard to explain. But on our side,
besides the physical superiority, was a tower of moral

strength, namely, the king's name, "which they upon
the adverse faction wanted." Passing them without an
effort, as it seemed, we threw them into the rear with so
lengthening an interval between us as proved in itself
the bitterest mockery of their presumption ; whilst our 5
guard blew back a shattering blast of triumph that
was really too painfully full of derision.

I mention this little incident for its connection with
what followed. A Welsh rustic, sitting behind me,
asked if I had not felt my heart burn within me during 10
the progress of the race ? I said, with philosophic
calmness, *No* ; because we were not racing with a
mail, so that no glory could be gained. In fact, it
was sufficiently mortifying that such a Birmingham
thing should dare to challenge us. The Welshman 15
replied that he didn't see *that* ; for that a cat might
look at a king, and a Brummagem coach might law-
fully race the Holyhead mail. " *Race* us, if you like,"
I replied, " though even *that* has an air of sedition ;
but not *beat* us. This would have been treason ; and 20
for its own sake I am glad that the 'Tallyho' was
disappointed." So dissatisfied did the Welshman seem
with this opinion that at last I was obliged to tell him
a very fine story from one of our elder dramatists :
viz. that once, in some far Oriental kingdom, when the 25
sultan of all the land, with his princes, ladies, and chief
omrahs, were flying their falcons, a hawk suddenly
flew at a majestic eagle, and, in defiance of the eagle's
natural advantages, in contempt also of the eagle's
traditional royalty, and before the whole assembled 30
field of astonished spectators from Agra and Lahore,
killed the eagle on the spot. Amazement seized the
sultan at the unequal contest, and burning admiration
for its unparalleled result. He commanded that the

hawk should be brought before him; he caressed the
bird with enthusiasm; and he ordered that, for the
commemoration of his matchless courage, a diadem
of gold and rubies should be solemnly placed on the
5 hawk's head, but then that, immediately after this
solemn coronation, the bird should be led off to execution, as the most valiant indeed of traitors, but not
the less a traitor, as having dared to rise rebelliously
against his liege lord and anointed sovereign, the eagle.
10 " Now," said I to the Welshman, " to you and me, as
men of refined sensibilities, how painful it would have
been that this poor Brummagem brute, the ' Tallyho,'
in the impossible case of a victory over us, should
have been crowned with Birmingham tinsel, with paste
15 diamonds and Roman pearls, and then led off to instant
execution." The Welshman doubted if that could be
warranted by law. And, when I hinted at the 6th
of Edward Longshanks, chap. 18, for regulating the
precedency of coaches, as being probably the statute
20 relied on for the capital punishment of such offences,
he replied drily that, if the attempt to pass a mail
really were treasonable, it was a pity that the " Tallyho "
appeared to have so imperfect an acquaintance with
law.

25 The modern modes of travelling cannot compare
with the old mail-coach system in grandeur and power.
They boast of more velocity—not, however, as a
consciousness, but as a fact of our lifeless knowledge,
resting upon *alien* evidence : as, for instance, because
30 somebody *says* that we have gone fifty miles in the hour,
though we are far from feeling it as a personal experience ; or upon the evidence of a result, as that actually
we find ourselves in York four hours after leaving
London. Apart from such an assertion, or such a

result, I myself am little aware of the pace. But, seated on the old mail-coach, we needed no evidence out of ourselves to indicate the velocity. On this system the word was not *magna loquimur*, as upon railways, but *vivimus*. Yes, " magna *vivimus* " ; we do not make verbal ostentation of our grandeurs, we realise our grandeurs in act, and in the very experience of life. The vital experience of the glad animal sensibilities made doubts impossible on the question of our speed ; we heard our speed, we saw it, we felt it as a thrilling ; and this speed was not the product of blind insensate agencies, that had no sympathy to give, but was incarnated in the fiery eyeballs of the noblest amongst brutes, in his dilated nostril, spasmodic muscles, and thunder-beating hoofs. The sensibility of the horse, uttering itself in the maniac light of his eye, might be the last vibration of such a movement ; the glory of Salamanca might be the first. But the intervening links that connected them, that spread the earthquake of battle into the eyeballs of the horse, were the heart of man and its electric thrillings— kindling in the rapture of the fiery strife, and then propagating its own tumults by contagious shouts and gestures to the heart of his servant the horse. But now, on the new system of travelling, iron tubes and boilers have disconnected man's heart from the ministers of his locomotion. Nile nor Trafalgar has power to raise an extra bubble in a steam kettle. The galvanic cycle is broken up for ever ; man's imperial nature no longer sends itself forward through the electric sensibility of the horse ; the inter-agencies are gone in the mode of communication between the horse and his master out of which grew so many aspects of sublimity under accidents of mists that hid, or sudden

blazes that revealed, of mobs that agitated, or midnight
solitudes that awed.   Tidings fitted to convulse all
nations must henceforwards travel by culinary process ;
and the trumpet that once announced from afar the
5 laurelled mail, heart-shaking when heard screaming on
the wind and proclaiming itself through the darkness
to every village or solitary house on its route, has now
given way for ever to the pot-wallopings of the boiler.
Thus have perished multiform openings for public
10 expressions of interest, scenical yet natural, in great
national tidings—for revelations of faces and groups
that could not offer themselves amongst the fluctuating
mobs of a railway station.   The gatherings of gazers
about a laurelled mail had one centre, and acknow-
15 ledged one sole interest.   But the crowds attending
at a railway station have as little unity as running
water, and own as many centres as there are separate
carriages in the train.

Going Down with Victory

But the grandest chapter of our experience within the
20 whole mail-coach service was on those occasions when we
went down from London with the news of victory.   A
period of about ten years stretched from Trafalgar to
Waterloo ;   the second and third years of which period
(1806 and 1807) were comparatively sterile ;   but the
25 other nine (from 1805 to 1815 inclusively) furnished a
long succession of victories, the least of which, in such
a contest of Titans, had an inappreciable value of
position :   partly for its absolute interference with the
plans of our enemy, but still more from its keeping
30 alive through central Europe the sense of a deep-seated
vulnerability in France.   Even to tease the coasts of

our enemy, to mortify them by continual blockades, to insult them by capturing if it were but a baubling schooner under the eyes of their arrogant armies, repeated from time to time a sullen proclamation of power lodged in one quarter to which the hopes of Christendom turned in secret. How much more loudly must this proclamation have spoken in the audacity of having bearded the *élite* of their troops, and having beaten them in pitched battles ! Five years of life it was worth paying down for the privilege of an outside place on a mail-coach, when carrying down the first tidings of any such event. And it is to be noted that, from our insular situation, and the multitude of our frigates disposable for the rapid transmission of intelligence, rarely did any unauthorised rumour steal away a prelibation from the first aroma of the regular despatches. The government news was generally the earliest news.

From eight P.M. to fifteen or twenty minutes later imagine the mails assembled on parade in Lombard Street ; where, at that time, and not in St Martin's-le-Grand, was seated the General Post-Office. In what exact strength we mustered I do not remember ; but, from the length of each separate *attelage*, we filled the street, though a long one, and though we were drawn up in double file. On *any* night the spectacle was beautiful. The absolute perfection of all the appointments about the carriages and the harness, their strength, their brilliant cleanliness, their beautiful simplicity—but, more than all, the royal magnificence of the horses— were what might first have fixed the attention. Every carriage on every morning in the year was taken down to an official inspector for examination : wheels, axles, linchpins, pole, glasses, lamps, were all critically

probed and tested. Every part of every carriage had
been cleaned, every horse had been groomed, with as
much rigour as if they belonged to a private gentleman ;
and that part of the spectacle offered itself always.
But the night before us is a night of victory ; and,
behold ! to the ordinary display what a heart-shaking
addition !—horses, men, carriages, all are dressed in
laurels and flowers, oak-leaves and ribbons. The
guards, as being officially his Majesty's servants, and of
the coachmen such as are within the privilege of the
post-office, wear the royal liveries of course ; and, as
it is summer (for all the *land* victories were naturally
won in summer), they wear, on this fine evening, these
liveries exposed to view, without any covering of upper
coats. Such a costume, and the elaborate arrangement of the laurels in their hats, dilate their hearts, by
giving to them openly a personal connection with the
great news in which already they have the general
interest of patriotism. That great national sentiment
surmounts and quells all sense of ordinary distinctions.
Those passengers who happen to be gentlemen are now
hardly to be distinguished as such except by dress ;
for the usual reserve of their manner in speaking to
the attendants has on this night melted away. One
heart, one pride, one glory, connects every man by the
transcendent bond of his national blood. The spectators, who are numerous beyond precedent, express
their sympathy with these fervent feelings by continual
hurrahs. Every moment are shouted aloud by the
post-office servants, and summoned to draw up, the
great ancestral names of cities known to history through
a thousand years—Lincoln, Winchester, Portsmouth,
Gloucester, Oxford, Bristol, Manchester, York, New-
castle, Edinburgh, Glasgow, Perth, Stirling, Aberdeen

—expressing the grandeur of the empire by the antiquity of its towns, and the grandeur of the mail establishment by the diffusive radiation of its separate
missions.   Every moment you hear the thunder of lids
locked down upon the mail-bags.   That sound to each
individual mail is the signal for drawing off; which process is the finest part of the entire spectacle.   Then come
the horses into play.   Horses! can these be horses
that bound off with the action and gestures of leopards?
What stir!—what sea-like ferment!—what a thunder-
ing of wheels!—what a trampling of hoofs!—what a
sounding of trumpets!—what farewell cheers—what
redoubling peals of brotherly congratulation, connecting the name of the particular mail—" Liverpool for
ever!"—with the name of the particular victory—
" Badajoz for ever!" or " Salamanca for ever!"
The half-slumbering consciousness that all night long,
and all the next day—perhaps for even a longer period
—many of these mails, like fire racing along a train
of gunpowder, will be kindling at every instant new
successions of burning joy, has an obscure effect of
multiplying the victory itself, by multiplying to the
imagination into infinity the stages of its progressive
diffusion.   A fiery arrow seems to be let loose, which
from that moment is destined to travel, without
intermission, westwards for three hundred miles—
northwards for six hundred; and the sympathy of our
Lombard Street friends at parting is exalted a hundred-
fold by a sort of visionary sympathy with the yet
slumbering sympathies which in so vast a succession
we are going to awake.

Liberated from the embarrassments of the city, and
issuing into the broad uncrowded avenues of the
northern suburbs, we soon begin to enter upon our

natural pace of ten miles an hour.   In the broad light
of the summer evening, the sun, perhaps, only just at
the point of setting, we are seen from every storey of
every house.   Heads of every age crowd to the windows ;
5 young and old understand the language of our victorious
symbols ;   and rolling volleys of sympathising cheers
run along us, behind us, and before us.   The beggar,
rearing himself against the wall, forgets his lameness—
real or assumed—thinks not of his whining trade, but
10 stands erect, with bold exulting smiles, as we pass him.
The victory has healed him, and says, Be thou whole !
Women and children, from garrets alike and cellars,
through infinite London, look down or look up with
loving eyes upon our gay ribbons and our martial
15 laurels ;   sometimes kiss their hands ;   sometimes hang
out, as signals of affection, pocket-handkerchiefs,
aprons, dusters, anything that, by catching the summer
breezes, will express an aerial jubilation.   On the
London side of Barnet, to which we draw near within
20 a few minutes after nine, observe that private carriage
which is approaching us.   The weather being so warm,
the glasses are all down ;   and one may read, as on the
stage of a theatre, everything that goes on within.   It
contains three ladies—one likely to be " mamma," and
25 two of seventeen or eighteen, who are probably her
daughters.   What lovely animation, what beautiful
unpremeditated pantomime, explaining to us every
syllable that passes, in these ingenuous girls !   By the
sudden start and raising of the hands on first discover-
30 ing our laurelled equipage, by the sudden movement
and appeal to the elder lady from both of them, and by
the heightened colour on their animated countenances,
we can almost hear them saying, " See, see !   Look at
their laurels !   Oh, mamma !   there has been a great

battle in Spain ; and it has been a great victory." In
a moment we are on the point of passing them. We
passengers—I on the box, and the two on the roof
behind me—raise our hats to the ladies ; the coachman
makes his professional salute with the whip ; the guard 5
even, though punctilious on the matter of his dignity
as an officer under the crown, touches his hat. The
ladies move to us, in return, with a winning gracious-
ness of gesture ; all smile on each side in a way that
nobody could misunderstand, and that nothing short 10
of a grand national sympathy could so instantaneously
prompt. Will these ladies say that we are nothing to
them ? Oh no ; they will not say *that*. They cannot
deny—they do not deny—that for this night they are
our sisters ; gentle or simple, scholar or illiterate 15
servant, for twelve hours to come, we on the outside
have the honour to be their brothers. Those poor
women, again, who stop to gaze upon us with delight
at the entrance of Barnet, and seem, by their air of
weariness, to be returning from labour—do you mean 20
to say that they are washerwomen and charwomen ?
Oh, my poor friend, you are quite mistaken. I assure
you they stand in a far higher rank ; for this one night
they feel themselves by birthright to be daughters of
England, and answer to no humbler title. 25

Every joy, however, even rapturous joy—such is the
sad law of earth—may carry with it grief, or fear of
grief, to some. Three miles beyond Barnet, we see
approaching us another private carriage, nearly repeating the circumstances of the former case. Here, also, 30
the glasses are all down ; here, also, is an elderly lady
seated ; but the two daughters are missing ; for the
single young person sitting by the lady's side seems to
be an attendant—so I judge from her dress, and her

air of respectful reserve. The lady is in mourning ; and her countenance expresses sorrow. At first she does not look up ; so that I believe she is not aware of our approach, until she hears the measured beating of
5 our horses' hoofs. Then she raises her eyes to settle them painfully on our triumphal equipage. Our decorations explain the case to her at once ; but she beholds them with apparent anxiety, or even with terror. Some time before this, I, finding it difficult to
10 hit a flying mark when embarrassed by the coachman's person and reins intervening, had given to the guard a *Courier* evening paper, containing the gazette, for the next carriage that might pass. Accordingly he tossed it in, so folded that the huge capitals expressing some
15 such legend as GLORIOUS VICTORY might catch the eye at once. To see the paper, however, at all, interpreted as it was by our ensigns of triumph, explained every-thing ; and, if the guard were right in thinking the lady to have received it with a gesture of horror, it could not
20 be doubtful that she had suffered some deep personal affliction in connection with this Spanish war.

Here, now, was the case of one who, having formerly suffered, might, erroneously perhaps, be distressing herself with anticipations of another similar suffering.
25 That same night, and hardly three hours later, occurred the reverse case. A poor woman, who too probably would find herself, in a day or two, to have suffered the heaviest of afflictions by the battle, blindly allowed herself to express an exultation so unmeasured in the
30 news and its details as gave to her the appearance which amongst Celtic Highlanders is called *fey*. This was at some little town where we changed horses an hour or two after midnight. Some fair or wake had kept the people up out of their beds, and had occasioned a partial

illumination of the stalls and booths, presenting an
unusual but very impressive effect. We saw many
lights moving about as we drew near ; and perhaps the
most striking scene on the whole route was our reception at this place. The flashing of torches and the
beautiful radiance of blue lights (technically, Bengal
lights) upon the heads of our horses ; the fine effect of
such a showery and ghostly illumination falling upon
our flowers and glittering laurels ; whilst all around
ourselves, that formed a centre of light, the darkness
gathered on the rear and flanks in massy blackness :
these optical splendours, together with the prodigious
enthusiasm of the people, composed a picture at once
scenical and affecting, theatrical and holy. As we
stayed for three or four minutes, I alighted ; and immediately from a dismantled stall in the street, where no
doubt she had been presiding through the earlier part
of the night, advanced eagerly a middle-aged woman.
The sight of my newspaper it was that had drawn her
attention upon myself. The victory which we were
carrying down to the provinces on *this* occasion was
the imperfect one of Talavera—imperfect for its results,
such was the virtual treachery of the Spanish general,
Cuesta, but not imperfect in its ever-memorable hero-
ism. I told her the main outline of the battle. The
agitation of her enthusiasm had been so conspicuous
when listening, and when first applying for information, that I could not but ask her if she had not some
relative in the Peninsular army. Oh yes ; her only son
was there. In what regiment ? He was a trooper in
the 23rd Dragoons. My heart sank within me as she
made that answer. This sublime regiment, which an
Englishman should never mention without raising his
hat to their memory, had made the most memorable

and effective charge recorded in military annals. They
leaped their horses—*over* a trench where they could ;
into it, and with the result of death or mutilation, when
they could *not*. What proportion cleared the trench is
5 nowhere stated. Those who *did* closed up and went
down upon the enemy with such divinity of fervour (I
use the word *divinity* by design : the inspiration of God
must have prompted this movement for those whom
even then He was calling to His presence) that two
10 results followed. As regarded the enemy, this 23rd
Dragoons, not, I believe, originally three hundred and
fifty strong, paralysed a French column six thousand
strong, then ascended the hill, and fixed the gaze of
the whole French army. As regarded themselves, the
15 23rd were supposed at first to have been barely not
annihilated ; but eventually, I believe, about one in
four survived. And this, then, was the regiment—a
regiment already for some hours glorified and hallowed
to the ear of all London, as lying stretched, by a large
20 majority, upon one bloody aceldama—in which the
young trooper served whose mother was now talking
in a spirit of such joyous enthusiasm. Did I tell her
the truth ? Had I the heart to break up her dreams ?
No. To-morrow, said I to myself—to-morrow, or the
25 next day, will publish the worst. For one night more
wherefore should she not sleep in peace ? After to-
morrow the chances are too many that peace will
forsake her pillow. This brief respite, then, let her owe
to *my* gift and *my* forbearance. But, if I told her not
30 of the bloody price that had been paid, not therefore
was I silent on the contributions from her son's regiment
to that day's service and glory. I showed her not the
funeral banners under which the noble regiment was
sleeping. I lifted not the overshadowing laurels from

the bloody trench in which horse and rider lay mangled together. But I told her how these dear children of England, officers and privates, had leaped their horses over all obstacles as gaily as hunters to the morning's chase. I told her how they rode their horses into the midst of death—saying to myself, but not saying to *her*, " and laid down their young lives for thee, O mother England ! as willingly—poured out their noble blood as cheerfully—as ever, after a long day's sport, when infants, they had rested their weary heads upon their mother's knees, or had sunk to sleep in her arms." Strange it is, yet true, that she seemed to have no fears for her son's safety, even after this knowledge that the 23rd Dragoons had been memorably engaged ; but so much was she enraptured by the knowledge that *his* regiment, and therefore that *he*, had rendered conspicuous service in the dreadful conflict—a service which had actually made them, within the last twelve hours, the foremost topic of conversation in London—so absolutely was fear swallowed up in joy—that, in the mere simplicity of her fervent nature, the poor woman threw her arms round my neck, as she thought of her son, and gave to *me* the kiss which secretly was meant for *him*.

SECTION II—THE VISION OF SUDDEN DEATH

What is to be taken as the predominant opinion of man, reflective and philosophic, upon SUDDEN DEATH ? It is remarkable that, in different conditions of society, sudden death has been variously regarded as the consummation of an earthly career most fervently to be desired, or, again, as that consummation which is with most horror to be deprecated. Cæsar the Dictator, at

his last dinner-party (*cœna*), on the very evening before
his assassination, when the minutes of his earthly career
were numbered, being asked what death, in *his* judgment, might be pronounced the most eligible, replied
5 " That which should be most sudden." On the other
hand, the divine Litany of our English Church, when
breathing forth supplications, as if in some representative character, for the whole human race prostrate
before God, places such a death in the very van of
10 horrors : " From lightning and tempest ; from plague,
pestilence, and famine ; from battle and murder, and
from SUDDEN DEATH—*Good Lord, deliver us.*" Sudden
death is here made to crown the climax in a grand
ascent of calamities ; it is ranked among the last of
15 curses ; and yet by the noblest of Romans it was ranked
as the first of blessings. In that difference most readers
will see little more than the essential difference between
Christianity and Paganism. But this, on consideration,
I doubt. The Christian Church may be right in its
20 estimate of sudden death ; and it is a natural feeling,
though after all it may also be an infirm one, to wish
for a quiet dismissal from life, as that which *seems* most
reconcilable with meditation, with penitential retro-
spects, and with the humilities of farewell prayer.

25   The incident, so memorable in itself by its features
of horror, and so scenical by its grouping for the eye,
which furnished the text for this reverie upon *Sudden
Death* occurred to myself in the dead of night, as a
solitary spectator, when seated on the box of the
30 Manchester and Glasgow mail, in the second or third
summer after Waterloo. I find it necessary to relate
the circumstances, because they are such as could not
have occurred unless under a singular combination of

accidents. In those days, the oblique and lateral communications with many rural post-offices were so
arranged, either through necessity or through defect
of system, as to make it requisite for the main north-
western mail (*i.e.* the *down* mail) on reaching Manchester to halt for a number of hours ; how many, I
do not remember ; six or seven, I think ; but the
result was that, in the ordinary course, the mail recommenced its journey northwards about midnight.
Wearied with the long detention at a gloomy hotel, I
walked out about eleven o'clock at night for the sake
of fresh air ; meaning to fall in with the mail and
resume my seat at the post-office. The night, however,
being yet dark, as the moon had scarcely risen, and the
streets being at that hour empty, so as to offer no opportunities for asking the road, I lost my way, and did not
reach the post-office until it was considerably past midnight ; but, to my great relief (as it was important for
me to be in Westmoreland by the morning), I saw in
the huge saucer eyes of the mail, blazing through the
gloom, an evidence that my chance was not yet lost.
Past the time it was ; but, by some rare accident, the
mail was not even yet ready to start. I ascended to
my seat on the box, where my cloak was still lying
as it had lain at the Bridgewater Arms. I had left it
there in imitation of a nautical discoverer, who leaves
a bit of bunting on the shore of his discovery, by way
of warning off the ground the whole human race, and
notifying to the Christian and the heathen worlds, with
his best compliments, that he has hoisted his pocket-
handkerchief once and for ever upon that virgin soil :
thenceforward claiming the *jus dominii* to the top of
the atmosphere above it, and also the right of driving
shafts to the centre of the earth below it ; so that all

people found after this warning either aloft in upper
chambers of the atmosphere, or groping in subterraneous shafts, or squatting audaciously on the surface
of the soil, will be treated as trespassers—kicked, that
5 is to say, or decapitated, as circumstances may suggest,
by their very faithful servant, the owner of the said
pocket-handkerchief. In the present case, it is probable
that my cloak might not have been respected, and the
jus gentium might have been cruelly violated in my
10 person—for, in the dark, people commit deeds of darkness, gas being a great ally of morality ; but it so
happened that on this night there was no other outside
passenger ; and thus the crime, which else was but too
probable, missed fire for want of a criminal.

15   Having mounted the box, I took a small quantity of
laudanum, having already travelled two hundred and
fifty miles—viz. from a point seventy miles beyond
London. In the taking of laudanum there was nothing
extraordinary. But by accident it drew upon me the
20 special attention of my assessor on the box, the coachman. And in *that* also there was nothing extraordinary.
But by accident, and with great delight, it drew my
own attention to the fact that this coachman was a
monster in point of bulk, and that he had but one eye.
25 In fact, he had been foretold by Virgil as

Monstrum horrendum, informe, ingens, cui lumen ademptum.

He answered to the conditions in every one of the items :
1. a monster he was ; 2. dreadful ; 3. shapeless ;
4. huge ; 5. who had lost an eye. But why should
30 *that* delight me ? Had he been one of the Calendars
in the *Arabian Nights*, and had paid down his eye as
the price of his criminal curiosity, what right had *I* to
exult in his misfortune ? I did *not* exult ; I delighted

in no man's punishment, though it were even merited.
But these personal distinctions (Nos. 1, 2, 3, 4, 5)
identified in an instant an old friend of mine whom I
had known in the south for some years as the most
masterly of mail-coachmen. He was the man in all
Europe that could (if *any* could) have driven six-in-
hand full gallop over *Al Sirat*—that dreadful bridge
of Mahomet, with no side battlements, and of *extra*
room not enough for a razor's edge—leading right
across the bottomless gulf. Under this eminent man,
whom in Greek I cognominated Cyclops *Diphrélates*
(Cyclops the Charioteer), I, and others known to me,
studied the diphrelatic art. Excuse, reader, a word
too elegant to be pedantic. As a pupil, though I paid
extra fees, it is to be lamented that I did not stand
high in his esteem. It showed his dogged honesty
(though, observe, not his discernment) that he could
not see my merits. Let us excuse his absurdity in this
particular by remembering his want of an eye. Doubtless *that* made him blind to my merits. In the art of
conversation, however, he admitted that I had the
whip-hand of him. On the present occasion great joy
was at our meeting. But what was Cyclops doing
here ? Had the medical men recommended northern
air, or how ? I collected, from such explanations as he
volunteered, that he had an interest at stake in some
suit-at-law now pending at Lancaster ; so that probably he had got himself transferred to this station for
the purpose of connecting with his professional pursuits
an instant readiness for the calls of his lawsuit.

Meantime, what are we stopping for ? Surely we
have now waited long enough. Oh, this procrastinating
mail, and this procrastinating post-office ! Can't they
take a lesson upon that subject from *me* ? Some people

have called *me* procrastinating. Yet you are witness,
reader, that I was here kept waiting for the post-office.
Will the post-office lay its hand on its heart, in its
moments of sobriety, and assert that ever it waited for
me? What are they about? The guard tells me that
there is a large extra accumulation of foreign mails this
night, owing to irregularities caused by war, by wind,
by weather, in the packet service, which as yet does not
benefit at all by steam. For an *extra* hour, it seems,
the post-office has been engaged in threshing out the
pure wheaten correspondence of Glasgow, and winnowing it from the chaff of all baser intermediate towns.
But at last all is finished. Sound your horn, guard!
Manchester, good-bye! we've lost an hour by your
criminal conduct at the post-office: which, however,
though I do not mean to part with a serviceable ground
of complaint, and one which really *is* such for the horses,
to me secretly is an advantage, since it compels us to
look sharply for this lost hour amongst the next eight
or nine, and to recover it (if we can) at the rate of one
mile extra per hour. Off we are at last, and at eleven
miles an hour; and for the moment I detect no changes
in the energy or in the skill of Cyclops.

From Manchester to Kendal, which virtually (though
not in law) is the capital of Westmoreland, there were
at this time seven stages of eleven miles each. The
first five of these, counting from Manchester, terminate
in Lancaster; which is therefore fifty-five miles north
of Manchester, and the same distance exactly from
Liverpool. The first three stages terminate in Preston
(called, by way of distinction from other towns of that
name, *Proud* Preston); at which place it is that the
separate roads from Liverpool and from Manchester
to the north become confluent. Within these first

three stages lay the foundation, the progress, and termination of our night's adventure. During the first
stage, I found out that Cyclops was mortal : he was
liable to the shocking affection of sleep—a thing which
previously I had never suspected. If a man indulges 5
in the vicious habit of sleeping, all the skill in aurigation of Apollo himself, with the horses of Aurora to
execute his notions, avails him nothing. " Oh,
Cyclops ! " I exclaimed, " thou art mortal. My friend,
thou snorest." Through the first eleven miles, how- 10
ever, this infirmity—which I grieve to say that he
shared with the whole Pagan Pantheon—betrayed itself
only by brief snatches. On waking up, he made an
apology for himself which, instead of mending matters,
laid open a gloomy vista of coming disasters. The 15
summer assizes, he reminded me, were now going on at
Lancaster : in consequence of which for three nights
and three days he had not lain down on a bed. During
the day he was waiting for his own summons as a witness
on the trial in which he was interested, or else, lest he 20
should be missing at the critical moment, was drinking
with the other witnesses under the pastoral surveillance
of the attorneys. During the night, or that part of
it which at sea would form the middle watch, he was
driving. This explanation certainly accounted for his 25
drowsiness, but in a way which made it much more
alarming ; since now, after several days' resistance to
this infirmity, at length he was steadily giving way.
Throughout the second stage he grew more and more
drowsy. In the second mile of the third stage he sur- 30
rendered himself finally and without a struggle to his
perilous temptation. All his past resistance had but
deepened the weight of this final oppression. Seven
atmospheres of sleep rested upon him ; and, to con-

summate the case, our worthy guard, after singing
" Love amongst the Roses " for perhaps thirty times,
without invitation and without applause, had in
revenge moodily resigned himself to slumber—not so
5 deep, doubtless, as the coachman's, but deep enough
for mischief. And thus at last, about ten miles from
Preston, it came about that I found myself left in
charge of his Majesty's London and Glasgow mail, then
running at the least twelve miles an hour.

10 What made this negligence less criminal than else it
must have been thought was the condition of the roads
at night during the assizes. At that time, all the law
business of populous Liverpool, and also of populous
Manchester, with its vast cincture of populous rural
15 districts, was called up by ancient usage to the tribunal
of Lilliputian Lancaster. To break up this old traditional usage required, (1) a conflict with powerful
established interests ; (2) a large system of new arrangements ; and (3) a new parliamentary statute. But as
20 yet this change was merely in contemplation. As things
were at present, twice in the year so vast a body of
business rolled northwards from the southern quarter
of the county that for a fortnight at least it occupied
the severe exertions of two judges in its despatch. The
25 consequence of this was that every horse available for
such a service, along the whole line of road, was exhausted in carrying down the multitudes of people who
were parties to the different suits. By sunset, therefore, it usually happened that, through utter exhaustion
30 amongst men and horses, the road sank into profound
silence. Except the exhaustion in the vast adjacent
county of York from a contested election, no such
silence succeeding to no such fiery uproar was ever
witnessed in England.

On this occasion the usual silence and solitude prevailed along the road. Not a hoof nor a wheel was
to be heard. And, to strengthen this false luxurious
confidence in the noiseless roads, it happened also that
the night was one of peculiar solemnity and peace. 5
For my own part, though slightly alive to the possi-
bilities of peril, I had so far yielded to the influence of
the mighty calm as to sink into a profound reverie.
The month was August ; in the middle of which lay
my own birthday—a festival to every thoughtful man 10
suggesting solemn and often sigh-born thoughts. The
county was my own native county—upon which, in its
southern section, more than upon any equal area known
to man past or present, had descended the original
curse of labour in its heaviest form, not mastering the 15
bodies only of men, as of slaves, or criminals in mines,
but working through the fiery will. Upon no equal
space of earth was, or ever had been, the same energy
of human power put forth daily. At this particular
season also of the assizes, that dreadful hurricane of 20
flight and pursuit, as it might have seemed to a stranger,
which swept to and from Lancaster all day long, hunting the county up and down, and regularly subsiding
back into silence about sunset, could not fail (when
united with this permanent distinction of Lancashire 25
as the very metropolis and citadel of labour) to point
the thoughts pathetically upon that counter-vision of
rest, of saintly repose from strife and sorrow, towards
which, as to their secret haven, the profounder aspirations of man's heart are in solitude continually travel- 30
ling. Obliquely upon our left we were nearing the sea ;
which also must, under the present circumstances, be
repeating the general state of halcyon repose. The sea,
the atmosphere, the light, bore each an orchestral part

in this universal lull. Moonlight and the first timid
tremblings of the dawn were by this time blending ;
and the blendings were brought into a still more
exquisite state of unity by a slight silvery mist, motion-
5 less and dreamy, that covered the woods and fields,
but with a veil of equable transparency. Except the
feet of our own horses—which, running on a sandy
margin of the road, made but little disturbance—there
was no sound abroad. In the clouds and on the earth
10 prevailed the same majestic peace ; and, in spite of
all that the villain of a schoolmaster has done for the
ruin of our sublimer thoughts, which are the thoughts
of our infancy, we still believe in no such nonsense as
a limited atmosphere. Whatever we may swear with
15 our false feigning lips, in our faithful hearts we still
believe, and must for ever believe, in fields of air
traversing the total gulf between earth and the central
heavens. Still, in the confidence of children that tread
without fear *every* chamber in their father's house, and
20 to whom no door is closed, we, in that Sabbatic vision
which sometimes is revealed for an hour upon nights
like this, ascend with easy steps from the sorrow-
stricken fields of earth upwards to the sandals of God.

Suddenly, from thoughts like these I was awakened
25 to a sullen sound, as of some motion on the distant road.
It stole upon the air for a moment ; I listened in awe ;
but then it died away. Once roused, however, I could
not but observe with alarm the quickened motion of
our horses. Ten years' experience had made my eye
30 learned in the valuing of motion ; and I saw that we
were now running thirteen miles an hour. I pretend
to no presence of mind. On the contrary, my fear is
that I am miserably and shamefully deficient in that
quality as regards action. The palsy of doubt and dis-

traction hangs like some guilty weight of dark unfathomed remembrances upon my energies when the
signal is flying for *action*. But, on the other hand, this
accursed gift I have, as regards *thought*, that in the first
step towards the possibility of a misfortune I see its
total evolution ; in the radix of the series I see too
certainly and too instantly its entire expansion ; in
the first syllable of the dreadful sentence I read already
the last. It was not that I feared for ourselves. *Us*
our bulk and impetus charmed against peril in any
collision. And I had ridden through too many hundreds of perils that were frightful to approach, that
were matter of laughter to look back upon, the first
face of which was horror, the parting face a jest—for
any anxiety to rest upon *our* interests. The mail was
not built, I felt assured, nor bespoke, that could betray
me who trusted to its protection. But any carriage
that we could meet would be frail and light in comparison of ourselves. And I remarked this ominous
accident of our situation—we were on the wrong side
of the road. But then, it may be said, the other party,
if other there was, might also be on the wrong side ;
and two wrongs might make a right. *That* was not
likely. The same motive which had drawn *us* to the
right-hand side of the road—viz. the luxury of the
soft beaten sand as contrasted with the paved centre
—would prove attractive to others. The two adverse
carriages would therefore, to a certainty, be travelling
on the same side ; and from this side, as not being ours
in law, the crossing over to the other would, of course,
be looked for from *us*. Our lamps, still lighted, would
give the impression of vigilance on our part. And
every creature that met us would rely upon *us* for
quartering. All this, and if the separate links of the

anticipation had been a thousand times more, I saw, not discursively, or by effort, or by succession, but by one flash of horrid simultaneous intuition.

Under this steady though rapid anticipation of the evil which *might* be gathering ahead, ah ! what a sullen mystery of fear, what a sigh of woe, was that which stole upon the air, as again the far-off sound of a wheel was heard ! A whisper it was—a whisper from, perhaps, four miles off—secretly announcing a ruin that, being foreseen, was not the less inevitable ; that, being known, was not therefore healed. What could be done—who was it that could do it—to check the storm-flight of these maniacal horses ? Could I not seize the reins from the grasp of the slumbering coachman ? You, reader, think that it would have been in *your* power to do so. And I quarrel not with your estimate of yourself. But, from the way in which the coachman's hand was viced between his upper and lower thigh, this was impossible. Easy was it ? See, then, that bronze equestrian statue. The cruel rider has kept the bit in his horse's mouth for two centuries. Unbridle him for a minute, if you please, and wash his mouth with water. Easy was it ? Unhorse me, then, that imperial rider ; knock me those marble feet from those marble stirrups of Charlemagne.

The sounds ahead strengthened, and were now too clearly the sounds of wheels. Who and what could it be ? Was it industry in a taxed cart ? Was it youthful gaiety in a gig ? Was it sorrow that loitered, or joy that raced ? For as yet the snatches of sound were too intermitting, from distance, to decipher the character of the motion. Whoever were the travellers, something must be done to warn them. Upon the other party rests the active responsibility, but upon *us*

—and, woe is me! that *us* was reduced to my frail
opium-shattered self—rests the responsibility of warning. Yet, how should this be accomplished? Might
I not sound the guard's horn? Already, on the first
thought, I was making my way over the roof to the
guard's seat. But this, from the accident which I have
mentioned, of the foreign mails being piled upon the
roof, was a difficult and even dangerous attempt to
one cramped by nearly three hundred miles of outside
travelling. And, fortunately, before I had lost much
time in the attempt, our frantic horses swept round
an angle of the road which opened upon us that final
stage where the collision must be accomplished and the
catastrophe sealed. All was apparently finished. The
court was sitting; the case was heard; the judge had
finished; and only the verdict was yet in arrear.

Before us lay an avenue straight as an arrow, six
hundred yards, perhaps, in length; and the umbrageous trees, which rose in a regular line from either side,
meeting high overhead, gave to it the character of a
cathedral aisle. These trees lent a deeper solemnity
to the early light; but there was still light enough to
perceive, at the further end of this Gothic aisle, a frail
reedy gig, in which were seated a young man, and by
his side a young lady. Ah, young sir! what are you
about? If it is requisite that you should whisper your
communications to this young lady—though really I
see nobody, at an hour and on a road so solitary, likely
to overhear you—is it therefore requisite that you
should carry your lips forward to hers? The little
carriage is creeping on at one mile an hour; and the
parties within it, being thus tenderly engaged, are
naturally bending down their heads. Between them
and eternity, to all human calculation, there is but a

minute and a half. Oh heavens! what is it that I
shall do? Speaking or acting, what help can I offer?
Strange it is, and to a mere auditor of the tale might
seem laughable, that I should need a suggestion from
5 the *Iliad* to prompt the sole resource that remained.
Yet so it was. Suddenly I remembered the shout of
Achilles, and its effect. But could I pretend to shout
like the son of Peleus, aided by Pallas? No: but then
I needed not the shout that should alarm all Asia
10 militant; such a shout would suffice as might carry
terror into the hearts of two thoughtless young people
and one gig-horse. I shouted—and the young man
heard me not. A second time I shouted—and now he
heard me, for now he raised his head.

15 Here, then, all had been done that, by me, *could* be
done; more on *my* part was not possible. Mine had
been the first step; the second was for the young man;
the third was for God. If, said I, this stranger is a
brave man, and if indeed he loves the young girl at
20 his side—or, loving her not, if he feels the obligation,
pressing upon every man worthy to be called a man, of
doing his utmost for a woman confided to his protection—he will at least make some effort to save her. If
that fails, he will not perish the more, or by a death
25 more cruel, for having made it; and he will die as a
brave man should, with his face to the danger, and with
his arm about the woman that he sought in vain to
save. But, if he makes no effort—shrinking without
a struggle from his duty—he himself will not the less
30 certainly perish for this baseness of poltroonery. He
will die no less: and why not? Wherefore should we
grieve that there is one craven less in the world? No;
let him perish, without a pitying thought of ours wasted
upon him; and, in that case, all our grief will be

reserved for the fate of the helpless girl who now, upon
the least shadow of failure in *him*, must by the fiercest
of translations—must without time for a prayer—must
within seventy seconds—stand before the judgment-
seat of God.   5

But craven he was not : sudden had been the call
upon him, and sudden was his answer to the call.   He
saw, he heard, he comprehended, the ruin that was
coming down : already its gloomy shadow darkened
above him ; and already he was measuring his strength 10
to deal with it.   Ah ! what a vulgar thing does courage
seem when we see nations buying it and selling it for a
shilling a-day : ah ! what a sublime thing does courage
seem when some fearful summons on the great deeps
of life carries a man, as if running before a hurricane, 15
up to the giddy crest of some tumultuous crisis from
which lie two courses, and a voice says to him audibly,
" One way lies hope ; take the other, and mourn for
ever ! "   How grand a triumph if, even then, amidst the
raving of all around him, and the frenzy of the danger, 20
the man is able to confront his situation—is able to
retire for a moment into solitude with God, and to
seek his counsel from *Him* !

For seven seconds, it might be, of his seventy, the
stranger settled his countenance steadfastly upon us, as 25
if to search and value every element in the conflict
before him.   For five seconds more of his seventy he
sat immovably, like one that mused on some great
purpose.   For five more, perhaps, he sat with eyes
upraised, like one that prayed in sorrow, under some 30
extremity of doubt, for light that should guide him
to the better choice.   Then suddenly he rose ; stood
upright ; and, by a powerful strain upon the reins,
raising his horse's fore-feet from the ground, he slewed

him round on the pivot of his hind-legs, so as to plant
the little equipage in a position nearly at right angles
to ours. Thus far his condition was not improved ;
except as a first step had been taken towards the
possibility of a second. If no more were done, nothing
was done ; for the little carriage still occupied the very
centre of our path, though in an altered direction.
Yet even now it may not be too late : fifteen of the
seventy seconds may still be unexhausted ; and one
almighty bound may avail to clear the ground. Hurry,
then, hurry ! for the flying moments—*they* hurry.
Oh, hurry, hurry, my brave young man ! for the cruel
hoofs of our horses—*they* also hurry ! Fast are the
flying moments, faster are the hoofs of our horses.
But fear not for *him*, if human energy can suffice ;
faithful was he that drove to his terrific duty ; faithful
was the horse to *his* command. One blow, one impulse
given with voice and hand, by the stranger, one rush
from the horse, one bound as if in the act of rising to
a fence, landed the docile creature's forefeet upon the
crown or arching centre of the road. The larger half of
the little equipage had then cleared our overtowering
shadow : *that* was evident even to my own agitated
sight. But it mattered little that one wreck should
float off in safety if upon the wreck that perished were
embarked the human freightage. The rear part of the
carriage—was *that* certainly beyond the line of absolute ruin ? What power could answer the question ?
Glance of eye, thought of man, wing of angel, which of
these had speed enough to sweep between the question
and the answer, and divide the one from the other ?
Light does not tread upon the steps of light more
indivisibly than did our all-conquering arrival upon the
escaping efforts of the gig. *That* must the young man

have felt too plainly. His back was now turned to
us ; not by sight could he any longer communicate
with the peril ; but, by the dreadful rattle of our harness, too truly had his ear been instructed that all
was finished as regarded any effort of *his*. Already in 5
resignation he had rested from his struggle ; and perhaps in his heart he was whispering, " Father, which
art in heaven, do Thou finish above what I on earth
have attempted." Faster than ever millrace we ran
past them in our inexorable flight. Oh, raving of 10
hurricanes that must have sounded in their young ears
at the moment of our transit ! Even in that moment
the thunder of collision spoke aloud. Either with the
swingle-bar, or with the haunch of our near leader, we
had struck the off-wheel of the little gig ; which stood 15
rather obliquely, and not quite so far advanced as to
be accurately parallel with the near-wheel. The blow,
from the fury of our passage, resounded terrifically.
I rose in horror, to gaze upon the ruins we might have
caused. From my elevated station I looked down, 20
and looked back upon the scene ; which in a moment
told its own tale, and wrote all its records on my heart
for ever.

Here was the map of the passion that now had
finished. The horse was planted immovably, with 25
his fore-feet upon the paved crest of the central road.
He of the whole party might be supposed untouched
by the passion of death. The little cany carriage—
partly, perhaps, from the violent torsion of the wheels
in its recent movement, partly from the thundering 30
blow we had given to it—as if it sympathised with
human horror, was all alive with tremblings and shiver-
ings. The young man trembled not, nor shivered. He
sat like a rock. But *his* was the steadiness of agitation

frozen into rest by horror. As yet he dared not to look round ; for he knew that, if anything remained to do, by him it could no longer be done. And as yet he knew not for certain if their safety were accomplished. But
5 the lady——

But the lady—— ! Oh, heavens ! will that spectacle ever depart from my dreams, as she rose and sank upon her seat, sank and rose, threw up her arms wildly to heaven, clutched at some visionary object in the air,
10 fainting, praying, raving, despairing ? Figure to yourself, reader, the elements of the case ; suffer me to recall before your mind the circumstances of that unparalleled situation. From the silence and deep peace of this saintly summer night—from the pathetic blending of
15 this sweet moonlight, dawnlight, dreamlight—from the manly tenderness of this flattering, whispering, murmuring love—suddenly as from the woods and fields— suddenly as from the chambers of the air opening in revelation—suddenly as from the ground yawning at
20 her feet, leaped upon her, with the flashing of cataracts, Death the crowned phantom, with all the equipage of his terrors, and the tiger roar of his voice.

The moments were numbered ; the strife was finished ; the vision was closed. In the twinkling of an eye, our
25 flying horses had carried us to the termination of the umbrageous aisle ; at the right angles we wheeled into our former direction ; the turn of the road carried the scene out of my eyes in an instant, and swept it into my dreams for ever.

Section III—Dream-Fugue:

FOUNDED ON THE PRECEDING THEME OF SUDDEN DEATH

> Whence the sound
> Of instruments, that made melodious chime,
> Was heard, of harp and organ ; and who moved
> Their stops and chords was seen ; his volant touch
> Instinct through all proportions, low and high,   5
> Fled and pursued transverse the resonant fugue.
> *Par. Lost*, Bk. XI.

Tumultuosissimamente

PASSION of sudden death ! that once in youth I read and interpreted by the shadows of thy averted signs ! —rapture of panic taking the shape (which amongst tombs in churches I have seen) of woman bursting 10 her sepulchral bonds—of woman's Ionic form bending forward from the ruins of her grave with arching foot, with eyes upraised, with clasped adoring hands— waiting, watching, trembling, praying for the trumpet's call to rise from dust for ever ! Ah, vision too fearful 15 of shuddering humanity on the brink of almighty abysses !—vision that didst start back, that didst reel away, like a shrivelling scroll from before the wrath of fire racing on the wings of the wind ! Epilepsy so brief of horror, wherefore is it that thou canst not die ? 20 Passing so suddenly into darkness, wherefore is it that still thou sheddest thy sad funeral blights upon the gorgeous mosaics of dreams ? Fragment of music too passionate, heard once, and heard no more, what aileth thee, that thy deep rolling chords come up at intervals 25 through all the worlds of sleep, and after forty years have lost no element of horror ?

I

Lo, it is summer—almighty summer! The ever-lasting gates of life and summer are thrown open wide; and on the ocean, tranquil and verdant as a savannah, the unknown lady from the dreadful vision and I myself are floating—she upon a fairy pinnace, and I upon an English three-decker. Both of us are wooing gales of festal happiness within the domain of our common country, within that ancient watery park, within the pathless chase of ocean, where England takes her pleasure as a huntress through winter and summer, from the rising to the setting sun. Ah, what a wilderness of floral beauty was hidden, or was suddenly revealed, upon the tropic islands through which the pinnace moved! And upon her deck what a bevy of human flowers: young women how lovely, young men how noble, that were dancing together, and slowly drifting towards *us* amidst music and incense, amidst blossoms from forests and gorgeous corymbi from vintages, amidst natural carolling, and the echoes of sweet girlish laughter. Slowly the pinnace nears us, gaily she hails us, and silently she disappears beneath the shadow of our mighty bows. But then, as at some signal from heaven, the music, and the carols, and the sweet echoing of girlish laughter—all are hushed. What evil has smitten the pinnace, meeting or over-taking her? Did ruin to our friends couch within our own dreadful shadow? Was our shadow the shadow of death? I looked over the bow for an answer, and, behold! the pinnace was dismantled; the revel and the revellers were found no more; the glory of the vintage was dust; and the forests with their beauty were left without a witness upon the seas. "But where," and I turned to our crew—"where are the lovely women that danced beneath the awning of flowers and clustering corymbi? Whither have fled the noble young men that danced with *them*?" Answer there was none. But suddenly the man at the mast-head, whose countenance darkened with alarm, cried out, "Sail on the weather beam! Down she comes upon us: in seventy seconds she also will founder."

II

I looked to the weather side, and the summer had departed. The sea was rocking, and shaken with gathering wrath. Upon its surface sat mighty mists, which grouped themselves into arches and long cathedral aisles. Down one of these, with the fiery pace of a quarrel from a cross-bow, ran a frigate right athwart our course. "Are they mad?" some voice exclaimed from our deck. "Do they woo their ruin?" But in a moment, as she was close upon us, some impulse of a heady current or local vortex gave a wheeling bias to her course, and off she forged without a shock. As she ran past us, high aloft amongst the shrouds stood the lady of the pinnace. The deeps opened ahead in malice to receive her, towering surges of foam ran after her, the billows were fierce to catch her. But far away she was borne into desert spaces of the sea: whilst still by sight I followed her, as she ran before the howling gale, chased by angry sea-birds and by maddening billows; still I saw her, as at the moment when she ran past us, standing amongst the shrouds, with her white draperies streaming before the wind. There she stood, with hair dishevelled, one hand clutched amongst the tackling—rising, sinking, fluttering,

trembling, praying; there for leagues I saw her as she
stood, raising at intervals one hand to heaven, amidst
the fiery crests of the pursuing waves and the raving of
the storm; until at last, upon a sound from afar of
5 malicious laughter and mockery, all was hidden for ever
in driving showers; and afterwards, but when I knew
not, nor how.

III

Sweet funeral bells from some incalculable distance,
wailing over the dead that die before the dawn, awakened
10 me as I slept in a boat moored to some familiar shore.
The morning twilight even then was breaking; and,
by the dusky revelations which it spread, I saw a girl,
adorned with a garland of white roses about her head
for some great festival, running along the solitary
15 strand in extremity of haste. Her running was the
running of panic; and often she looked back as to some
dreadful enemy in the rear. But, when I leaped ashore,
and followed on her steps to warn her of a peril in front,
alas! from me she fled as from another peril, and vainly
20 I shouted to her of quicksands that lay ahead. Faster
and faster she ran; round a promontory of rocks she
wheeled out of sight; in an instant I also wheeled
round it, but only to see the treacherous sands gathering
above her head. Already her person was buried; only
25 the fair young head and the diadem of white roses
around it were still visible to the pitying heavens; and,
last of all, was visible one white marble arm. I saw
by the early twilight this fair young head, as it was
sinking down to darkness—saw this marble arm, as it
30 rose above her head and her treacherous grave, tossing,
faltering, rising, clutching, as at some false deceiving
hand stretched out from the clouds—saw this marble

arm uttering her dying hope, and then uttering her dying despair. The head, the diadem, the arm—these all had sunk ; at last over these also the cruel quicksand had closed ; and no memorial of the fair young girl remained on earth, except my own solitary tears, and the funeral bells from the desert seas, that, rising again more softly, sang a requiem over the grave of the buried child, and over her blighted dawn.

I sat, and wept in secret the tears that men have ever given to the memory of those that died before the dawn, and by the treachery of earth, our mother. But suddenly the tears and funeral bells were hushed by a shout as of many nations, and by a roar as from some great king's artillery, advancing rapidly along the valleys, and heard afar by echoes from the mountains. " Hush ! " I said, as I bent my ear earthwards to listen—" hush ! —this either is the very anarchy of strife, or else "— and then I listened more profoundly, and whispered as I raised my head—" or else, oh heavens ! it is *victory* that is final, victory that swallows up all strife."

IV

Immediately, in trance, I was carried over land and sea to some distant kingdom, and placed upon a triumphal car, amongst companions crowned with laurel. The darkness of gathering midnight, brooding over all the land, hid from us the mighty crowds that were weaving restlessly about ourselves as a centre : we heard them, but saw them not. Tidings had arrived, within an hour, of a grandeur that measured itself against centuries ; too full of pathos they were, too full of joy, to utter themselves by other language than by tears, by restless anthems, and *Te Deums* reverberated

from the choirs and orchestras of earth. These tidings
we that sat upon the laurelled car had it for our privilege to publish amongst all nations. And already, by
signs audible through the darkness, by snortings and
5 tramplings, our angry horses, that knew no fear or
fleshly weariness, upbraided us with delay. Wherefore
was it that we delayed? We waited for a secret word,
that should bear witness to the hope of nations as now
accomplished for ever. At midnight the secret word
10 arrived; which word was—*Waterloo and Recovered
Christendom!* The dreadful word shone by its own
light; before us it went; high above our leaders'
heads it rode, and spread a golden light over the paths
which we traversed. Every city, at the presence of
15 the secret word, threw open its gates. The rivers were
conscious as we crossed. All the forests, as we ran
along their margins, shivered in homage to the secret
word. And the darkness comprehended it.

Two hours after midnight we approached a mighty
20 Minster. Its gates, which rose to the clouds, were
closed. But, when the dreadful word that rode before
us reached them with its golden light, silently they
moved back upon their hinges; and at a flying gallop
our equipage entered the grand aisle of the cathedral.
25 Headlong was our pace; and at every altar, in the
little chapels and oratories to the right hand and left
of our course, the lamps, dying or sickening, kindled
anew in sympathy with the secret word that was
flying past. Forty leagues we might have run in the
30 cathedral, and as yet no strength of morning light had
reached us, when before us we saw the aerial galleries
of organ and choir. Every pinnacle of fretwork, every
station of advantage amongst the traceries, was crested
by white-robed choristers that sang deliverance; that

wept no more tears, as once their fathers had wept ; but at intervals that sang together to the generations, saying,

Chant the deliverer's praise in every tongue,

and receiving answers from afar, 5

Such as once in heaven and earth were sung.

And of their chanting was no end ; of our headlong pace was neither pause nor slackening.

Thus as we ran like torrents—thus as we swept with bridal rapture over the Campo Santo of the cathedral 10 graves—suddenly we became aware of a vast necropolis rising upon the far-off horizon—a city of sepulchres, built within the saintly cathedral for the warrior dead that rested from their feuds on earth. Of purple granite was the necropolis ; yet, in the first minute, it 15 lay like a purple stain upon the horizon, so mighty was the distance. In the second minute it trembled through many changes, growing into terraces and towers of wondrous altitude, so mighty was the pace. In the third minute already, with our dreadful gallop, we were 20 entering its suburbs. Vast sarcophagi rose on every side, having towers and turrets that, upon the limits of the central aisle, strode forward with haughty intrusion, that ran back with mighty shadows into answering recesses. Every sarcophagus showed many bas-reliefs 25 —bas-reliefs of battles and of battle-fields ; battles from forgotten ages, battles from yesterday ; battle-fields that, long since, nature had healed and reconciled to herself with the sweet oblivion of flowers ; battle-fields that were yet angry and crimson with carnage. Where the terraces 30 ran, there did *we* run ; where the towers curved, there did *we* curve. With the flight of swallows our horses

swept round every angle.   Like rivers in flood wheeling
round headlands, like hurricanes that ride into the
secrets of forests, faster than ever light unwove the
mazes of darkness, our flying equipage carried earthly
5 passions, kindled warrior instincts, amongst the dust
that lay around us—dust oftentimes of our noble
fathers that had slept in God from Crécy to Trafalgar.
And now had we reached the last sarcophagus, now were
we abreast of the last bas-relief, already had we recovered
10 the arrow-like flight of the illimitable central aisle, when
coming up this aisle to meet us we beheld afar off a
female child, that rode in a carriage as frail as flowers.
The mists which went before her hid the fawns that
drew her, but could not hide the shells and tropic
15 flowers with which she played—but could not hide the
lovely smiles by which she uttered her trust in the
mighty cathedral, and in the cherubim that looked
down upon her from the mighty shafts of its pillars.
Face to face she was meeting us ; face to face she rode,
20 as if danger there were none.   " Oh, baby ! " I exclaimed, " shalt thou be the ransom for Waterloo ?
Must we, that carry tidings of great joy to every people,
be messengers of ruin to thee ! "   In horror I rose at
the thought ; but then also, in horror at the thought,
25 rose one that was sculptured on a bas-relief—a Dying
Trumpeter.   Solemnly from the field of battle he rose
to his feet ; and, unslinging his stony trumpet, carried
it, in his dying anguish, to his stony lips—sounding once, and yet once again ; proclamation that,
30 in *thy* ears, oh baby ! spoke from the battlements of
death.   Immediately deep shadows fell between us,
and aboriginal silence.   The choir had ceased to sing.
The hoofs of our horses, the dreadful rattle of our
harness, the groaning of our wheels, alarmed the graves

no more. By horror the bas-relief had been unlocked unto life. By horror we, that were so full of life, we men and our horses, with their fiery fore-legs rising in mid-air to their everlasting gallop, were frozen to a bas-relief. Then a third time the trumpet sounded; the seals were taken off all pulses; life, and the frenzy of life, tore into their channels again; again the choir burst forth in sunny grandeur, as from the muffling of storms and darkness; again the thunderings of our horses carried temptation into the graves. One cry burst from our lips, as the clouds, drawing off from the aisle, showed it empty before us.—" Whither has the infant fled?—is the young child caught up to God?" Lo! afar off, in a vast recess, rose three mighty windows to the clouds; and on a level with their summits, at height insuperable to man, rose an altar of purest alabaster. On its eastern face was trembling a crimson glory. A glory was it from the reddening dawn that now streamed *through* the windows? Was it from the crimson robes of the martyrs painted *on* the windows? Was it from the bloody bas-reliefs of earth? There, suddenly, within that crimson radiance, rose the apparition of a woman's head, and then of a woman's figure. The child it was—grown up to woman's height. Clinging to the horns of the altar, voiceless she stood— sinking, rising, raving, despairing; and behind the volume of incense that, night and day, streamed upwards from the altar, dimly was seen the fiery font, and the shadow of that dreadful being who should have baptised her with the baptism of death. But by her side was kneeling her better angel, that hid his face with wings; that wept and pleaded for *her*; that prayed when *she* could *not*; that fought with Heaven by tears for *her* deliverance; which also, as he raised his immortal countenance from his wings, I saw, by the glory in his eye, that from Heaven he had won at last.

V

Then was completed the passion of the mighty fugue. The golden tubes of the organ, which as yet had but muttered at intervals—gleaming amongst clouds and surges of incense—threw up, as from fountains unfathomable, columns of heart-shattering music. Choir and anti-choir were filling fast with unknown voices. Thou also, Dying Trumpeter, with thy love that was victorious, and thy anguish that was finishing, didst enter the tumult; trumpet and echo—farewell love, and farewell anguish—rang through the dreadful *sanctus*. Oh, darkness of the grave! that from the crimson altar and from the fiery font wert visited and searched by the effulgence in the angel's eye—were these indeed thy children? Pomps of life, that, from the burials of centuries, rose again to the voice of perfect joy, did ye indeed mingle with the festivals of Death? Lo! as I looked back for seventy leagues through the mighty cathedral, I saw the quick and the dead that sang together to God, together that sang to the generations of man. All the hosts of jubilation, like armies that ride in pursuit, moved with one step. Us, that, with laurelled heads, were passing from the cathedral, they overtook, and, as with a garment, they wrapped us round with thunders greater than our own. As brothers we moved together; to the dawn that advanced, to the stars that fled; rendering thanks to God in the highest—that, having hid His face through one generation behind thick clouds of War, once again was ascending, from the Campo Santo of Waterloo was

ascending, in the visions of Peace ; rendering thanks
for thee, young girl ! whom having overshadowed with
His ineffable passion of death, suddenly did God relent,
suffered thy angel to turn aside His arm, and even in
thee, sister unknown ! shown to me for a moment only 5
to be hidden for ever, found an occasion to glorify His
goodness. A thousand times, amongst the phantoms
of sleep, have I seen thee entering the gates of the
golden dawn, with the secret word riding before thee,
with the armies of the grave behind thee—seen thee 10
sinking, rising, raving, despairing ; a thousand times
in the worlds of sleep have I seen thee followed by
God's angel through storms, through desert seas,
through the darkness of quicksands, through dreams
and the dreadful revelations that are in dreams ; only 15
that at the last, with one sling of His victorious arm,
He might snatch thee back from ruin, and might
emblazon in thy deliverance the endless resurrections
of His love !

BIOGRAPHY

JOAN OF ARC

WHAT is to be thought of *her* ? What is to be thought
of the poor shepherd girl from the hills and forests of
Lorraine, that—like the Hebrew shepherd boy from the
hills and forests of Judea—rose suddenly out of the
5 quiet, out of the safety, out of the religious inspiration,
rooted in deep pastoral solitudes, to a station in the
van of armies, and to the more perilous station at the
right hand of kings ? The Hebrew boy inaugurated
his patriotic mission by an *act*, by a victorious *act*, such
10 as no man could deny. But so did the girl of Lorraine,
if we read her story as it was read by those who saw
her nearest. Adverse armies bore witness to the boy
as no pretender ; but so they did to the gentle girl.
Judged by the voices of all who saw them *from a station
15 of good will*, both were found true and loyal to any
promises involved in their first acts. Enemies it was
that made the difference between their subsequent
fortunes. The boy rose to a splendour and a noonday
prosperity, both personal and public, that rang through
20 the records of his people, and became a byword among
his posterity for a thousand years, until the sceptre was
departing from Judah. The poor, forsaken girl, on the
contrary, drank not herself from that cup of rest which
she had secured for France. She never sang together
25 with the songs that rose in her native Domrémy as
echoes to the departing steps of invaders. She mingled
not in the festal dances at Vaucouleurs which celebrated

in rapture the redemption of France. No! for her voice was then silent; no! for her feet were dust. Pure, innocent, noble-hearted girl! whom, from earliest youth, ever I believed in as full of truth and self-sacrifice, this was amongst the strongest pledges for *thy* truth, that never once—no, not for a moment of weakness—didst thou revel in the vision of coronets and honour from man. Coronets for thee! Oh, no! Honours, if they come when all is over, are for those that share thy blood. Daughter of Domrémy, when the gratitude of thy king shall awaken, thou wilt be sleeping the sleep of the dead. Call her, King of France, but she will not hear thee. Cite her by the apparitors to come and receive a robe of honour, but she will be found *en contumace*. When the thunders of universal France, as even yet may happen, shall proclaim the grandeur of the poor shepherd girl that gave up all for her country, thy ear, young shepherd girl, will have been deaf for five centuries. To suffer and to do, that was thy portion in this life; that was thy destiny; and not for a moment was it hidden from thyself. Life, thou saidst, is short; and the sleep which is in the grave is long; let me use that life, so transitory, for the glory of those heavenly dreams destined to comfort the sleep which is so long! This pure creature—pure from every suspicion of even a visionary self-interest, even as she was pure in senses more obvious—never once did this holy child, as regarded herself, relax from her belief in the darkness that was travelling to meet her. She might not prefigure the very manner of her death; she saw not in vision, perhaps, the aerial altitude of the fiery scaffold, the spectators without end, on every road, pouring into Rouen as to a coronation, the surging smoke, the volleying flames, the hostile faces

all around, the pitying eye that lurked but here and there, until nature and imperishable truth broke loose from artificial restraints—these might not be apparent through the mists of the hurrying future. But the
5 voice that called her to death, *that* she heard for ever.

Great was the throne of France even in those days, and great was he that sat upon it; but well Joanna knew that not the throne, nor he that sat upon it, was for *her* ; but, on the contrary, that she was for *them* ;
10 not she by them, but they by her, should rise from the dust. Gorgeous were the lilies of France, and for centuries had the privilege to spread their beauty over land and sea, until, in another century, the wrath of God and man combined to wither them ; but well
15 Joanna knew, early at Domrémy she had read that bitter truth, that the lilies of France would decorate no garland for *her*. Flower nor bud, bell nor blossom, would ever bloom for *her* !

.   .   .   .

The education of this poor girl was mean according
20 to the present standard : was ineffably grand, according to a purer philosophic standard : and only not good for our age because for us it would be unattainable. She read nothing, for she could not read ; but she had heard others read parts of the Roman martyrology.
25 She wept in sympathy with the sad *Misereres* of the Romish Church ; she rose to heaven with the glad triumphant *Te Deums* of Rome ; she drew her comfort and her vital strength from the rites of the same Church. But, next after these spiritual advantages, she owed
30 most to the advantages of her situation. The fountain of Domrémy was on the brink of a boundless forest ; and it was haunted to that degree by fairies that the parish priest (*curé*) was obliged to read mass there once

a year, in order to keep them in any decent bounds.
Fairies are important, even in a statistical view : certain
weeds mark poverty in the soil ; fairies mark its
solitude. As surely as the wolf retires before cities
does the fairy sequester herself from the haunts of
the licensed victualler. A village is too much for her
nervous delicacy ; at most, she can tolerate a distant
view of a hamlet. We may judge, therefore, by the
uneasiness and extra trouble which they gave to the
parson, in what strength the fairies mustered at
Domrémy, and, by a satisfactory consequence, how
thinly sown with men and women must have been that
region even in its inhabited spots. But the forests of
Domrémy—those were the glories of the land : for in
them abode mysterious powers and ancient secrets that
towered into tragic strength. " Abbeys there were,
and abbey windows "—" like Moorish temples of the
Hindoos "—that exercised even princely power both in
Lorraine and in the German Diets. These had their
sweet bells that pierced the forests for many a league
at matins or vespers, and each its own dreamy legend.
Few enough, and scattered enough, were these abbeys,
so as in no degree to disturb the deep solitude of the
region ; yet many enough to spread a network or awning of Christian sanctity over what else might have
seemed a heathen wilderness. This sort of religious
talisman being secured, a man the most afraid of ghosts
(like myself, suppose, or the reader) becomes armed into
courage to wander for days in their sylvan recesses.
The mountains of the Vosges, on the eastern frontier
of France, have never attracted much notice from
Europe, except in 1813-14 for a few brief months, when
they fell within Napoleon's line of defence against the
Allies. But they are interesting for this among other

features, that they do not, like some loftier ranges, repel
woods ; the forests and the hills are on sociable terms.
" Live and let live " is their motto. For this reason,
in part, these tracts in Lorraine were a favourite
5 hunting-ground with the Carlovingian princes. About
six hundred years before Joanna's childhood, Charlemagne was known to have hunted there. That, of
itself, was a grand incident in the traditions of a forest
or a chase. In these vast forests, also, were to be found
10 (if anywhere to be found) those mysterious fawns that
tempted solitary hunters into visionary and perilous
pursuits. Here was seen (if anywhere seen) that
ancient stag who was already nine hundred years old,
but possibly a hundred or two more, when met by
15 Charlemagne ; and the thing was put beyond doubt
by the inscription upon his golden collar. I believe
Charlemagne knighted the stag ; and, if ever he is met
again by a king, he ought to be made an earl, or, being
upon the marches of France, a marquis. Observe, I
20 don't absolutely vouch for all these things : my own
opinion varies. On a fine breezy forenoon I am audaciously sceptical ; but as twilight sets in my credulity
grows steadily, till it becomes equal to anything that
could be desired. And I have heard candid sportsmen
25 declare that, outside of these very forests, they laughed
loudly at all the dim tales connected with their haunted
solitudes, but, on reaching a spot notoriously eighteen
miles deep within them, they agreed with Sir Roger
de Coverley that a good deal might be said on both
30 sides.

Such traditions, or any others that (like the stag)
connect distant generations with each other, are, for
that cause, sublime ; and the sense of the shadowy,
connected with such appearances that reveal them-

selves or not according to circumstances, leaves a colouring of sanctity over ancient forests, even in those minds
that utterly reject the legend as a fact.

But, apart from all distinct stories of that order, in
any solitary frontier between two great empires—as
here, for instance, or in the desert between Syria and
the Euphrates—there is an inevitable tendency, in
minds of any deep sensibility, to people the solitudes
with phantom images of powers that were of old so
vast. Joanna, therefore, in her quiet occupation of a
shepherdess, would be led continually to brood over
the political condition of her country by the traditions
of the past no less than by the mementoes of the local
present.

It is not requisite for the honour of Joanna, nor is
there in this place room, to pursue her brief career of
action. That, though wonderful, forms the earthly
part of her story; the spiritual part is the saintly
passion of her imprisonment, trial, and execution. It
is sufficient, as concerns *this* section of Joanna's life, to
say that she fulfilled, to the height of her promises, the
restoration of the prostrate throne. France had become
a province of England, and for the ruin of both, if
such a yoke could be maintained. Dreadful pecuniary
exhaustion caused the English energy to droop; and
that critical opening La Pucelle used with a corresponding felicity of audacity and suddenness (that were in
themselves portentous) for introducing the wedge of
French native resources, for rekindling the national
pride, and for planting the dauphin once more upon
his feet. When Joanna appeared, he had been on the
point of giving up the struggle with the English, distressed as they were, and of flying to the south of France.

She taught him to blush for such abject counsels. She
liberated Orleans, that great city, so decisive by its
fate for the issue of the war, and then beleaguered by
the English with an elaborate application of engineering
5 skill unprecedented in Europe. Entering the city after
sunset on the 29th of April, she sang Mass on Sunday,
8th May, for the entire disappearance of the besieging
force. On the 29th of June she fought and gained over
the English the decisive battle of Patay; on the 9th of
10 July she took Troyes by a *coup-de-main* from a mixed
garrison of English and Burgundians; on the 15th of
that month she carried the dauphin into Rheims; on
Sunday the 17th she crowned him; and there she
rested from her labour of triumph. All that was to be
15 *done* she had now accomplished; what remained was—
to *suffer*.

All this forward movement was her own; excepting
one man, the whole council was against her. Her
enemies were all that drew power from earth. Her
20 supporters were her own strong enthusiasm, and the
headlong contagion by which she carried this sublime
frenzy into the hearts of women, of soldiers, and of all
who lived by labour. Henceforward she was thwarted;
and the worst error that she committed was to lend
25 the sanction of her presence to counsels which she had
ceased to approve. But she had now accomplished the
capital objects which her own visions had dictated.
These involved all the rest. Errors were now less
important; and doubtless it had now become more
30 difficult for herself to pronounce authentically what
were errors. The noble girl had achieved, as by a
rapture of motion, the capital end of clearing out a free
space around her sovereign, giving him the power to
move his arms with effect, and, secondly, the inappreci-

able end of winning for that sovereign what seemed to all France the heavenly ratification of his rights, by crowning him with the ancient solemnities. She had made it impossible for the English now to step before her. They were caught in an irretrievable blunder, owing partly to discord among the uncles of Henry VI, partly to a want of funds, but partly to the very impossibility which they believed to press with tenfold force upon any French attempt to forestall theirs. They laughed at such a thought ; and, while they laughed, she *did* it. Henceforth the single redress for the English of this capital oversight, but which never *could* have redressed it effectually, was to vitiate and taint the coronation of Charles VII as the work of a witch. That policy, and not malice (as M. Michelet is so happy to believe), was the moving principle in the subsequent prosecution of Joanna. Unless they unhinged the force of the first coronation in the popular mind by associating it with power given from hell, they felt that the sceptre of the invader was broken.

But she, the child that, at nineteen, had wrought wonders so great for France, was she not elated ? Did she not lose, as men so often *have* lost, all sobriety of mind when standing upon the pinnacle of success so giddy ? Let her enemies declare. During the progress of her movement, and in the centre of ferocious struggles, she had manifested the temper of her feelings by the pity which she had everywhere expressed for the suffering enemy. She forwarded to the English leaders a touching invitation to unite with the French, as brothers, in a common crusade against infidels— thus opening the road for a soldierly retreat. She interposed to protect the captive or the wounded ; she mourned over the excesses of her countrymen ; she

threw herself off her horse to kneel by the dying English
soldier, and to comfort him with such ministrations,
physical or spiritual, as his situation allowed. " Nolebat," says the evidence, " uti ense suo, aut quemquam
5 interficere." She sheltered the English that invoked
her aid in her own quarters. She wept as she beheld,
stretched on the field of battle, so many brave enemies
that had died without confession. And, as regarded
herself, her elation expressed itself thus : on the day
10 when she had finished her work, she wept ; for she knew
that, when her *triumphal* task was done, her end must
be approaching. Her aspirations pointed only to a
place which seemed to her more than usually full of
natural piety, as one in which it would give her pleasure
15 to die. And she uttered, between smiles and tears, as
a wish that inexpressibly fascinated her heart, and yet
was half fantastic, a broken prayer that God would
return her to the solitudes from which He had drawn
her, and suffer her to become a shepherdess once more.
20 It was a natural prayer, because nature has laid a
necessity upon every human heart to seek for rest and
to shrink from torment. Yet, again, it was a half-
fantastic prayer, because, from childhood upward,
visions that she had no power to mistrust, and the
25 voices which sounded in her ear for ever, had long since
persuaded her mind that for *her* no such prayer could be
granted. Too well she felt that her mission must be
worked out to the end, and that the end was now at
hand. All went wrong from this time. She herself
30 had created the *funds* out of which the French restoration should grow ; but she was not suffered to witness
their development or their prosperous application.
More than one military plan was entered upon which
she did not approve. But she still continued to expose

her person as before. Severe wounds had not taught her caution. And at length, in a sortie from Compiègne (whether through treacherous collusion on the part of her own friends is doubtful to this day), she was made prisoner by the Burgundians, and finally surrendered 5 to the English.

Now came her trial. This trial, moving of course under English influence, was conducted in chief by the Bishop of Beauvais. He was a Frenchman, sold to English interests, and hoping, by favour of the 10 English leaders, to reach the highest preferment. " Bishop that art, Archbishop that shalt be, Cardinal that mayest be," were the words that sounded continually in his ear ; and doubtless a whisper of visions still higher, of a triple crown, and feet upon the necks 15 of kings, sometimes stole into his heart. M. Michelet is anxious to keep us in mind that this bishop was but an agent of the English. True. But it does not better the case for his countryman that, being an accomplice in the crime, making himself the leader in 20 the persecution against the helpless girl, he was willing to be all this in the spirit, and with the conscious vileness of a cat's-paw. Never from the foundations of the earth was there such a trial as this, if it were laid open in all its beauty of defence and all its hellish- 25 ness of attack. Oh, child of France ! shepherdess, peasant girl ! trodden under foot by all around thee, how I honour thy flashing intellect, quick as God's lightning, and true as God's lightning to its mark, that ran before France and laggard Europe by many a 30 century, confounding the malice of the ensnarer, and making dumb the oracles of falsehood ! Is it not scandalous, is it not humiliating to civilisation, that, even at this day, France exhibits the horrid spectacle

of judges examining the prisoner against himself;
seducing him, by fraud, into treacherous conclusions
against his own head; using the terrors of their power
for extorting confessions from the frailty of hope;
5 nay (which is worse), using the blandishments of con-
descension and snaky kindness for thawing into com-
pliances of gratitude those whom they had failed to
freeze into terror? Wicked judges! barbarian jurisprudence!—that, sitting in your own conceit on the
10 summits of social wisdom, have yet failed to learn the
first principles of criminal justice—sit ye humbly and
with docility at the feet of this girl from Domrémy,
that tore your webs of cruelty into shreds and dust.
" Would you examine me as a witness against myself?"
15 was the question by which many times she defied their
arts. Continually she showed that their interrogations
were irrelevant to any business before the court, or
that entered into the ridiculous charges against her.
General questions were proposed to her on points of
20 casuistical divinity; two-edged questions, which not
one of themselves could have answered, without, on
the one side, landing himself in heresy (as then interpreted), or, on the other, in some presumptuous expression of self-esteem. Next came a wretched Dominican,
25 that pressed her with an objection, which, if applied
to the Bible, would tax every one of its miracles
with unsoundness. The monk had the excuse of never
having read the Bible. M. Michelet has no such excuse;
and it makes one blush for him, as a philosopher, to
30 find him describing such an argument as " weighty,"
whereas it is but a varied expression of rude Mahometan
metaphysics. Her answer to this, if there were room
to place the whole in a clear light, was as shattering
as it was rapid. Another thought to entrap her by

asking what language the angelic visitors of her solitude
had talked—as though heavenly counsels could want
polyglot interpreters for every word, or that God
needed language at all in whispering thoughts to a
human heart. Then came a worse devil, who asked 5
her whether the Archangel Michael had appeared
naked. Not comprehending the vile insinuation,
Joanna, whose poverty suggested to her simplicity
that it might be the *costliness* of suitable robes which
caused the demur, asked them if they fancied God, 10
who clothed the flowers of the valleys, unable to find
raiment for his servants. The answer of Joanna
moves a smile of tenderness, but the disappointment of
her judges makes one laugh exultingly. Others succeeded by troops, who upbraided her with leaving her 15
father ; as if that greater Father, whom she believed
herself to have been serving, did not retain the power of
dispensing with his own rules, or had not said that for
a less cause than martyrdom man and woman should
leave both father and mother. 20

On Easter Sunday, when the trial had been long
proceeding, the poor girl fell so ill as to cause a belief
that she had been poisoned. It was not poison.
Nobody had any interest in hastening a death so
certain. M. Michelet, whose sympathies with all feel- 25
ings are so quick that one would gladly see them always
as justly directed, reads the case most truly. Joanna
had a twofold malady. She was visited by a paroxysm
of the complaint called *homesickness*. The cruel nature
of her imprisonment, and its length, could not but 30
point her solitary thoughts, in darkness and in chains
(for chained she was), to Domrémy. And the season,
which was the most heavenly period of the spring,
added stings to this yearning. That was one of her

maladies—*nostalgia*, as medicine calls it ; the other was
weariness and exhaustion from daily combats with
malice.   She saw that everybody hated her and thirsted
for her blood ; nay, many kind-hearted creatures that
would have pitied her profoundly, as regarded all
political charges, had their natural feelings warped by
the belief that she had dealings with fiendish powers.
She knew she was to die ; that was *not* the misery ! the
misery was that this consummation could not be reached
without so much intermediate strife, as if she were
contending for some chance (where chance was none) of
happiness, or were dreaming for a moment of escaping
the inevitable.   Why, then, *did* she contend ?   Knowing
that she would reap nothing from answering her per-
secutors, why did she not retire by silence from the
superfluous contest ?   It was because her quick and
eager loyalty to truth would not suffer her to see it
darkened by frauds which *she* could expose, but others,
even of candid listeners, perhaps, could not ; it was
through that imperishable grandeur of soul which
taught her to submit meekly and without a struggle
to her punishment, but taught her *not* to submit—
no, not for a moment—to calumny as to facts, or to
misconstruction as to motives.   Besides, there were
secretaries all around the court taking down her words.
That was meant for no good to *her*.   But the end does
not always correspond to the meaning.   And Joanna
might say to herself, " These words that will be used
against me to-morrow and the next day, perhaps, in
some nobler generation, may rise again for my justification."   Yes, Joanna, they *are* rising even now in
Paris, and for more than justification !

Woman, sister, there are some things which you do
not execute as well as your brother, man ; no, nor ever

will. Pardon me if I doubt whether you will ever produce a great poet from your choirs, or a Mozart, or a Phidias, or a Michael Angelo, or a great philosopher, or a great scholar. By which last is meant—not one who depends simply on an infinite memory, but also on an infinite and electrical power of combination ; bringing together from the four winds, like the angel of the resurrection, what else were dust from dead men's bones, into the unity of breathing life. If you *can* create yourselves into any of these great creators, why have you not ?

Yet, sister woman, though I cannot consent to find a Mozart or a Michael Angelo in your sex, cheerfully, and with the love that burns in depths of admiration, I acknowledge that you can do one thing as well as the best of us men—a greater thing than even Milton is known to have done, or Michael Angelo ; you can die grandly, and as goddesses would die, were goddesses mortal. If any distant worlds (which *may* be the case) are so far ahead of us Tellurians in optical resources as to see distinctly through their telescopes all that we do on earth, what is the grandest sight to which we ever treat them ? St Peter's at Rome, do you fancy, on Easter Sunday, or Luxor, or perhaps the Himalayas ? Oh, no ! my friend ; suggest something better ; these are baubles to *them* ; they see in other worlds, in their own, far better toys of the same kind. These, take my word for it, are nothing. Do you give it up ? The finest thing, then, we have to show them is a scaffold on the morning of execution. I assure you there is a strong muster in those far telescopic worlds, on any such morning, of those who happen to find themselves occupying the right hemisphere for a peep at *us*. How, then, if it be announced in some such telescopic

world by those who make a livelihood of catching
glimpses at our newspapers, whose language they have
long since deciphered, that the poor victim in the
morning's sacrifice is a woman ?   How, if it be pub-
5 lished in that distant world that the sufferer wears
upon her head, in the eyes of many, the garlands of
martyrdom ? How, if it should be some Marie
Antoinette, the widowed queen, coming forward on
the scaffold, and presenting to the morning air her
10 head, turned grey by sorrow—daughter of Cæsars
kneeling down humbly to kiss the guillotine, as one
that worships death ? How, if it were the noble
Charlotte Corday, that in the bloom of youth, that with
the loveliest of persons, that with homage waiting
15 upon her smiles wherever she turned her face to scatter
them—homage that followed those smiles as surely
as the carols of birds, after showers in spring, follow
the reappearing sun and the racing of sunbeams over
the hills—yet thought all these things cheaper than the
20 dust upon her sandals, in comparison of deliverance
from hell for her dear suffering France ! Ah ! these
were spectacles indeed for those sympathising people
in distant worlds ; and some, perhaps, would suffer a
sort of martyrdom themselves, because they could not
25 testify their wrath, could not bear witness to the
strength of love and to the fury of hatred that burned
within them at such scenes, could not gather into
golden urns some of that glorious dust which rested
in the catacombs of earth.

30   Bishop of Beauvais ! thy victim died in fire upon a
scaffold—thou upon a down bed. But, for the departing minutes of life, both are oftentimes alike. At the
farewell crisis, when the gates of death are opening,

and flesh is resting from its struggles, oftentimes the tortured and the torturer have the same truce from carnal torment; both sink together into sleep; together both sometimes kindle into dreams. When the mortal mists were gathering fast upon you two, 5 bishop and shepherd girl—when the pavilions of life were closing up their shadowy curtains about you— let us try, through the gigantic glooms, to decipher the flying features of your separate visions.

The shepherd girl that had delivered France—she, 10 from her dungeon, she, from her baiting at the stake, she, from her duel with fire, as she entered her last dream—saw Domrémy, saw the fountain of Domrémy, saw the pomp of forests in which her childhood had wandered. That Easter festival which man had denied 15 to her languishing heart—that resurrection of spring-time, which the darkness of dungeons had intercepted from *her*, hungering after the glorious liberty of forests —were by God given back into her hands as jewels that had been stolen from her by robbers. With 20 those, perhaps (for the minutes of dreams can stretch into ages), was given back to her by God the bliss of childhood. By special privilege for *her* might be created, in this farewell dream, a second childhood, innocent as the first; but not, like *that*, sad with the 25 gloom of a fearful mission in the rear. This mission had now been fulfilled. The storm was weathered; the skirts even of that mighty storm were drawing off. The blood that she was to reckon for had been exacted; the tears that she was to shed in secret had been paid 30 to the last. The hatred to herself in all eyes had been faced steadily, had been suffered, had been survived. And in her last fight upon the scaffold she had triumphed gloriously; victoriously she had tasted the

stings of death.   For all, except this comfort from her
farewell dream, she had died—died amid the tears of
ten thousand enemies—died amid the drums and
trumpets of armies—died amid peals redoubling upon
5 peals, volleys upon volleys, from the saluting clarions
of martyrs.

Bishop of Beauvais! because the guilt-burdened man
is in dreams haunted and waylaid by the most frightful
of his crimes, and because upon that fluctuating mirror
10 —rising (like the mocking mirrors of *mirage* in Arabian
deserts) from the fens of death—most of all are reflected
the sweet countenances which the man has laid in
ruins; therefore I know, bishop, that you also, entering your final dream, saw Domrémy.   That fountain,
15 of which the witnesses spoke so much, showed itself to
your eyes in pure morning dews; but neither dews,
nor the holy dawn, could cleanse away the bright spots
of innocent blood upon its surface.   By the fountain,
bishop, you saw a woman seated, that hid her face.
20 But, as *you* draw near, the woman raises her wasted
features.   Would Domrémy know them again for the
features of her child?   Ah, but *you* know them, bishop,
well!   Oh, mercy! what a groan was *that* which the
servants, waiting outside the bishop's dream at his bed-
25 side, heard from his labouring heart, as at this moment
he turned away from the fountain and the woman,
seeking rest in the forests afar off.   Yet not *so* to escape
the woman, whom once again he must behold before
he dies.   In the forests to which he prays for pity, will
30 he find a respite?   What a tumult, what a gathering
of feet is there!   In glades where only wild deer should
run armies and nations are assembling; towering in
the fluctuating crowd are phantoms that belong to
departed hours.   There is the great English Prince,

Regent of France. There is my Lord of Winchester,
the princely cardinal, that died and made no sign.
There is the bishop of Beauvais, clinging to the shelter
of thickets. What building is that which hands so
rapid are raising ? Is it a martyr's scaffold ? Will 5
they burn the child of Domrémy a second time ? No ;
it is a tribunal that rises to the clouds ; and two
nations stand around it, waiting for a trial. Shall my
Lord of Beauvais sit again upon the judgment-seat,
and again number the hours for the innocent ? Ah, 10
no ! he is the prisoner at the bar. Already all is waiting : the mighty audience is gathered, the Court is
hurrying to their seats, the witnesses are arrayed, the
trumpets are sounding, the judge is taking his place.
Oh, but this is sudden ! My lord, have you no counsel ? 15
" Counsel I have none ; in heaven above, or on earth
beneath, counsellor there is none now that would take
a brief from *me* : all are silent." Is it, indeed, come to
this ? Alas ! the time is short, the tumult is wondrous,
the crowd stretches away into infinity ; but yet I will 20
search in it for somebody to take your brief ; I know
of somebody that will be your counsel. Who is this
that cometh from Domrémy ? Who is she in bloody
coronation robes from Rheims ? Who is she that
cometh with blackened flesh from walking the furnaces 25
of Rouen ? This is she, the shepherd girl, counsellor
that had none for herself, whom I choose, bishop, for
yours. She it is, I engage, that shall take my lord's
brief. She it is, bishop, that would plead for you ;
yes, bishop, *she*—when heaven and earth are silent. 30

HISTORY

Revolt of the Tartars

OR, FLIGHT OF THE KALMUCK KHAN AND HIS PEOPLE FROM THE RUSSIAN TERRITORIES TO THE FRONTIERS OF CHINA

THERE is no great event in modern history, or, perhaps it may be said more broadly, none in all history, from its earliest records, less generally known, or more striking to the imagination, than the flight eastwards of a
5 principal Tartar nation across the boundless steppes of Asia in the latter half of the last century. The *terminus a quo* of this flight, and the *terminus ad quem*, are equally magnificent ; the mightiest of Christian thrones being the one, the mightiest of Pagan the other. And the
10 grandeur of these two terminal objects is harmoniously supported by the romantic circumstances of the flight. In the abruptness of its commencement, and the fierce velocity of its execution, we read the wild barbaric character of those who conducted the movement. In
15 the unity of purpose connecting this myriad of wills, and in the blind but unerring aim at a mark so remote, there is something which recalls to the mind those almighty instincts that propel the migrations of the swallow and the lemming, or the life-withering marches
20 of the locust. Then again, in the gloomy vengeance of Russia and her vast artillery, which hung upon the rear and the skirts of the fugitive vassals, we are reminded of Miltonic images—such, for instance, as that of the solitary hand pursuing through desert spaces and

through ancient chaos a rebellious host, and overtaking with volleying thunders those who believed themselves already within the security of darkness and of distance.

On the 21st of January, 1761, the young Prince Oubacha assumed the sceptre of the Kalmucks upon the death of his father. Some part of the power attached to this dignity he had already wielded since his fourteenth year, in quality of Vice-Khan, by the express appointment and with the avowed support of the Russian Government. He was now about eighteen years of age, amiable in his personal character, and not without titles to respect in his public character as a sovereign prince. In times more peaceable, and amongst a people more entirely civilised, or more humanised by religion, it is even probable that he might have discharged his high duties with considerable distinction. But his lot was thrown upon stormy times, and a most difficult crisis amongst tribes, whose native ferocity was exasperated by debasing forms of superstition, and by a nationality as well as an inflated conceit of their own merit absolutely unparalleled, whilst the circumstances of their hard and trying position under the jealous surveillance of an irresistible lord paramount, in the person of the Russian Czar, gave a fiercer edge to the natural unamiableness of the Kalmuck disposition, and irritated its gloomier qualities into action under the restless impulses of suspicion and permanent distrust. No prince could hope for a cordial allegiance from his subjects, or a peaceful reign under the circumstances of the case ; for the dilemma in which a Kalmuck ruler stood at present was of this nature : *wanting* the sanction and support of the Czar, he was inevitably too weak from without to command

confidence from his subjects, or resistance to his com-
petitors ; on the other hand, *with* this kind of support,
and deriving his title in any degree from the favour of
the Imperial Court, he became almost in that extent an
5 object of hatred at home, and within the whole compass
of his own territory. He was at once an object of
hatred for the past, being a living monument of national
independence, ignominiously surrendered, and an object
of jealousy for the future, as one who had already adver-
10 tised himself to be a fitting tool for the ultimate purposes
(whatsoever those might prove to be) of the Russian
Court. Coming himself to the Kalmuck sceptre under
the heaviest weight of prejudice from the unfortunate
circumstances of his position, it might have been
15 expected that Oubacha would have been pre-eminently
an object of detestation ; for, besides his known dependence upon the Cabinet of St Petersburg, the direct line
of succession had been set aside, and the principle of
inheritance violently suspended, in favour of his own
20 father, so recently as nineteen years before the era
of his own accession, consequently within the lively
remembrance of the existing generation. He therefore,
almost equally with his father, stood within the full
current of the national prejudices, and might have
25 anticipated the most pointed hostility. But it was not
so : such are the caprices in human affairs, that he was
even, in a moderate sense, popular—a benefit which
wore the more cheering aspect, and the promises of
permanence, inasmuch as he owed it exclusively to his
30 personal qualities of kindness and affability, as well as
to the beneficence of his government. On the other
hand, to balance this unlooked-for prosperity at the
outset of his reign, he met with a rival in popular favour
—almost a competitor—in the person of Zebek-Dorchi,

a prince with considerable pretensions to the throne,
and perhaps, it might be said, with equal pretensions.
Zebek-Dorchi was a direct descendant of the same royal
house as himself, through a different branch. On public
grounds his claim stood, perhaps, on a footing equally
good with that of Oubacha, whilst his personal qualities,
even in those aspects which seemed to a philosophical
observer most odious and repulsive, promised the most
effectual aid to the dark purposes of an intriguer or a
conspirator, and were generally fitted to win a popular
support precisely in those points where Oubacha was
most defective. He was much superior in external
appearance to his rival on the throne, and so far better
qualified to win the good opinion of a semi-barbarous
people ; whilst his dark intellectual qualities of Machiavellian dissimulation, profound hypocrisy, and perfidy
which knew no touch of remorse, were admirably
calculated to sustain any ground which he might win
from the simple-hearted people with whom he had to
deal—and from the frank carelessness of his unconscious
competitor.

At the very outset of his treacherous career, Zebek-
Dorchi was sagacious enough to perceive that nothing
could be gained by open declaration of hostility to the
reigning prince. A triple vengeance was what he meditated : (1) upon the Russian Cabinet for having under-
valued his own pretensions to the throne ; (2) upon his
amiable rival for having supplanted him ; and (3) upon
all those of the nobility who had manifested their sense
of his weakness by their neglect, or their sense of
his perfidious character by their suspicions. Here
was a colossal outline of wickedness ; and by one in
his situation, feeble (as it might seem) for the accomplishment of its humblest parts, how was the total

edifice to be reared in its comprehensive grandeur?
He, a worm as he was, could he venture to assail the
mighty behemoth of Muscovy, the potentate who
counted three hundred languages around the footsteps
5 of his throne, and from whose "lion ramp" recoiled
alike "baptised and infidel"—Christendom on the one
side, strong by her intellect and her organisation, and
the "barbaric East" on the other, with her unnumbered
numbers? The match was a monstrous one; but in
10 its very monstrosity there lay this germ of encourage-
ment, that it could not be suspected. The very hope-
lessness of the scheme grounded his hopes, and he
resolved to execute a vengeance which should involve,
as it were, in the unity of a well-laid tragic fable, all
15 whom he judged to be his enemies. That vengeance
lay in detaching from the Russian empire the whole
Kalmuck nation, and breaking up that system of intercourse which had thus far been beneficial to both. This
last was a consideration which moved him but little.
20 True it was, that Russia to the Kalmucks had secured
lands and extensive pasturage; true it was, that the
Kalmucks reciprocally to Russia had furnished a powerful cavalry. But the latter loss would be part of his
triumph, and the former might be more than compen-
25 sated in other climates under other sovereigns. Here
was a scheme which, in its final accomplishment, would
avenge him bitterly on the Czarina, and in the course
of its accomplishment might furnish him with ample
occasions for removing his other enemies. It may be
30 readily supposed, indeed, that he who could deliberately
raise his eyes to the Russian autocrat as an antagonist
in single duel with himself, was not likely to feel much
anxiety about Kalmuck enemies of whatever rank. He
took his resolution, therefore, sternly and irrevocably to

effect this astonishing translation of an ancient people
across the pathless deserts of Central Asia, intersected
continually by rapid rivers, rarely furnished with
bridges, and of which the fords were known only to
those who might think it for their interest to conceal
them, through many nations inhospitable or hostile ;
frost and snow around them (from the necessity of commencing their flight in winter), famine in their front,
and the sabre, or even the artillery of an offended and
mighty empress, hanging upon their rear for thousands
of miles. But what was to be their final mark—the
port of shelter after so fearful a course of wandering ?
Two things were evident : it must be some power at a
great distance from Russia, so as to make return even
in that view hopeless ; and it must be a power of sufficient rank to ensure them protection from any hostile
efforts on the part of the Czarina for reclaiming them,
or for chastising their revolt. Both conditions were
united obviously in the person of Kien Long, the
reigning Emperor of China, who was further recommended to them by his respect for the head of
their religion. To China, therefore, and, as their first
rendezvous, to the shadow of the great Chinese Wall,
it was settled by Zebek that they should direct their
flight.

It is contended by many persons who have reviewed
the affair with a command of all the documents bearing
on the case, more especially the letters or minutes of
Council subsequently discovered in the handwriting
of Zebek-Dorchi, and the important evidence of the
Russian captive Weseloff, who was carried off by the
Kalmucks in their flight, that beyond all doubt Oubacha
was powerless for any purpose of impeding or even of
delaying the revolt. He himself, indeed, was under

religious obligations of the most terrific solemnity never
to flinch from the enterprise, or even to slacken in
his zeal : for Zebek-Dorchi, distrusting the firmness
of his resolution under any unusual pressure of alarm
5 or difficulty, had, in the very earliest stage of the
conspiracy, availed himself of the Khan's well-known
superstition to engage him, by means of previous concert
with the priests and their head the Lama, in some dark
and mysterious rites of consecration, terminating in
10 oaths under such terrific sanctions as no Kalmuck would
have courage to violate. As far, therefore, as regarded
the personal share of the Khan in what was to come,
Zebek was entirely at his ease ; he knew him to be so
deeply pledged by religious terrors to the prosecution of
15 the conspiracy, that no honours within the Czarina's
gift could have possibly shaken his adhesion : and then,
as to threats from the same quarter, he knew him to be
sealed against those fears by others of a gloomier character, and better adapted to his peculiar temperament.
20 For Oubacha was a brave man as respected all bodily
enemies or the dangers of human warfare, but was as
sensitive and as timid as the most superstitious of old
women in facing the frowns of a priest, or under the
vague anticipations of ghostly retributions. But, had
25 it been otherwise, and had there been any reason to
apprehend an unsteady demeanour on the part of this
prince at the approach of the critical moment, such
were the changes already effected in the state of their
domestic politics amongst the Tartars, by the under-
30 mining arts of Zebek-Dorchi and his ally the Lama, that
very little importance would have attached to that
doubt. All power was now effectually lodged in the
hands of Zebek-Dorchi. He was the true and absolute
wielder of the Kalmuck sceptre ; all measures of import-

ance were submitted to his discretion ; and nothing was
finally resolved but under his dictation. This result he
had brought about, in a year or two, by means sufficiently simple ; first of all, by availing himself of the
prejudice in his favour, so largely diffused amongst the 5
lowest of the Kalmucks, that his own title to the throne,
in quality of great-grandson in a direct line from Ajouka,
the most illustrious of all the Kalmuck Khans, stood
upon a better basis than that of Oubacha, who derived
from a collateral branch ; secondly, with respect to 10
that sole advantage which Oubacha possessed above
himself in the ratification of his title, by improving this
difference between their situations to the disadvantage
of his competitor, as one who had not scrupled to accept
that triumph from an alien power at the price of his 15
independence, which he himself (as he would have it
understood) disdained to court ; thirdly, by his own
talents and address, coupled with the ferocious energy
of his moral character ; fourthly—and perhaps in an
equal degree—by the criminal facility and good-nature 20
of Oubacha ; finally (which is remarkable enough, as
illustrating the character of the man), by that very new
modelling of the Sarga or Privy Council which he had
used as a principal topic of abuse and malicious insinuation against the Russian Government, whilst, in reality, 25
he first had suggested the alteration to the Empress,
and he chiefly appropriated the political advantages
which it was fitted to yield. For, as he was himself
appointed the chief of the Sargatchi, and as the pensions
to the inferior Sargatchi passed through his hands, 30
whilst in effect they owed their appointments to his
nomination, it may be easily supposed, that whatever
power existed in the state capable of controlling the
Khan, being held by the Sarga under its new organisa-

tion, and this body being completely under his influence, the final result was to throw all the functions of the state, whether nominally in the Prince or in the Council, substantially into the hands of this one man ; whilst,
5 at the same time, from the strict league which he maintained with the Lama, all the thunders of the spiritual power were always ready to come in aid of the magistrate, or to supply his incapacity in cases which he could not reach.

10   But the time was now rapidly approaching for the mighty experiment. The day was drawing near on which the signal was to be given for raising the standard of revolt, and by a combined movement on both sides of the Wolga for spreading the smoke of one vast
15 conflagration, that should wrap in a common blaze their own huts and the stately cities of their enemies, over the breadth and length of those great provinces in which their flocks were dispersed. The Year of the Tiger was now within one little month of its com-
20 mencement ; the fifth morning of that year was fixed for the fatal day when the fortunes and happiness of a whole nation were to be put upon the hazard of a dicer's throw ; and as yet that nation was in profound ignorance of the whole plan. The Khan, such was
25 the kindness of his nature, could not bring himself to make the revelation so urgently required. It was clear, however, that this could not be delayed ; and Zebek-Dorchi took the task willingly upon himself. But where or how should this notification be made, so as
30 to exclude Russian hearers ? After some deliberation, the following plan was adopted : Couriers, it was contrived, should arrive in furious haste, one upon the heels of another, reporting a sudden inroad of the Kirghises and Bashkirs upon the Kalmuck lands, at

a point distant about 120 miles. Thither all the
Kalmuck families, according to immemorial custom,
were required to send a separate representative ; and
there accordingly, within three days, all appeared.
The distance, the solitary ground appointed for the
rendezvous, the rapidity of the march, all tended to
make it almost certain that no Russian could be
present. Zebek-Dorchi then came forward. He did
not waste many words upon rhetoric. He unfurled an
immense sheet of parchment, visible from the uttermost distance at which any of this vast crowd could
stand ; the total number amounted to 80,000 ; all saw,
and many heard. They were told of the oppressions
of Russia ; of her pride and haughty disdain evidenced
towards them by a thousand acts ; of her contempt for
their religion ; of her determination to reduce them to
absolute slavery ; of the preliminary measures she had
already taken by erecting forts upon many of the
great rivers in their neighbourhood ; of the ulterior
intentions she thus announced to circumscribe their
pastoral lands, until they would all be obliged to
renounce their flocks, and to collect in towns like
Sarepta, there to pursue mechanical and servile trades
of shoemaker, tailor, and weaver, such as the free-born
Tartar had always disdained. " Then again," said the
subtle prince, " she increases her military levies upon
our population every year ; we pour out our blood as
young men in her defence, or more often in support
of her insolent aggressions ; and as old men, we reap
nothing from our sufferings, nor benefit by our survivor-
ship where so many are sacrificed." At this point of
his harangue, Zebek produced several papers (forged, as
it is generally believed, by himself and the Lama),
containing projects of the Russian court for a general

transfer of the eldest sons, taken *en masse* from the
greatest Kalmuck families, to the Imperial Court.
" Now let this be once accomplished," he argued, " and
there is an end of all useful resistance from that day
forwards. Petitions we might make, or even remon-
strances ; as men of words we might play a bold part ;
but for deeds, for that sort of language by which our
ancestors were used to speak—holding us by such a
chain, Russia would make a jest of our wishes, knowing
full well that we should not dare to make any effectual
movement."

Having thus sufficiently roused the angry passions
of his vast audience, and having alarmed their fears
by this pretended scheme against their first-born (an
artifice which was indispensable to his purpose, because
it met beforehand *every* form of amendment to his
proposal coming from the more moderate nobles, who
would not otherwise have failed to insist upon trying
the effect of bold addresses to the Empress, before
resorting to any desperate extremity), Zebek-Dorchi
opened his scheme of revolt, and, if so, of instant revolt ;
since any preparations reported at St Petersburg would
be a signal for the armies of Russia to cross into such
positions from all parts of Asia as would effectually
intercept their march. It is remarkable, however, that,
with all his audacity and his reliance upon the momentary excitement of the Kalmucks, the subtle prince did
not venture, at this stage of his seduction, to make so
startling a proposal as that of a flight to China. All
that he held out for the present was a rapid march
to the Temba or some other great river, which they were
to cross, and to take up a strong position on the farther
bank, from which, as from a post of conscious security,
they could hold a bolder language to the Czarina, and

one which would have a better chance of winning a favourable audience.

These things, in the irritated condition of the simple Tartars, passed by acclamation ; and all returned homewards to push forward with the most furious speed the preparations for their awful undertaking. Rapid and energetic these of necessity were ; and in that degree they became noticeable and manifest to the Russians who happened to be intermingled with the different hordes either on commercial errands, or as agents officially from the Russian Government, some in a financial, others in a diplomatic character.

Precisely on the 5th of January, the day so solemnly appointed under religious sanctions by the Lama, the Kalmucks on the east bank of the Wolga were seen at the earliest dawn of day assembling by troops and squadrons, and in the tumultuous movement of some great morning of battle. Tens of thousands continued moving off the ground at every half-hour's interval. Women and children, to the amount of two hundred thousand and upwards, were placed upon wagons, or upon camels, and drew off by masses of twenty thousand at once—placed under suitable escorts, and continually swelled in numbers by other outlying bodies of the horde, who kept falling in at various distances upon the first and second day's march. From sixty to eighty thousand of those who were the best mounted stayed behind the rest of the tribes, with purposes of devastation and plunder more violent than prudence justified, or the amiable character of the Khan could be supposed to approve. But in this, as in other instances, he was completely overruled by the malignant counsels of Zebek-Dorchi. The first tempest of the desolating fury of the Tartars discharged itself upon their own

habitations. But this, as cutting off all infirm looking
backward from the hardships of their march, had been
thought so necessary a measure by all the chieftains,
that even Oubacha himself was the first to authorise
the act by his own example. He seized a torch previously prepared with materials the most durable as
well as combustible, and steadily applied it to the
timbers of his own palace. Nothing was saved from the
general wreck except the portable part of the domestic
utensils, and that part of the woodwork which could
be applied to the manufacture of the long Tartar lances.
This chapter in their memorable day's work being
finished, and the whole of their villages throughout a district of ten thousand square miles in one simultaneous
blaze, the Tartars waited for further orders.

These, it was intended, should have taken a character of valedictory vengeance, and thus have left behind
to the Czarina a dreadful commentary upon the main
motives of their flight. It was the purpose of Zebek-
Dorchi that all the Russian towns, churches, and buildings of every description should be given up to pillage
and destruction, and such treatment applied to the
defenceless inhabitants as might naturally be expected
from a fierce people already infuriated by the spectacle of their own outrages, and by the bloody retalia-
tions which they must necessarily have provoked.
This part of the tragedy, however, was happily intercepted by a providential disappointment at the very
crisis of departure. It has been mentioned already,
that the motive for selecting the depth of winter as
the season of flight (which otherwise was obviously
the very worst possible), had been the impossibility of
effecting a junction sufficiently rapid with the tribes
on the west of the Wolga, in the absence of bridges,

unless by a natural bridge of ice. For this one advantage, the Kalmuck leaders had consented to aggravate by a thousandfold the calamities inevitable to a rapid flight over boundless tracts of country, with women, children, and herds of cattle—for this one single advantage ; and yet, after all, it was lost. The reason never has been explained satisfactorily, but the fact was such. Some have said that the signals were not properly concerted for marking the moment of absolute departure—that is, for signifying whether the settled intention of the Eastern Kalmucks might not have been suddenly interrupted by adverse intelligence. Others have supposed that the ice might not be equally strong on both sides of the river, and might even be generally insecure for the treading of heavy and heavily laden animals such as camels. But the prevailing notion is, that some accidental movements on the 3rd and 4th of January of Russian troops in the neighbourhood of the Western Kalmucks, though really having no reference to them or their plans, had been construed into certain signs that all was discovered ; and that the prudence of the Western chieftains, who, from situation, had never been exposed to those intrigues by which Zebek-Dorchi had practised upon the pride of the Eastern tribes, now stepped in to save their people from ruin. Be the cause what it might, it is certain that the Western Kalmucks were in some way prevented from forming the intended junction with their brethren of the opposite bank ; and the result was, that at least one hundred thousand of these Tartars were left behind in Russia. This accident it was which saved their Russian neighbours universally from the desolation which else awaited them. One general massacre and conflagration would assuredly have sur-

prised them, to the utter extermination of their pro-
perty, their houses, and themselves, had it not been
for this disappointment. But the Eastern chieftains
did not dare to put to hazard the safety of their brethren
5 under the first impulse of the Czarina's vengeance for
so dreadful a tragedy ; for, as they were well aware
of too many circumstances by which she might discover
the concurrence of the Western people in the general
scheme of revolt, they justly feared that she would
10 thence infer their concurrence also in the bloody events
which marked its outset.

Little did the Western Kalmucks guess what reasons
they also had for gratitude on account of an interposition so unexpected, and which at the moment they
15 so generally deplored. Could they but have witnessed
the thousandth part of the sufferings which overtook
their Eastern brethren in the first month of their sad
flight, they would have blessed Heaven for their own
narrow escape ; and yet these sufferings of the first
20 month were but a prelude or foretaste comparatively
slight of those which afterwards succeeded.

For now began to unroll the most awful series of
calamities, and the most extensive, which is anywhere
recorded to have visited the sons and daughters of
25 men. It is possible that the sudden inroads of destroying nations, such as the Huns, or the Avars, or the
Mongol Tartars, may have inflicted misery as extensive ; but there the misery and the desolation would be
sudden, like the flight of volleying lightning. Those who
30 were spared at first would generally be spared to the
end ; those who perished at all would perish at once.
It is possible that the French retreat from Moscow may
have made some nearer approach to this calamity in
duration, though still a feeble and miniature approach ;

for the French sufferings did not commence in good earnest until about one month from the time of leaving Moscow ; and though it is true that afterwards the vials of wrath were emptied upon the devoted army for six or seven weeks in succession, yet what is that to this Kalmuck tragedy, which lasted for more than as many months ? But the main feature of horror by which the Tartar march was distinguished from the French, lies in the accompaniment of women and children. There were both, it is true, with the French army, but not so many as to bear any marked proportion to the total numbers concerned. The French, in short, were merely an army—a host of professional destroyers, whose regular trade was bloodshed, and whose regular element was danger and suffering. But the Tartars were a nation carrying along with them more than two hundred and fifty thousand women and children, utterly unequal, for the most part, to any contest with the calamities before them. The Children of Israel were in the same circumstances as to the accompaniment of their families; but they were released from the pursuit of their enemies in a very early stage of their flight ; and their subsequent residence in the Desert was not a march, but a continued halt, and under a continued interposition of Heaven for their comfortable support. Earthquakes, again, however comprehensive in their ravages, are shocks of a moment's duration. A much nearer approach made to the wide range and the long duration of the Kalmuck tragedy may have been in a pestilence such as that which visited Athens in the Peloponnesian War, or London in the reign of Charles II. There also the martyrs were counted by myriads, and the period of the desolation was counted by months. But, after all, the total amount of destruction was on a smaller scale ; and there was this feature of alleviation to the *conscious* pressure of the calamity—that the misery was withdrawn from public notice into private chambers and hospitals. 5 The siege of Jerusalem by Vespasian and his son, taken in its entire circumstances, comes nearest of all— for breadth and depth of suffering, for duration, for the exasperation of the suffering from without by internal feuds, and, finally, for that last most appalling expres- 10 sion of the furnace-heat of the anguish in its power to extinguish the natural affections even of maternal love. But, after all, each case had circumstances of romantic misery peculiar to itself—circumstances with- out precedent, and (wherever human nature is ennobled 15 by Christianity), it may be confidently hoped, never to be repeated.

The first point to be reached, before any hope of repose could be encouraged, was the River Jaik. This was not above 300 miles from the main point of de- 20 parture on the Wolga ; and if the march thither was to be a forced one, and a severe one, it was alleged, on the other hand, that the suffering would be the more brief and transient ; one summary exertion, not to be repeated, and all was achieved. Forced the march 25 was, and severe beyond example : there the forewarn- ing proved correct ; but the promised rest proved a mere phantom of the wilderness—a visionary rainbow, which fled before their hope-sick eyes, across these interminable solitudes, for seven months of hardship 30 and calamity, without a pause. These sufferings, by their very nature, and the circumstances under which they arose, were (like the scenery of the steppes) somewhat monotonous in their colouring and external features ; what variety, however, there was, will be most naturally exhibited by tracing historically the successive stages of the general misery, exactly as it unfolded itself under the double agency of weakness still increasing from within, and hostile pressure from without. Viewed in this manner, under the real order of development, it is remarkable that these sufferings of the Tartars, though under the moulding hands of accident, arrange themselves almost with a scenical propriety. They seem combined, as with the skill of an artist ; the intensity of the misery advancing regularly with the advances of the march, and the stages of the calamity corresponding to the stages of the route ; so that, upon raising the curtain which veils the great catastrophe, we behold one vast climax of anguish, towering upwards by regular gradations, as if constructed artificially for picturesque effect—a result which might not have been surprising had it been reasonable to anticipate the same rate of speed, and even an accelerated rate, as prevailing through the later stages of the expedition. But it seemed, on the contrary, most reasonable to calculate upon a continual decrement in the rate of motion according to the increasing distance from the headquarters of the pursuing enemy. This calculation, however, was defeated by the extraordinary circumstance, that the Russian armies did not begin to close in very fiercely upon the Kalmucks until after they had accomplished a distance of full 2000 miles : 1000 miles farther on the assaults became even more tumultuous and murderous : and already the great shadows of the Chinese Wall were dimly descried, when the frenzy and *acharnement* of the pursuers, and the bloody desperation of the miserable fugitives, had reached its uttermost extremity. Let us briefly rehearse the main stages of the misery, and trace the

ascending steps of the tragedy, according to the great
divisions of the route marked out by the central rivers
of Asia.

The first stage, we have already said, was from the
5 Wolga to the Jaik; the distance about 300 miles; the
time allowed seven days. For the first week, therefore,
the rate of marching averaged about 43 English miles
a day. The weather was cold, but bracing; and, at a
more moderate pace, this part of the journey might
10 have been accomplished without much distress by a
people as hardy as the Kalmucks: as it was, the cattle
suffered greatly from over-driving; milk began to fail
even for the children; the sheep perished by wholesale;
and the children themselves were saved only by the
15 innumerable camels.

The Cossacks, who dwelt upon the banks of the Jaik,
were the first among the subjects of Russia to come into
collision with the Kalmucks. Great was their surprise
at the suddenness of the irruption, and great also their
20 consternation; for, according to their settled custom,
by far the greater part of their number was absent
during the winter months at the fisheries upon the
Caspian. Some who were liable to surprise at the most
exposed points, fled in crowds to the fortress of Koula-
25 gina, which was immediately invested, and summoned
by Oubacha. He had, however, in his train only a
few light pieces of artillery; and the Russian Com-
mandant at Koulagina, being aware of the hurried circumstances in which the Khan was placed, and that
30 he stood upon the very edge, as it were, of a renewed
flight, felt encouraged by these considerations to a more
obstinate resistance than might else have been advisable, with an enemy so little disposed to observe the
usages of civilised warfare. The period of his anxiety

was not long : on the fifth day of the siege, he descried
from the walls a succession of Tartar couriers, mounted
upon fleet Bactrian camels, crossing the vast plains
around the fortress at a furious pace, and riding into
the Kalmuck encampment at various points. Great
agitation appeared immediately to follow : orders were
soon after dispatched in all directions ; and it became
speedily known that upon a distant flank of the Kalmuck movement a bloody and exterminating battle
had been fought the day before, in which one entire
tribe of the Khan's dependants, numbering not less
than 9000 fighting-men, had perished to the last man.
This was the *ouloss*, or clan, called Feka-Zechorr,
between whom and the Cossacks there was a feud of
ancient standing. In selecting, therefore, the points
of attack, on occasion of the present hasty inroad, the
Cossack chiefs were naturally eager so to direct their
efforts as to combine with the service of the Empress
some gratification to their own party hatreds : more
especially as the present was likely to be their final
opportunity for revenge, if the Kalmuck evasion should
prosper. Having, therefore, concentrated as large a
body of Cossack cavalry as circumstances allowed, they
attacked the hostile *ouloss* with a precipitation which
denied to it all means for communicating with Oubacha ;
for the necessity of commanding an ample range of
pasturage, to meet the necessities of their vast flocks
and herds, had separated this *ouloss* from the Khan's
headquarters by an interval of 80 miles ; and thus it
was, and not from oversight, that it came to be thrown
entirely upon its own resources. These had proved
insufficient : retreat, from the exhausted state of their
horses and camels, no less than from the prodigious
encumbrances of their live stock, was absolutely out

of the question : quarter was disdained on the one
side, and would not have been granted on the other :
and thus it had happened that the setting sun of that
one day (the thirteenth from the first opening of the
5 revolt) threw his parting rays upon the final agonies
of an ancient *ouloss*, stretched upon a bloody field,
who on that day's dawning had held and styled themselves an independent nation.

Universal consternation was diffused through the wide
10 borders of the Khan's encampment by this disastrous
intelligence ; not so much on account of the numbers
slain, or the total extinction of a powerful ally, as
because the position of the Cossack force was likely
to put to hazard the future advances of the Kalmucks,
15 or at least to retard and hold them in check until the
heavier columns of the Russian army should arrive
upon their flanks. The siege of Koulagina was instantly
raised ; and that signal, so fatal to the happiness of
the women and their children, once again resounded
20 through the tents—the signal for flight, and this time
for a flight more rapid than ever. About 150 miles
ahead of their present position, there arose a tract of
hilly country, forming a sort of margin to the vast
sea-like expanse of champaign savannahs, steppes, and
25 occasionally of sandy deserts, which stretched away
on each side of this margin both eastwards and westwards. Pretty nearly in the centre of this hilly range
lay a narrow defile, through which passed the nearest
and the most practicable route to the river Torgau
30 (the farther bank of which river offered the next great
station of security for a general halt). It was the more
essential to gain this pass before the Cossacks, inasmuch
as not only would the delay in forcing the pass give
time to the Russian pursuing columns for combining

their attacks, and for bringing up their artillery, but also because (even if all enemies in pursuit were thrown out of the question) it was held by those best acquainted with the difficult and obscure geography of these pathless steppes—that the loss of this one narrow strait amongst the hills would have the effect of throwing them (as their only alternative in a case where so wide a sweep of pasturage was required) upon a circuit of at least 500 miles extra; besides that, after all, this circuitous route would carry them to the Torgau at a point ill fitted for the passage of their heavy baggage. The defile in the hills, therefore, it was resolved to gain; and yet, unless they moved upon it with the velocity of light cavalry, there was little chance but it would be found preoccupied by the Cossacks. They also, it is true, had suffered greatly in the bloody action with the defeated *ouloss*; but the excitement of victory, and the intense sympathy with their unexampled triumph, had again swelled their ranks, and would probably act with the force of a vortex to draw in their simple countrymen from the Caspian. The question, therefore, of preoccupation was reduced to a race. The Cossacks were marching upon an oblique line not above 50 miles longer than that which led to the same point from the Kalmuck headquarters before Koulagina; and therefore, without the most furious haste on the part of the Kalmucks, there was not a chance for them, burdened and "trashed" as they were, to anticipate so agile a light cavalry as the Cossacks in seizing this important pass.

Dreadful were the feelings of the poor women on hearing this exposition of the case. For they easily understood that too capital an interest (the *summa rerum*) was now at stake, to allow of any regard to

minor interests, or what would be considered such in
their present circumstances. The dreadful week already
passed—their inauguration in misery—was yet fresh
in their remembrance. The scars of suffering were
5 impressed not only upon their memories, but upon their
very persons and the persons of their children. And
they knew that, where no speed had much chance of
meeting the cravings of the chieftains, no test would
be accepted, short of absolute exhaustion, that as much
10 had been accomplished as could have been accomplished.
Weseloff, the Russian captive, has recorded the silent
wretchedness with which the women and elder boys
assisted in drawing the tent-ropes. On the 5th of
January all had been animation, and the joyousness of
15 indefinite expectation ; now, on the contrary, a brief
but bitter experience had taught them to take an
amended calculation of what it was that lay before
them.

One whole day and far into the succeeding night had
20 the renewed flight continued ; the sufferings had been
greater than before ; for the cold had been more
intense ; and many perished out of the living creatures
through every class, except only the camels—whose
powers of endurance seemed equally adapted to cold
25 and to heat. The second morning, however, brought
an alleviation to the distress. Snow had begun to fall ;
and though not deep at present, it was easily foreseen
that it soon would be so ; and that, as a halt would in
that case become unavoidable, no plan could be better
30 than that of staying where they were ; especially as the
same cause would check the advance of the Cossacks.
Here then was the last interval of comfort which
gleamed upon the unhappy nation during their whole
migration. For ten days the snow continued to fall

with little intermission. At the end of that time keen
bright frosty weather succeeded ; the drifting had
ceased ; in three days the smooth expanse became firm
enough to support the treading of the camels ; and the
flight was recommenced. But during the halt much 5
domestic comfort had been enjoyed ; and for the last
time universal plenty. The cows and oxen had perished
in such vast numbers on the previous marches, that an
order was now issued to turn what remained to account
by slaughtering the whole, and salting whatever part 10
should be found to exceed the immediate consumption.
This measure led to a scene of general banqueting and
even of festivity amongst all who were not incapacitated
for joyous emotions by distress of mind, by grief for
the unhappy experience of the few last days, and by 15
anxiety for the too gloomy future. Seventy thousand
persons of all ages had already perished ; exclusively
of the many thousand allies who had been cut down by
the Cossack sabre. And the losses in reversion were
likely to be many more. For rumours began now to 20
arrive from all quarters, by the mounted couriers whom
the Khan had dispatched to the rear and to each flank
as well as in advance, that large masses of the Imperial
troops were converging from all parts of Central Asia
to the fords of the river Torgau, as the most convenient 25
point for intercepting the flying tribes ; and it was by
this time well known that a powerful division was close
in their rear, and was retarded only by the numerous
artillery which had been judged necessary to support
their operations. New motives were thus daily arising 30
for quickening the emotions of the wretched Kalmucks,
and for exhausting those who were already but too
much exhausted.

It was not until the 2nd day of February that the

Khan's advanced guard came in sight of Ouchim, the defile among the hills of Mougaldchares, in which they anticipated so bloody an opposition from the Cossacks. A pretty large body of these light cavalry had, in fact, 5 preoccupied the pass by some hours ; but the Khan having two great advantages—namely, a strong body of infantry, who had been conveyed by sections of five on about 200 camels, and some pieces of light artillery which he had not yet been forced to abandon—soon 10 began to make a serious impression upon this unsupported detachment ; and they would probably at any rate have retired ; but at the very moment when they were making some dispositions in that view, Zebek-Dorchi appeared upon their rear with a body of trained 15 riflemen, who had distinguished themselves in the war with Turkey. These men had contrived to crawl unobserved over the cliffs which skirted the ravine, availing themselves of the dry beds of the summer torrents, and other inequalities of the ground, to conceal their 20 movement. Disorder and trepidation ensued instantly in the Cossack files ; the Khan, who had been waiting with the *élite* of his heavy cavalry, charged furiously upon them ; total overthrow followed to the Cossacks, and a slaughter such as in some measure avenged the 25 recent bloody extermination of their allies, the ancient *ouloss* of Feka-Zechorr. The slight horses of the Cossacks were unable to support the weight of heavy Polish dragoons and a body of trained *cameleers* (that is, cuirassiers mounted on camels) ; hardy they were, 30 but not strong, nor a match for their antagonists in weight ; and their extraordinary efforts through the last few days to gain their present position had greatly diminished their powers for effecting an escape. Very few, in fact, *did* escape ; and the bloody day at Ouchim became as memorable amongst the Cossacks as that which, about twenty days before, had signalised the complete annihilation of the Feka-Zechorr.

The road was now open to the river Irgitch, and as yet even far beyond it to the Torgau; but how long this state of things would continue, was every day more doubtful. Certain intelligence was now received that a large Russian army, well appointed in every arm, was advancing upon the Torgau, under the command of General Traubenberg. This officer was to be joined on his route by ten thousand Bashkirs, and pretty nearly the same amount of Kirghises—both hereditary enemies of the Kalmucks, both exasperated to a point of madness by the bloody trophies which Oubacha and Momotbacha had, in late years, won from such of their compatriots as served under the Sultan. The Czarina's yoke these wild nations bore with submissive patience, but not the hands by which it had been imposed; and, accordingly, catching with eagerness at the present occasion offered to their vengeance, they sent an assurance to the Czarina of their perfect obedience to her commands, and at the same time a message significantly declaring in what spirit they meant to execute them, viz. "that they would not trouble her Majesty with prisoners."

Here then arose, as before with the Cossacks, a race for the Kalmucks with the regular armies of Russia, and concurrently with nations as fierce and semi-humanised as themselves, besides that they had been stung into threefold activity by the furies of mortified pride and military abasement, under the eyes of the Turkish Sultan. The forces, and more especially the artillery, of Russia were far too overwhelming to bear the thought of a regular opposition in pitched battles,

even with a less dilapidated state of their resources
than they could reasonably expect at the period of their
arrival on the Torgau. In their speed lay their only
hope—in strength of foot, as before, and not in strength
5 of arm. Onward, therefore, the Kalmucks pressed,
marking the lines of their wide-extending march over
the sad solitudes of the steppes by a never-ending
chain of corpses. The old and the young, the sick
man on his couch, the mother with her baby—all were
10 dropping fast. Sights such as these, with the many
rueful aggravations incident to the helpless condition of
infancy—of disease and of female weakness abandoned
to the wolves amidst a howling wilderness, continued to
track their course through a space of full two thousand
15 miles; for so much, at the least, it was likely to prove,
including the circuits to which they were often compelled by rivers or hostile tribes, from the point of
starting on the Wolga, until they could reach their
destined halting-ground on the east bank of the Torgau.
20 For the first seven weeks of this march their sufferings
had been embittered by the excessive severity of the
cold; and every night—so long as wood was to be had
for fires, either from the lading of the camels, or from
the desperate sacrifice of their baggage-wagons, or (as
25 occasionally happened) from the forests which skirted
the banks of the many rivers which crossed their path
—no spectacle was more frequent than that of a circle,
composed of men, women, and children gathered by
hundreds round a central fire, all dead and stiff at
30 the return of morning light. Myriads were left behind
from pure exhaustion, of whom none had a chance,
under the combined evils which beset them, of surviving through the next twenty-four hours. Frost,
however, and snow at length ceased to persecute; the

vast extent of the march at length brought them into
more genial latitudes, and the unusual duration of the
march was gradually bringing them into more genial
seasons of the year.　Two thousand miles had at last
been traversed ; February, March, April, were gone ; 5
the balmy month of May had opened, vernal sights and
sounds came from every side to comfort the heart-
weary travellers ; and at last, in the latter end of May,
crossing the Torgau, they took up a position where
they hoped to find liberty to repose themselves for many 10
weeks in comfort as well as in security, and to draw
such supplies from the fertile neighbourhood as might
restore their shattered forces to a condition for execut-
ing, with less of wreck and ruin, the large remainder of
the journey.　　　　　　　　　　　　　　　　　　15

　　Yes ; it was true that two thousand miles of wandering had been completed, but in a period of nearly five
months, and with the terrific sacrifice of at least two
hundred and fifty thousand souls, to say nothing of
herds and flocks past all reckoning.　These had all 20
perished : ox, cow, horse, mule, ass, sheep, or goat,
not one survived—only the camels.　These arid and
adust creatures, looking like the mummies of some antediluvian animals, without the affections or sensibilities
of flesh and blood—these only still erected their speak- 25
ing eyes to the eastern heavens, and had to all appearance come out from this long tempest of trial un-
scathed and hardly diminished.　The Khan, knowing
how much he was individually answerable for the
misery which had been sustained, must have wept tears 30
even more bitter than those of Xerxes, when he threw
his eyes over the myriads whom he had assembled :
for the tears of Xerxes were unmingled with remorse.
Whatever amends were in his power the Khan resolved

to make, by sacrifices to the general good of all personal regards ; and accordingly even at this point of
their advance, he once more deliberately brought under
review the whole question of the revolt. The question
5 was formally debated before the Council, whether, even
at this point, they should untread their steps, and,
throwing themselves upon the Czarina's mercy, return
to their old allegiance ? In that case, Oubacha pro-
fessed himself willing to become the scapegoat for the
10 general transgression. This, he argued, was no fantastic scheme, but even easy of accomplishment ; for
the unlimited and sacred power of the Khan, so well
known to the Empress, made it absolutely iniquitous
to attribute any separate responsibility to the people
15 —upon the Khan rested the guilt, upon the Khan would
descend the Imperial vengeance. This proposal was
applauded for its generosity, but was energetically
opposed by Zebek-Dorchi. Were they to lose the
whole journey of two thousand miles ? Was their
20 misery to perish without fruit ? True it was that they
had yet reached only the half-way house ; but, in that
respect, the motives were evenly balanced for retreat
or for advance. Either way they would have pretty
nearly the same distance to traverse, but with this
25 difference—that, forwards, their route lay through
lands comparatively fertile ; backwards, through a
blasted wilderness, rich only in memorials of their
sorrow, and hideous to Kalmuck eyes by the trophies
of their calamity. Besides, though the Empress might
30 accept an excuse for the past, would she the less for-
bear to suspect for the future ? The Czarina's *pardon*
they might obtain, but could they ever hope to recover
her *confidence* ? Doubtless there would now be a standing presumption against them, an immortal ground of

jealousy ; and a jealous government would be but another name for a harsh one. Finally, whatever motives there ever had been for the revolt surely remained unimpaired by anything that had occurred. In reality, the revolt was, after all, no revolt, but (strictly speaking) a return to their old allegiance ; since, not above one hundred and fifty years ago (viz. in the year 1616), their ancestors had revolted from the Emperor of China. They had now tried both governments ; and for them China was the land of promise, and Russia the house of bondage.

Spite, however, of all that Zebek could say or do, the yearning of the people was strongly in behalf of the Khan's proposal ; the pardon of their prince, they persuaded themselves, would be readily conceded by the Empress : and there is little doubt that they would at this time have thrown themselves gladly upon the Imperial mercy ; when suddenly all was defeated by the arrival of two envoys from Traubenberg. This general had reached the fortress of Orsk, after a very painful march, on the 12th of April ; thence he set forwards towards Oriembourg, which he reached upon the 1st of June, having been joined on his route at various times during the month of May by the Kirghises and a corps of ten thousand Bashkirs. From Oriembourg he sent forward his official offers to the Khan, which were harsh and peremptory, holding out no specific stipulations as to pardon or impunity, and exacting unconditional submission as the preliminary price of any cessation from military operations. The personal character of Traubenberg, which was anything but energetic, and the condition of his army, disorganised in a great measure by the length and severity of the march, made it probable that, with a little time for negotiation, a more conciliatory tone would have been assumed. But, unhappily for all parties, sinister events occurred in the meantime, such as effectually put an end to every hope of the kind.

5 The two envoys sent forward by Traubenberg had reported to this officer that a distance of only ten days' march lay between his own headquarters and those of the Khan. Upon this fact transpiring, the Kirghises, by their prince Nourali, and the Bashkirs, entreated
10 the Russian general to advance without delay. Once having placed his cannon in position, so as to command the Kalmuck camp, the fate of the rebel Khan and his people would be in his own hands : and they would themselves form his advanced guard. Traubenberg,
15 however (*why* has not been certainly explained), refused to march, grounding his refusal upon the condition of his army, and their absolute need of refreshment. Long and fierce was the altercation ; but at length, seeing no chance of prevailing, and dreading above all
20 other events the escape of their detested enemy, the ferocious Bashkirs went off in a body by forced marches. In six days they reached the Torgau, crossed by swimming their horses, and fell upon the Kalmucks, who were dispersed for many a league in search of food
25 or provender for their camels. The first day's action was one vast succession of independent skirmishes, diffused over a field of thirty to forty miles in extent ; one party often breaking up into three or four, and again (according to the accidents of ground) three or
30 four blending into one ; flight and pursuit, rescue and total overthrow, going on simultaneously, under all varieties of form, in all quarters of the plain. The Bashkirs had found themselves obliged, by the scattered state of the Kalmucks, to split up into innumer-

able sections ; and thus, for some hours, it had been impossible for the most practised eye to collect the general tendency of the day's fortune. Both the Khan and Zebek-Dorchi were at one moment made prisoners, and more than once in imminent danger of being cut down ; but at length Zebek succeeded in rallying a strong column of infantry, which, with the support of the camel-corps on each flank, compelled the Bashkirs to retreat. Clouds, however, of these wild cavalry continued to arrive through the next two days and nights, followed or accompanied by the Kirghises. These being viewed as the advanced parties of Trauben-berg's army, the Kalmuck chieftains saw no hope of safety but in flight ; and in this way it happened that a retreat, which had so recently been brought to a pause, was resumed at the very moment when the unhappy fugitives were anticipating a deep repose without further molestation the whole summer through.

I now revert to the final scenes of the Kalmuck flight. These it would be useless to pursue circumstantially through the whole two thousand miles of suffering which remained ; for the character of that suffering was even more monotonous than on the former half of the flight, but also more severe. Its main elements were exces-sive heat, with the accompaniments of famine and thirst, but aggravated at every step by the murderous attacks of their cruel enemies the Bashkirs and the Kirghises.

These people, " more fell than anguish, hunger, or the sea," stuck to the unhappy Kalmucks like a swarm of enraged hornets. And very often, whilst *they* were attacking them in the rear, their advanced parties and flanks were attacked with almost equal fury by the

people of the country which they were traversing ; and
with good reason, since the law of self-preservation had
now obliged the fugitive Tartars to plunder provisions,
and to forage wherever they passed. In this respect
their condition was a constant oscillation of wretchedness ; for sometimes, pressed by grinding famine, they
took a circuit of perhaps a hundred miles, in order to
strike into a land rich in the comforts of life ; but in
such a land they were sure to find a crowded population,
of which every arm was raised in unrelenting hostility,
with all the advantages of local knowledge, and with
constant preoccupation of all the defensible positions, mountain passes, or bridges. Sometimes, again,
wearied out with this mode of suffering, they took a
circuit of perhaps a hundred miles, in order to strike
into a land with few or no inhabitants. But in such a
land they were sure to meet absolute starvation. Then,
again, whether with or without this plague of starvation,
whether with or without this plague of hostility in front,
whatever might be the " fierce varieties " of their misery
in this respect, no rest ever came to their unhappy rear ;
" post equitem sedet atra cura"; it was a torment like
the undying worm of conscience. And, upon the whole,
it presented a spectacle altogether unprecedented in the
history of mankind. Private and personal malignity
is not unfrequently immortal ; but rare indeed is it to
find the same pertinacity of malice in a nation. And
what embittered the interest was, that the malice was
reciprocal. Thus far the parties met upon equal terms ;
but that equality only sharpened the sense of their dire
inequality as to other circumstances. The Bashkirs
were ready to fight " from morn to dewy eve." The
Kalmucks, on the contrary, were always obliged to run.
Was it *from* their enemies as creatures whom they feared ?

No ; but *towards* their friends—towards that final haven of China—as what was hourly implored by the prayers of their wives, and the tears of their children. But, though they fled unwillingly, too often they fled in vain —being unwillingly recalled. There lay the torment. 5 Every day the Bashkirs fell upon them ; every day the same unprofitable battle was renewed ; as a matter of course, the Kalmucks recalled part of their advanced guard to fight them ; every day the battle raged for hours, and uniformly with the same result. For no 10 sooner did the Bashkirs find themselves too heavily pressed, and that the Kalmuck march had been retarded by some hours, than they retired into the boundless deserts, where all pursuit was hopeless. But if the Kalmucks resolved to press forward, regardless of their 15 enemies, in that case their attacks became so fierce and overwhelming, that the general safety seemed likely to be brought into question ; nor could any effectual remedy be applied to the case, even for each separate day, except by a most embarrassing halt, and by counter- 20 marches, that, to men in their circumstances, were almost worse than death. It will not be surprising, that the irritation of such a systematic persecution, superadded to a previous and hereditary hatred, and accompanied by the stinging consciousness of utter impotence as re- 25 garded all effectual vengeance, should gradually have inflamed the Kalmuck animosity into the wildest expression of downright madness and frenzy. Indeed, long before the frontiers of China were approached, the hostility of both sides had assumed the appearance much more of 30 a warfare amongst wild beasts, than amongst creatures acknowledging the restraints of reason or the claims of a common nature. The spectacle became too atrocious ; it was that of a host of lunatics pursued by a host of fiends.

On a fine morning in early autumn of the year 1771, Kien Long, the Emperor of China, was pursuing his amusements in a wild frontier district lying on the outside of the Great Wall. For many hundred square leagues the country was desolate of inhabitants, but rich in woods of ancient growth, and overrun with game of every description. In a central spot of this solitary region, the Emperor had built a gorgeous hunting lodge, to which he resorted annually for recreation and relief from the cares of government. Led onwards in pursuit of game, he had rambled to a distance of 200 miles or more from this lodge, followed at a little distance by a sufficient military escort, and every night pitching his tent in a different situation, until at length he had arrived on the very margin of the vast central deserts of Asia. Here he was standing by accident at an opening of his pavilion, enjoying the morning sunshine, when suddenly to the westwards there arose a vast cloudy vapour, which by degrees expanded, mounted, and seemed to be slowly diffusing itself over the whole face of the heavens. By and by this vast sheet of mist began to thicken towards the horizon, and to roll forward in billowy volumes. The Emperor's suite assembled from all quarters. The silver trumpets were sounded in the rear, and from all the glades and forest avenues began to trot forward towards the pavilion the yagers—half cavalry, half huntsmen—who composed the Imperial escort. Conjecture was on the stretch to divine the cause of this phenomenon, and the interest continually increased, in proportion as simple curiosity gradually deepened into the anxiety of uncertain danger. At first it had been imagined that some vast troops of deer or other wild animals of the chase had been disturbed in their forest haunts by the Emperor's movements, or possibly by wild beasts prowling for prey, and might be fetching a compass by way of re-entering the forest grounds at some remoter points secure from molestation. But this conjecture was dissipated by the slow increase of the cloud, and the steadiness of its motion. In the course of two hours the vast phenomenon had advanced to a point which was judged to be within five miles of the spectators, though all calculations of distance were difficult, and often fallacious, when applied to the endless expanses of the Tartar deserts. Through the next hour, during which the gentle morning breeze had a little freshened, the dusty vapour had developed itself far and wide into the appearance of huge aerial draperies, hanging in mighty volumes from the sky to the earth ; and at particular points, where the eddies of the breeze acted upon the pendulous skirts of these aerial curtains, rents were perceived, sometimes taking the form of regular arches, portals, and windows, through which began dimly to gleam the heads of camels " indorsed " with human beings—and at intervals the moving of men and horses in tumultuous array—and then through other openings or vistas at far distant points the flashing of polished arms. But sometimes, as the wind slackened or died away, all those openings, of whatever form, in the cloudy pall would slowly close, and for a time the whole pageant was shut up from view ; although the growing din, the clamours, shrieks, and groans, ascending from infuriated myriads, reported, in a language not to be misunderstood, what was going on behind the cloudy screen.

It was in fact the Kalmuck host, now in the last extremities of their exhaustion, and very fast approaching to that final stage of privation and killing misery, beyond which few or none could have lived, but also,

happily for themselves, fast approaching (in a literal
sense) that final stage of their long pilgrimage, at which
they would meet hospitality on a scale of royal magnificence, and full protection from their enemies.   These
5 enemies, however, as yet, were still hanging on their
rear as fiercely as ever, though this day was destined
to be the last of their hideous persecution.   The Khan
had, in fact, sent forward couriers with all the requisite
statements and petitions, addressed to the Emperor of
10 China.   These had been duly received, and preparations made in consequence to welcome the Kalmucks
with the most paternal benevolence.   But, as these
couriers had been dispatched from the Torgau at the
moment of arrival thither, and before the advance of
15 Traubenberg had made it necessary for the Khan to
order a hasty renewal of the flight, the Emperor had
not looked for their arrival on his frontiers until full
three months after the present time.   The Khan had
indeed expressly notified his intention to pass the
20 summer heats on the banks of the Torgau, and to re-
commence his retreat about the beginning of September.
The subsequent change of plan being unknown to Kien
Long, left him for some time in doubt as to the true
interpretation to be put upon this mighty apparition in
25 the desert ; but at length the savage clamours of hostile
fury, and the clangour of weapons, unveiled to the
Emperor the true nature of those unexpected calamities,
which had so prematurely precipitated the Kalmuck
measures.

30   Apprehending the real state of affairs, the Emperor
instantly perceived that the first act of his fatherly care
for these erring children (as he esteemed them), now
returning to their ancient obedience, must be—to
deliver them from their pursuers.   And this was less

difficult than might have been supposed. Not many miles in the rear was a body of well-appointed cavalry, with a strong detachment of artillery, who always attended the Emperor's motions. These were hastily summoned. Meantime it occurred to the train of courtiers that some danger might arise to the Emperor's person from the proximity of a lawless enemy ; and accordingly he was induced to retire a little to the rear. It soon appeared, however, to those who watched the vapoury shroud in the desert, that its motion was not such as would argue the direction of the march to be exactly upon the pavilion, but rather in a diagonal line, making an angle of full 45 degrees with that line in which the imperial *cortège* had been standing, and therefore with a distance continually increasing. Those who knew the country judged that the Kalmucks were making for a large fresh-water lake about seven or eight miles distant ; they were right ; and to that point the imperial cavalry was ordered up ; and it was precisely in that spot, and about three hours after, and at noonday on the 8th of September, that the great exodus of the Kalmuck Tartars was brought to a final close, and with a scene of such memorable and hellish fury, as formed an appropriate winding up to an expedition in all its parts and details so awfully disastrous. The Emperor was not personally present, or at least he saw whatever he *did* see from too great a distance to discriminate its individual features ; but he records in his written memorial the report made to him of this scene by some of his own officers.

The Lake of Tengis, near the dreadful desert of Kobi, lay in a hollow amongst hills of a moderate height, ranging generally from two to three thousand feet high. About eleven o'clock in the forenoon, the Chinese

cavalry reached the summit of a road which led through
a cradle-like dip in the mountains right down upon the
margin of the lake. From this pass, elevated about
two thousand feet above the level of the water, they
5 continued to descend, by a very winding and difficult
road, for an hour and a half; and during the whole of
this descent they were compelled to be inactive spectators of the fiendish spectacle below. The Kalmucks,
reduced by this time from about six hundred thousand
10 souls to two hundred and sixty thousand, and after
enduring for so long a time the miseries I have previously
described—outrageous heat, famine, and the destroying
scimitar of the Kirghises and the Bashkirs—had for the
last ten days been traversing a hideous desert, where no
15 vestiges were seen of vegetation, and no drop of water
could be found. Camels and men were already so over-
laden, that it was a mere impossibility that they should
carry a tolerable sufficiency for the passage of this
frightful wilderness. On the eighth day, the wretched
20 daily allowance, which had been continually diminish-
ing, failed entirely; and thus, for two days of insupportable fatigue, the horrors of thirst had been
carried to the fiercest extremity. Upon this last morning, at the sight of the hills and the forest scenery, which
25 announced to those who acted as guides the neighbourhood of the lake of Tengis, all the people rushed along
with maddening eagerness to the anticipated solace.
The day grew hotter and hotter, the people more and
more exhausted, and gradually, in the general rush
30 forwards to the lake, all discipline and command were
lost — all attempts to preserve a rearguard were
neglected—the wild Bashkirs rode in amongst the en-
cumbered people, and slaughtered them by wholesale,
and almost without resistance. Screams and tumultu-

ous shouts proclaimed the progress of the massacre ;
but none heeded—none halted ; all alike, pauper or
noble, continued to rush on with maniacal haste to the
waters—all with faces blackened by the heat preying
upon the liver, and with tongue drooping from the 5
mouth. The cruel Bashkir was affected by the same
misery, and manifested the same symptoms of his misery
as the wretched Kalmuck ; the murderer was oftentimes in the same frantic misery as his murdered
victim—many indeed (an ordinary effect of thirst) in 10
both nations had become lunatic, and in this state,
whilst mere multitude and condensation of bodies alone
opposed any check to the destroying scimitar and the
trampling hoof, the lake was reached ; and into that
the whole vast body of enemies together rushed, and 15
together continued to rush, forgetful of all things at
that moment but of one almighty instinct. This absorption of the thoughts in one maddening appetite lasted
for a single half-hour ; but in the next arose the final
scene of parting vengeance. Far and wide the waters 20
of the solitary lake were instantly dyed red with blood
and gore : here rode a party of savage Bashkirs, hewing
off heads as fast as the swathes fall before the mower's
scythe ; there stood unarmed Kalmucks in a death-
grapple with their detested foes, both up to the middle 25
in water, and oftentimes both sinking together below
the surface, from weakness or from struggles, and
perishing in each other's arms. Did the Bashkirs at
any point collect into a cluster for the sake of giving
impetus to the assault ? Thither were the camels 30
driven in fiercely by those who rode them, generally
women or boys ; and even these quiet creatures were
forced into a share in this carnival of murder, by
trampling down as many as they could strike prostrate

with the lash of their fore-legs. Every moment the water grew more polluted ; and yet every moment fresh myriads came up to the lake and rushed in, not able to resist their frantic thirst, and swallowing large draughts
5 of water, visibly contaminated with the blood of their slaughtered compatriots. Wheresoever the lake was shallow enough to allow of men raising their heads above the water, there, for scores of acres, were to be seen all forms of ghastly fear, of agonising struggle, of spasm, of
10 death, and the fear of death—revenge, and the lunacy of revenge—until the neutral spectators, of whom there were not a few, now descending the eastern side of the lake, at length averted their eyes in horror. This horror, which seemed incapable of further addition, was, how-
15 ever, increased by an unexpected incident : the Bash-kirs, beginning to perceive here and there the approach of the Chinese cavalry, felt it prudent—wheresoever they were sufficiently at leisure from the passions of the murderous scene—to gather into bodies. This
20 was noticed by the governor of a small Chinese fort, built upon an eminence above the lake ; and immedi-ately he threw in a broadside, which spread havoc amongst the Bashkir tribe. As often as the Bashkirs collected into " globes " and " turms," as their only
25 means of meeting the long lines of descending Chinese cavalry—so often did the Chinese governor of the fort pour in his exterminating broadside ; until at length the lake, at its lower end, became one vast seething cauldron of human bloodshed and carnage. The
30 Chinese cavalry had reached the foot of the hills : the Bashkirs, attentive to *their* movements, had formed ; skirmishes had been fought : and, with a quick sense that the contest was henceforwards rapidly becoming hopeless, the Bashkirs and Kirghises began to retire.

The pursuit was not as vigorous as the Kalmuck hatred
would have desired. But, at the same time, the very
gloomiest hatred could not but find, in their own
dreadful experience of the Asiatic deserts, and in
the certainty that these wretched Bashkirs had to
repeat that same experience a second time, for thousands of miles, as the price exacted by a retributary
Providence for their vindictive cruelty—not the very
gloomiest of the Kalmucks, or the least reflecting,
but found in all this a retaliatory chastisement more
complete and absolute than any which their swords
and lances could have obtained, or human vengeance
have devised.

Here ends the tale of the Kalmuck wanderings in the
Desert ; for any subsequent marches which awaited
them were neither long nor painful. Every possible
alleviation and refreshment for their exhausted bodies
had been already provided by Kien Long with the most
princely munificence ; and lands of great fertility were
immediately assigned to them in ample extent along
the River Ily, not very far from the point at which they
had first emerged from the wilderness of Kobi. Peace
and prosperity, under the gentle rule of a fatherly lord
paramount, redawned upon the tribes : their household *lares*, after so harsh a translation to distant
climates, found again a happy reinstatement in what
had in fact been their primitive abodes : they found
themselves settled in quiet sylvan scenes, rich in all the
luxuries of life, and endowed with the perfect loveliness of Arcadian beauty. But from the hills of this
favoured land, and even from the level grounds as they
approached its western border, they still look out upon
that fearful wilderness which once beheld a nation in

agony—the utter extirpation of nearly half a million
from amongst its numbers, and, for the remainder, a
storm of misery so fierce, that in the end (as happened
also at Athens during the Peloponnesian War, from a
5 different form of misery) very many lost their memory ;
all records of their past life were wiped out as with
a sponge—utterly erased and cancelled : and many
others lost their reason ; some in a gentle form of
pensive melancholy, some in a more restless form of
10 feverish delirium and nervous agitation, and others in
the fixed forms of tempestuous mania, raving frenzy,
or moping idiocy. Two great commemorative monuments arose in after years to mark the depth and permanence of the awe—the sacred and reverential grief
15 with which all persons looked back upon the dread
calamities attached to the Year of the Tiger—all who
had either personally shared in those calamities, and
had themselves drunk from that cup of sorrow, or who
had effectually been made witnesses to their results, and
20 associated with their relief ; two great monuments ;
one embodied in the religious solemnity, enjoined
by the Dalai Lama, called in the Tartar language a
Romanang—that is, a national commemoration, with
music the most rich and solemn, of all the souls who
25 departed to the rest of Paradise from the afflictions of
the Desert : this took place about six years after the
arrival in China. Secondly, another more durable and
more commensurate to the scale of the calamity and to
the grandeur of this national exodus, in the mighty
30 columns of granite and brass, erected by the Emperor
Kien Long, near the banks of the Ily : these columns
stand upon the very margin of the steppes ; and they
bear a short but emphatic inscription to the following
effect :—

By the Will of God,
Here, upon the brink of these Deserts,
Which from this point begin and stretch away
Pathless, treeless, waterless
For thousands of miles—and along the margins of many   5
      mighty nations,
Rested from their labours and from great afflictions
Under the shadow of the Chinese Wall,
And by the favour of KIEN LONG, God's Lieutenant upon
      Earth,   10
The ancient Children of the Wilderness—the Torgote
      Tartars—
Flying before the wrath of the Grecian Czar,
Wandering sheep who had strayed away from the Celestial
      Empire in the year 1616,   15
But are now mercifully gathered again, after infinite sorrow,
Into the fold of their forgiving Shepherd.
Hallowed be the spot for ever,
      and
Hallowed be the day—September 8, 1771 !   20
      Amen.

LITERARY CRITICISM

The Meaning of Literature

WHAT is it that we mean by *literature* ? Popularly, and
amongst the thoughtless, it is held to include everything that is printed in a book.   Little logic is required
to disturb *that* definition ; the most thoughtless person
5 is easily made aware, that in the idea of *literature*, one
essential element is—some relation to a general and
common interest of man, so that, what applies only to
a local, or professional, or merely personal interest,
even though presenting itself in the shape of a book,
10 will not belong to literature.   So far the definition is
easily narrowed ; and it is as easily expanded.   For
not only is much that takes a station in books not
literature ; but inversely, much that really *is* literature
never reaches a station in books.   The weekly sermons
15 of Christendom, that vast pulpit literature which acts
so extensively upon the popular mind—to warn, to
uphold, to renew, to comfort, to alarm, does not attain
the sanctuary of libraries in the ten-thousandth part of
its extent.   The drama again, as, for instance, the finest
20 of Shakespeare's plays in England, and all leading
Athenian plays in the noontide of the Attic stage,
operated as a literature on the public mind, and were
(according to the strictest letter of that term) *published*
through the audiences that witnessed their representa-
25 tion some time before they were published as things to
be read : and they were published in this scenical mode
of publication with much more effect than they could

have had as books, during ages of costly copying, or of costly printing.

Books, therefore, do not suggest an idea co-extensive and interchangeable with the idea of literature ; since much literature, scenic, forensic, or didactic (as from lecturers and public orators), may never come into books ; and much that *does* come into books may connect itself with no literary interest. But a far more important correction, applicable to the common vague idea of literature, is to be sought—not so much in a better definition of literature, as in a sharper distinction of the two functions which it fulfils. In that great social organ, which, collectively, we call literature, there may be distinguished two separate offices that may blend and often *do* so, but capable, severally, of a severe insulation, and naturally fitted for reciprocal repulsion. There is, first, the literature of *knowledge* ; and, secondly, the literature of *power*. The function of the first is—to *teach* ; the function of the second is—to *move* : the first is a rudder ; the second, an oar or a sail. The first speaks to the *mere* discursive understanding ; the second speaks ultimately, it may happen, to the higher understanding or reason, but always *through* affections of pleasure and sympathy. Remotely, it may travel towards an object seated in what Lord Bacon calls *dry* light ; but, proximately, it does and must operate, else it ceases to be a literature of *power*, on and through that *humid* light which clothes itself in the mists and glittering *iris* of human passions, desires, and genial emotions. Men have so little reflected on the higher functions of literature, as to find it a paradox if one should describe it as a mean or subordinate purpose of books to give information. But this is a paradox only in the sense which makes it honourable to be paradoxical. Whenever we talk in ordinary language of seeking information or gaining knowledge, we understand the words as connected with something of absolute novelty. But it is the grandeur of all truth, which *can* occupy a very high place in human interests, that it is never absolutely novel to the meanest of minds : it exists eternally by way of germ or latent principle in the lowest as in the highest, needing to be developed, but never to be planted. To be capable of transplantation is the immediate criterion of a truth that ranges on a lower scale. Besides which, there is a rarer thing than truth, namely, *power*, or deep sympathy with truth. What is the effect, for instance, upon society, of children ? By the pity, by the tenderness, and by the peculiar modes of admiration, which connect themselves with the helplessness, with the innocence, and with the simplicity of children, not only are the primal affections strengthened and continually renewed, but the qualities which are dearest in the sight of heaven—the frailty, for instance, which appeals to forbearance ; the innocence which symbolises the heavenly, and the simplicity which is most alien from the worldly, are kept up in perpetual remembrance, and their ideals are continually refreshed. A purpose of the same nature is answered by the higher literature, viz. the literature of power. What do you learn from *Paradise Lost* ? Nothing at all. What do you learn from a cookery-book ? Something new—something that you did not know before, in every paragraph. But would you therefore put the wretched cookery-book on a higher level of estimation than the divine poem ? What you owe to Milton is not any knowledge, of which a million separate items are still but a million of advancing steps on the same earthly level ; what you owe, is *power*, that is, exercise and expansion to your own latent capacity of sympathy with the infinite, where every pulse and each separate influx is a step upwards—a step ascending as upon a Jacob's ladder from earth to mysterious altitudes above the earth. *All* the steps of knowledge, from first to last, carry you further on the same plane, but could never raise you one foot above your ancient level of earth : whereas, the very *first* step in power is a flight—is an ascending movement into another element where earth is forgotten.

Were it not that human sensibilities are ventilated and continually called out into exercise by the great phenomena of infancy, or of real life as it moves through chance and change, or of literature as it recombines these elements in the mimicries of poetry, romance, etc., it is certain that, like any animal power or muscular energy falling into disuse, all such sensibilities would gradually drop and dwindle. It is in relation to these great *moral* capacities of man that the literature of power, as contradistinguished from that of knowledge, lives and has its field of action. It is concerned with what is highest in man ; for the Scriptures themselves never condescended to deal by suggestion or co-opera-tion, with the mere discursive understanding : when speaking of man in his intellectual capacity, the Scrip-tures speak not of the understanding, but of " *the understanding heart*"—making the heart, *i.e.* the great *intuitive* (or non-discursive) organ, to be the inter-changeable formula for man in his highest state of capacity for the infinite. Tragedy, romance, fairy tale, or epopee, all alike restore to man's mind the ideals of justice, of hope, of truth, of mercy, of retribution, which else (left to the support of daily life in its realities) would languish for want of sufficient illustration. What

is meant, for instance, by *poetic justice* ?—It does not mean a justice that differs by its object from the ordinary justice of human jurisprudence ; for then it must be confessedly a very bad kind of justice ; but it
5 means a justice that differs from common forensic justice by the degree in which it *attains* its object, a justice that is more omnipotent over its own ends, as dealing—not with the refractory elements of earthly life—but with the elements of its own creation, and with
10 materials flexible to its own purest preconceptions. It is certain that, were it not for the literature of power, these ideals would often remain amongst us as mere arid notional forms ; whereas, by the creative forces of man put forth in literature, they gain a vernal life
15 of restoration, and germinate into vital activities. The commonest novel, by moving in alliance with human fears and hopes, with human instincts of wrong and right, sustains and quickens those affections. Calling them into action, it rescues them from torpor. And
20 hence the pre-eminence over all authors that merely *teach*, of the meanest that *moves* ; or that teaches, if at all, indirectly *by* moving. The very highest work that has ever existed in the literature of knowledge, is but a *provisional* work : a book upon trial and sufferance, and
25 *quamdiu bene se gesserit*. Let its teaching be even partially revised, let it be but expanded, nay, even let its teaching be but placed in a better order, and instantly it is superseded. Whereas the feeblest works in the literature of power, surviving at all, survive as finished
30 and unalterable amongst men. For instance, the *Principia* of Sir Isaac Newton was a book *militant* on earth from the first. In all stages of its progress it would have to fight for its existence : first, as regards absolute truth ; secondly, when that combat was over, as regards

its form or mode of presenting the truth. And as soon as a La Place, or anybody else, builds higher upon the foundations laid by this book, effectually he throws it out of the sunshine into decay and darkness ; by weapons won from this book he superannuates and destroys this book, so that soon the name of Newton remains, as a mere *nominis umbra*, but his book, as a living power, has transmigrated into other forms. Now, on the contrary, the *Iliad*, the *Prometheus* of Aeschylus, —the *Othello* or *King Lear*,—the *Hamlet* or *Macbeth*,— and the *Paradise Lost*, are not militant but triumphant for ever as long as the languages exist in which they speak or can be taught to speak. They never *can* transmigrate into new incarnations. To reproduce *these* in new forms, or variations, even if in some things they should be improved, would be to plagiarise. A good steam-engine is properly superseded by a better. But one lovely pastoral valley is not superseded by another, nor a statue of Praxiteles by a statue of Michael Angelo. These things are separated not by imparity, but by disparity. They are not thought of as unequal under the same standard, but as different in *kind*, and if otherwise equal, as equal under a different standard. Human works of immortal beauty and works of nature in one respect stand on the same footing ; they never absolutely repeat each other ; never approach so near as not to differ ; and they differ not as better and worse, or simply by more and less : they differ by undecipherable and incommunicable differences, that cannot be caught by mimicries, that cannot be reflected in the mirror of copies, that cannot become ponderable in the scales of vulgar comparison.

Applying these principles to Pope, as a representative of fine literature in general, we would wish to remark the claim which he has, or which an equal writer has, to the attention and jealous winnowing of those critics, in particular, who watch over public morals. Clergymen, and all the organs of public criticism put in motion by clergymen, are more especially concerned in the just appreciation of such writers, if the two canons are remembered, which we have endeavoured to illustrate, viz. that all works in this class, as opposed to those in the literature of knowledge, first, work by far deeper agencies ; and, secondly, are more permanent ; in the strictest sense they are κτήματα ἐς ἀεί : and what evil they do, or what good they do, is commensurate with the national language, sometimes long after the nation has departed. At this hour, five hundred years since their creation, the tales of Chaucer, never equalled on this earth for their tenderness, and for life of picturesqueness, are read familiarly by many in the charming language of their natal day, and by others in the modernisations of Dryden, of Pope, and Wordsworth. At this hour, one thousand eight hundred years since their creation, the Pagan tales of Ovid, never equalled on this earth for the gaiety of their movement and the capricious graces of their narrative, are read by all Christendom. This man's people and their monuments are dust ; but *he* is alive : he has survived them, as he told us that he had it in his commission to do, by a thousand years ; "and *shall* a thousand more."

All the literature of knowledge builds only ground-nests, that are swept away by floods, or confounded by the plough ; but the literature of power builds nests in aërial altitudes of temples sacred from violation, or of forests inaccessible to fraud. *This* is a great prerogative of the *power* literature ; and it is a greater which lies in the mode of its influence. The *knowledge*

literature, like the fashion of this world, passeth away.
An Encyclopædia is its abstract ; and, in this respect,
it may be taken for its speaking symbol—that, before
one generation has passed, an Encyclopædia is superannuated ; for it speaks through the dead memory and
unimpassioned understanding, which have not the repose of higher faculties, but are continually enlarging
and varying their phylacteries. But all literature,
properly so called—literature κατ᾽ ἐξοχήν, for the very
same reason that it is so much more durable than the
literature of knowledge, is (and by the very same proportion it is) more intense and electrically searching in
its impressions. The directions in which the tragedy
of this planet has trained our human feelings to play,
and the combinations into which the poetry of this
planet has thrown our human passions of love and
hatred, of admiration and contempt, exercise a power
bad or good over human life, that cannot be contemplated, when stretching through many generations,
without a sentiment allied to awe. And of this let
every one be assured—that he owes to the impassioned
books which he has read, many a thousand more of
emotions than he can consciously trace back to them.
Dim by their origination, these emotions yet arise in
him, and mould him through life like forgotten incidents
of his childhood.

On the Knocking at the Gate in *Macbeth*

From my boyish days I had always felt a great perplexity on one point in *Macbeth*. It was this : the
knocking at the gate, which succeeds to the murder of
Duncan, produced to my feelings an effect for which
I never could account. The effect was, that it reflected

back upon the murder a peculiar awfulness and a depth
of solemnity ; yet, however obstinately I endeavoured
with my understanding to comprehend this, for many
years I never could see *why* it should produce such an
5 effect.

Here I pause for one moment, to exhort the reader
never to pay any attention to his understanding, when
it stands in opposition to any other faculty of his mind.
The mere understanding, however useful and indis-
10 pensable, is the meanest faculty in the human mind
and the most to be distrusted ; and yet the great
majority of people trust to nothing else ; which may
do for ordinary life, but not for philosophic purposes.
Of this out of ten thousand instances that I might
15 produce, I will cite one. Ask of any person whatsoever, who is not previously prepared for the demand
by a knowledge of the perspective, to draw in the
rudest way the commonest appearance which depends
upon the laws of that science ; as, for instance, to
20 represent the effect of two walls standing at right
angles to each other, or the appearance of the houses
on each side of a street, as seen by a person looking
down the street from one extremity. Now in all cases,
unless the person has happened to observe in pictures
25 how it is that artists produce these effects, he will
be utterly unable to make the smallest approximation
to it. Yet why ? For he has actually seen the effect
every day of his life. The reason is—that he allows
his understanding to overrule his eyes. His under-
30 standing, which includes no intuitive knowledge of the
laws of vision, can furnish him with no reason why a
line which is known and can be proved to be a horizontal line, should not *appear* a horizontal line ; a line
that made any angle with the perpendicular, less than

a right angle, would seem to him to indicate that his houses were all tumbling down together.   Accordingly, he makes the line of his houses a horizontal line, and fails, of course, to produce the effect demanded.   Here, then, is one instance out of many, in which not only the under-   5 standing is allowed to overrule the eyes, but where the understanding is positively allowed to obliterate the eyes, as it were ; for not only does the man believe the evidence of his understanding in opposition to that of his eyes, but (what is monstrous !) the idiot is not aware   10 that his eyes ever gave such evidence.   He does not know that he has seen (and therefore *quoad* his consciousness has *not* seen) that which he *has* seen every day of his life.

But to return from this digression, my understanding   15 could furnish no reason why the knocking at the gate in *Macbeth* should produce any effect, direct or reflected. In fact, my understanding said positively that it could *not* produce any effect.   But I knew better ; I felt that it did : and I waited and clung to the problem until   20 further knowledge should enable me to solve it.   At length, in 1812, Mr Williams made his *début* on the stage of Ratcliffe Highway, and executed those unparalleled murders which have procured for him such a brilliant and undying reputation.   On which murders, by the   25 way, I must observe, that in one respect they have had an ill effect, by making the connoisseur in murder very fastidious in his taste, and dissatisfied by anything that has been since done in that line.   All other murders look pale by the deep crimson of his ; and, as an   30 amateur once said to me in a querulous tone, " There has been absolutely nothing *doing* since his time, or nothing that's worth speaking of."   But this is wrong ; for it is unreasonable to expect all men to be great artists, and born with the genius of Mr Williams. Now it will be remembered, that in the first of these murders (that of the Marrs), the same incident (of a knocking at the door soon after the work of extermination was complete) did actually occur, which the genius of Shakespeare has invented ; and all good judges and the most eminent dilettanti acknowledged the felicity of Shakespeare's suggestion, as soon as it was actually realised. Here, then, was a fresh proof that I was right in relying on my own feeling, in opposition to my understanding ; and again I set myself to study the problem ; at length I solved it to my own satisfaction ; and my solution is this. Murder, in ordinary cases, where the sympathy is wholly directed to the case of the murdered person, is an incident of coarse and vulgar horror ; and for this reason—that it flings the interest exclusively upon the natural but ignoble instinct by which we cleave to life ; an instinct which, as being indispensable to the primal law of self-preservation, is the same in kind (though different in degree) amongst all living creatures : this instinct, therefore, because it annihilates all distinctions, and degrades the greatest of men to the level of " the poor beetle that we tread on," exhibits human nature in its most abject and humiliating attitude. Such an attitude would little suit the purposes of the poet. What then must he do ? He must throw the interest on the murderer. Our sympathy must be with *him* ; (of course I mean a sympathy of comprehension, a sympathy by which we enter into his feelings, and are made to understand them,—not a sympathy of pity or approbation). In the murdered person, all strife of thought, all flux and reflux of passion and of purpose, are crushed by one overwhelming panic ; the fear of instant death smites him " with its petrific mace." But in the murderer, such a murderer as a poet will condescend to, there must be raging some great storm of passion—jealousy, ambition, vengeance, hatred—which will create a hell within him ; and into this hell we are to look.

In *Macbeth*, for the sake of gratifying his own enormous and teeming faculty of creation, Shakespeare has introduced two murderers : and, as usual in his hands, they are remarkably discriminated : but,—though in Macbeth the strife of mind is greater than in his wife, the tiger spirit not so awake, and his feelings caught chiefly by contagion from her,—yet, as both were finally involved in the guilt of murder, the murderous mind of necessity is finally to be presumed in both. This was to be expressed ; and on its own account, as well as to make it a more proportionable antagonist to the unoffending nature of their victim, " the gracious Duncan," and adequately to expound " the deep damnation of his taking off," this was to be expressed with peculiar energy. We were to be made to feel that the human nature, *i.e.* the divine nature of love and mercy, spread through the hearts of all creatures, and seldom utterly withdrawn from man—was gone, vanished, extinct ; and that the fiendish nature had taken its place. And, as this effect is marvellously accomplished in the *dialogues* and *soliloquies* themselves, so it is finally consummated by the expedient under consideration ; and it is to this that I now solicit the reader's attention. If the reader has ever witnessed a wife, daughter, or sister in a fainting fit, he may chance to have observed that the most affecting moment in such a spectacle is *that* in which a sigh and a stirring announce the recommencement of suspended life. Or, if the reader has ever been present in a vast metropolis, on the day when some great national idol was carried in funeral pomp to his grave, and chancing to walk near the course through which it passed, has felt powerfully in the silence and desertion of the streets, and in the 5 stagnation of ordinary business, the deep interest which at that moment was possessing the heart of man—if all at once he should hear the death-like stillness broken up by the sound of wheels rattling away from the scene, and making known that the transitory vision was dis- 10 solved, he will be aware that at no moment was his sense of the complete suspension and pause in ordinary human concerns so full and affecting, as at that moment when the suspension ceases, and the goings-on of human life are suddenly resumed. All action in any direction 15 is best expounded, measured, and made apprehensible, by reaction. Now apply this to the case of *Macbeth*. Here, as I have said, the retiring of the human heart and the entrance of the fiendish heart was to be ex- pressed and made sensible. Another world has stept 20 in ; and the murderers are taken out of the region of human things, human purposes, human desires. They are transfigured : Lady Macbeth is " unsexed " ; Macbeth has forgot that he was born of woman ; both are conformed to the image of devils ; and the world 25 of devils is suddenly revealed. But how shall this be conveyed and made palpable ? In order that a new world may step in, this world must for a time dis- appear. The murderers and the murder must be in- sulated—cut off by an immeasurable gulf from the 30 ordinary tide and succession of human affairs—locked up and sequestered in some deep recess ; we must be made sensible that the world of ordinary life is suddenly arrested—laid asleep—tranced—racked into a dread armistice ; time must be annihilated ; relation

to things without abolished ; and all must pass self
withdrawn into a deep syncope and suspension of
earthly passion. Hence it is, that when the deed is
done, when the work of darkness is perfect, then the
world of darkness passes away like a pageantry in the 5
clouds : the knocking at the gate is heard ; and it
makes known audibly that the reaction has commenced ; the human has made its reflux upon the
fiendish ; the pulses of life are beginning to beat again ;
and the re-establishment of the goings-on of the world 10
in which we live, first makes us profoundly sensible of
the awful parenthesis that had suspended them.

O mighty poet ! Thy works are not as those of other
men, simply and merely great works of art ; but are
also like the phenomena of nature, like the sun and the 15
sea, the stars and the flowers ; like frost and snow,
rain and dew, hailstorm and thunder, which are to be
studied with entire submission of our faculties, and
in the perfect faith that in them there can be no too
much or too little, nothing useless or inert—but that, 20
the further we press in our discoveries, the more we
shall see proofs of design and self-supporting arrangement where the careless eye had seen nothing but
accident !

NOTES

(The heavy figures at the beginning of individual notes refer to pages, the light figures to lines)

AUTOBIOGRAPHY

DE QUINCEY'S SCHOOLDAYS

All the autobiographical extracts in this section are taken from the *Confessions of an English Opium-Eater*. Two versions of this book exist : the original form in two contributions to the *London Magazine* in 1821, and a new version which appeared in 1856 in De Quincey's *Selections Grave and Gay*. The latter, from which these extracts are taken, was enlarged to nearly three times the original size, chiefly by additions to the account of his early life and character.

The *Confessions* are arranged in three parts : the *Preliminary Confessions*, or introductory narrative of the youthful adventures which laid the foundation of the writer's habit of opium-eating in after life, and which furnish a key to some parts of the imagery of the dreams ; the *Pleasures of Opium*, outlining his introduction to the drug ; and the *Pains of Opium*, which narrates the nightmare visions.

Though this book is generally admitted to be one of the finest examples of introspective biography, two points should be remembered in reading the account of the writer's childhood—that the narrative was written many years after the events (twenty years in the case of the first version, and over fifty in the second), and that De Quincey's handling of facts is frequently arbitrary, imaginative, and fragmentary. The Opium-Eater is essentially a literary creation, and to keep the facts in proportion the section of the Introduction dealing with the life of De Quincey (pp. ix-xvi) should be read first.

1 3 Manchester Grammar School : founded by Hugh Oldham in 1515 to meet the needs of the new middle class. In De Quincey's time there were about 200 pupils, one-third of whom

were boarders.   Most of the day-boys were drawn from the professional and trading classes.   The school was moved in 1931 from
its buildings in Long Millgate to Rusholme, a suburb of the city.

Mr Charles Lawson was Second Master from 1749 to 1767, and
High Master from then until 1807.   He was a staunch Jacobite,
and, although a deacon, never proceeded to priest's orders, as
he would not take the necessary oath of allegiance to George II.
He was a successful High Master, but the school declined in his
old age.   A monument to him stands in the Cathedral.

1 15 **lazaretto :** public hospital for diseased persons.

1 22 **Pisistratus :** three times Tyrant of Athens, between 560
and 527 B.C.   He encouraged architecture and literature, and
there is a doubtful legend, to which De Quincey refers here, that
the Greek epic songs and lays were not written by Homer, but
were first united and written down as the *Iliad* and *Odyssey* by
Pisistratus.

1 24 **the Athenian captives in Sicily :** in his *Life of Nicias*
Plutarch relates that, during the Peloponnesian War, Athens
declared war against Syracuse.   Nicias led an expedition against
the city, but was disastrously defeated, and many Athenian
captives were put to work in the stone quarries of Syracuse.   It
appears that the dramas of Euripides were especially popular in
Sicily, but that only a few fragments of his works had reached the
island.   Any of the captives, therefore, who could recite the works
of the dramatist were released and held in honour (*see also* Thucydides, VII.).   Browning's *Balaustion's Adventure* is based on
this story.

1 26-27 **"Repeated air Of sad Electra's poet"** : Milton's sonnet,
When the Assault was intended to the City.   Euripides (480-406 B.C.)
in one of his tragedies deals with the history of Electra, a daughter
of Agamemnon.   There is a story that a chance hearing of the
repetition of a chorus from this play moved the Spartans to spare
Athens when it was conquered in 404 B.C.

2 11-12 **"the great Emathian conqueror"** : Alexander the
Great, King of Macedonia, of which Emathia was a province,
destroyed the whole city of Thebes in 336 B.C., as punishment for
a revolt, except the temples and the house of Pindar.   Pindar
(522-442 B.C.) was the greatest lyric poet of Greece.   The quota-
tion is from the same sonnet of Milton.

2 19-20 **Ecbatana, Babylon, Susa, Persepolis :** important cities
in the ancient Persian Empire.

2 21 **nuzzur :** a present made to a superior ; tribute. (Arab. *nazr*.)

2 27-28 **" riding up to the Soldan's chair " :** Milton, *Par. Lost*, I. 762. Soldan is the same as Sultan, the head of the Ottoman Empire.

2 30-31 **archididascalus :** head teacher. Latinised form of Greek διδάσκω, I teach, and αρχεῖν, to be first.

3 22 **Horne Tooke's case :** Horne Tooke (1736-1812) was prevented from practising at the Bar and also from entering Parliament because he was in Holy Orders. A Bill was passed to exclude anyone in Holy Orders from being elected to Parliament.

4 7 **alumni :** pupils ; lit. foster children. Lat. *alo*, I nourish.

4 11 **Horace :** Latin lyric and satirical poet (65-8 B.C.).

4 13 **plagosus Orbilius :** " the beating Orbilius," Hor. 2 *Ep.* I. 70, 71 : " the things which I remember, Orbilius, who was fond of flogging, made me learn when little."

4 23 **Sycophancy :** obsequious flattery, servility.

6 15 **Lord Bacon :** see Essay *Of Counsell* : "A long Table and a square Table, or Seats about the Walls, seeme Things of Forme, but are Things of Substance ; For at a long Table, a few at the upper end, in effect, sway all the Businesse ; but in the other Forme there is more use of the Counsellours' Opinions that sit lower."

6 18-19 **perihelion :** the part of a planet's orbit which is at its least distance from the sun ; *aphelion*, at its greatest distance.

6 23 **Lucifer :** the name given by Milton to Satan, the leader of the fallen angels.

6 26 **Atlas :** in one story, one of the Titans who warred on Jove and who, as a punishment, was forced to bear the world on his shoulders. In later Greek mythology he is represented as a wealthy king, the owner of the Garden of the Hesperides, whom Perseus, with the head of the Gorgon, turned into a mountain for his inhospitality.

6 29 **John o' Groat's house :** a house erected on the north coast of Caithness, Scotland (regarded as the most northerly point of Great Britain), by a Dutchman named Groot in 1600. The story goes that to avoid disputes among his family about precedence John built an octagonal house, with eight doors, so that each of the eight Groots could enter by his own door.

7 1 **King Arthur :** *i.e.* in founding the Order of the Round Table.

7 1 Charlemagne : ruler of the Franks (742-814) and founder of the Holy Roman Empire. He was famous for his victories against the Moors and the Saxons on behalf of Christianity.

7 2 paladin : one of the twelve peers of Charlemagne's household.

7 5 Harrington (1611-77) : author of *Oceana* (1656), a political allegory depicting an ideal commonwealth.

8 29 Suetonius : Roman historian (A.D. 70-140) ; author of *Lives of the Cæsars* and *De Illustribus Grammaticis*, or lives of famous poets, orators, and historians.

8 31-32 Flavian family : the Roman emperors Vespasian and his sons Titus and Domitian, belonging to the house of Flavius.

9 26-27 Bath Grammar School : *see* Introduction, p. **x.**

9 28 Lord Altamont : De Quincey made the acquaintance of Lord Altamont, afterwards Marquis of Sligo, at Bath, and accompanied him on a tour of England and Ireland in 1800. He tried to obtain Lord Altamont's guarantee in his transactions with moneylenders in London, after which there is no further reference to the friendship in De Quincey's writings.

10 18 Dr Cooke Taylor : English scholar (1800-49), author of *Memoirs of the House of Orleans* and *Notes of a Tour in Lancashire*, to the latter of which De Quincey is probably referring.

10 25 Handel : famous German musician (1685-1759). He spent most of his life in England, composing many operas and oratorios, the best known of which is the *Messiah.*

12 29-30 Chateaubriand : French author and politician (1768-1848). He lived in England during the Revolution, and from 1822 to 1824 he was ambassador at London for the restored Bourbon régime. He was one of the leaders of the Romantic movement in French literature, and De Quincey's reference here is to *Sketches of English Literature*, dealing largely with Milton.

13 4 testimony of Balaam : Balaam was a semi-heathen magician mentioned in the Old Testament. He was bribed by the King of Moab to curse Israel, but, against his will, he uttered blessings and foretold the defeat of Moab. See *Num.* xxii.-xxiv.

14 4 polemics : ecclesiastical controversy.

14 29 Froissart . . . Lord Berners : Froissart (*c.* 1338-1404), the French historian and poet, was the author of the *Chronicles*, a history of the main events in England, France, and Spain, from 1325-1400 ―― one of the greatest medieval historical works. The first English translation was made by Lord Berners in 1525.

16 3 **professor of tigrology**: an apothecary who regularly prescribed for De Quincey's illness a mixture "that must have suggested itself to him when prescribing for a tiger."

16 20-23 **Wordsworth . . . "the senselessness of joy"**: Sonnet on *Calais, Aug.* 15, 1802. Wordsworth was an enthusiastic supporter of the early stages of the French Revolution.

16 31 **Already I trod by anticipation . . .**: the close of this paragraph is an excellent example of De Quincey's exquisite diction.

17 15 **Lady Carbery**: of Laxton, Northants, wife of Baron Carbery, Co. Cork. She had been a friend of De Quincey from his childhood, and he visited her to teach her Greek.

18 23 **vails**: form of "avail"—help, profit: money given to servants by a visitor.

19 15 **sub judice**: under trial; not yet decided.

20 12 **Anne Radcliffe**: British romantic novelist (1764-1823) and a leading exponent of the School of Terror; author of *The Mysteries of Udolpho*.

20 26 **Arcadia**: district of Central Greece, which, according to Virgil, was the home of pastoral simplicity and happiness.

20 26 **Sicily**: the home of several famous pastoral poets, *e.g.* Theocritus, who wrote many descriptions of the beauty of Sicilian country life.

21 10 **Mecca**: the holy city of the Mohammedans.

21 11 **St Peter's**: Cathedral at Rome; the chief church of Roman Catholic Christendom.

21 21 **barouche**: a four-wheeled carriage.

21 30 **phrenologically**: phrenology is the science of the human mind, dealing with the feelings and intellect.

22 8 **ladies of the Hesperides**: the daughters of Hesperus, who, on an island in the far west, guarded the golden apples given by Terra (Earth) to Juno on her marriage to Jupiter.

22 12 **Pausanias**: a Greek traveller and geographer (*c.* A.D. 150); his *Itinerary of Greece* describes the myths and legends of the Greek people. De Quincey's reference can be found in Pausanias, i. 15, 3, and i. 32, 4.

22 13 **Marathon**: a village 10 miles from Athens, where a small army of Athenians under Miltiades defeated the enormous invading army of Persians in 490 B.C.

22 19 **Falstaff :** see *The Merry Wives of Windsor*, V. v. The people who torment Falstaff are the wives and their friends in disguise.

23 34 **the foreign letter :** a letter from abroad containing a large sum of money, and addressed to a *Monsieur De Quincey*, which Thomas received on the eve of his departure. The problem of whether to take the money, which was probably meant for some obscure connection of the family, or not, occupied his mind for some time.

24 10 **remark of Dr Johnson's :** *The Idler*, paper 103.

24 32 **prayer against the perils of darkness :** the third collect in the Evening Prayer of the English Liturgy : '' Lighten our darkness, we beseech thee, O Lord . . .''

26 12-13 **ancient collegiate church :** now Manchester Cathedral.

26 31 **" pensive citadel " :** Wordsworth's sonnet beginning '' Nuns fret not at their convent's narrow room.''

THE BORE AT CHESTER

27 23 **earliest parade :** De Quincey in a note says, '' It was a very scenical parade, for somewhere along this reach of the Dee—viz. immediately below St John's Priory—Edgar, the first sovereign of all England, was rowed by nine vassal *reguli* '' [in A.D. 973].

27 27 **Parkgate :** a small town on the estuary of the Dee, a few miles from Chester.

28 1 **Cop :** probably from the Celtic, meaning the head or top of a thing, especially the top of a hill.

29 18-19 **morass of Solway :** a district of Cumberland. Several villages were destroyed in 1771 through the overflowing of the waters of the bog after excessive rain.

29 19-20 **ἄνω ποτάμων of Euripides :** *Medea*, 409 : '' The streams of the sacred rivers flow backwards.''

30 4 **Deucalion and Pyrrha :** in classical legend, the sole survivors of a flood by which Jupiter destroyed the world. They were ordered to repeople the earth by throwing stones behind them, Deucalion's stones becoming men, and Pyrrha's, women.

31 34 **Vesuvius :** volcano near Naples, Italy.

32 16 **County Palatine :** Cheshire. After the Conquest the earls of certain counties (Cheshire, Lancashire, and Durham) were given special privileges and royal rights, these counties being known as the Counties Palatine (Lat. *palatinum* = belonging to the palace).

32 18 παῤῥησία : parrhesia : freeness in speaking.

32 28 **The Bore :** in certain funnel-shaped estuaries (*e.g.* the Amazon, the Seine, and the Severn), where the advancing tidal wave is concentrated on a narrowing front, a wave is sometimes produced which rushes upstream like a wall of foaming water, several feet in height. This is known as the Bore.

FAREWELL TO WALES

For the circumstances of De Quincey's tour in North Wales, *see* Introduction, p. xi.

33 4 **Oswestry :** market town of Shropshire, 17 miles from Shrewsbury.

33 7 **Jessica's moonlight :** see *Merchant of Venice*, V. i. 54. The words referred to are actually spoken by Lorenzo, not Jessica.

33 19 **lambent :** flickering on the surface.

34 27 **locus penitentiæ :** place for repentance.

34 30 **pié poudré :** court of justice held at fairs to settle disputes between buyers and sellers ; Fr. *pied-poudreux*, dusty-footed, a vagabond.

35 19 **smart-money :** money paid by a prisoner to the jailer to secure preferential treatment.

35 20 **comme il faut :** as it should be.

35 23-24 **Grecian phrase,** ἐπομπεύε : moved in state, *i.e.* in solemn procession.

35 26 **Cæsar semper Augustus :** the ever-to-be-worshipped Cæsar. The title Augustus was conferred by the Roman Senate on Octavian in 27 B.C., but it was taken by all the succeeding emperors, whether descended from Octavian or not.

35 27 **avatars :** appearances as an object of worship ; originally the descent of a Hindu deity in visible form.

35 29-30 **one of the twelve Cæsars :** Vespasian. His dying words are recorded in Bacon's Essay *Of Death*.

35 32 **metamorphosis :** change of form.

36 9 **apotheosis :** ascension to glory ; especially the formal attribution of divine honours to a deceased Roman emperor.

36 17-18 " **sounds that live in darkness** " : *Excursion*, I. 289-91. The following paragraphs are a good example of De Quincey's treatment of scenery.

38 5 " **the inside of a wolf's throat** " : a common similitude for pitch dark.

38 13 **Acherontis avari** : of greedy Acheron. Virgil, *Georgics*, II. 492. Acheron is one of the five rivers of the underworld ; often used for the lower regions themselves.

38 13 **Whispering gallery** : a gallery in the dome of St Paul's Cathedral, London, from which whispers are strangely magnified in sound.

38 20-21 **camera obscura** : dark-chamber. An apparatus in which the images of external objects, received through a double convex lens, are exhibited distinctly, and in their natural colours, on a white surface placed at the focus of the lens.

39 19 **Lombard Street** : a London street which took its name from the Italian bankers of Lombardy who settled there. In De Quincey's time the G.P.O. was situated in Lombard Street.

LONDON

40 13 **mei juris** : of my own right, *i.e.* my own master.

42 2-3 **officina diplomatum** : workshop of the documents.

44 4-5 **Wordsworth records** : see *Goody Blake and Harry Gill*. Several of Wordsworth's poems are located in the Dorsetshire district.

45 24 **dog-sleep** : dozing like a dog, *i.e.* watchful.

46 25-26 **the plan of Cromwell** : there are various reports, probably exaggerated, that after the dissolution of his last parliament Cromwell took elaborate precautions against royalist assassins, including frequent changes of residence. *See* Clarendon, *Hist. of Rebellion*, XV.

46 33 **esculent** : eatable. Lat. *edere*, to eat.

47 18 **Bluebeard room** : in the old Bluebeard story, he permits his wife to enter any room in the palace except one, to which, however, he gives her a golden key. Curiosity getting the better of her, she opens the door, and finds the bodies of wives murdered previously for similar curiosity. *See* Perrault, *Contes du Temps Passé*.

47 28 **Tartarus** : in classical mythology the place of punishment in the Lower World ; hence often used for the Lower World itself.

49 8 **Dr Johnson has recorded :** *See* Mrs Piozzo's *Anecdotes of the late Samuel Johnson.* She relates that he was uncommonly fond of peaches, and although he ate seven or eight each morning before breakfast, he protested that he never had as many as he wished.

49 18-19 **" The world was all before us " :** cf. *Paradise Lost*, XII. 646-47.

DREAM-PHANTASIES

INTRODUCTION TO OPIUM

For De Quincey's introduction to opium, and the part played by the drug in his dream-faculty, *see* Introduction, pp. xii, xxiii.

50 25 **manna :** the food miraculously supplied to the Israelites in the wilderness. See *Ex.* xvi, 15.

50 25 **ambrosia :** the fabled food of the gods which made its recipients immortal.

51 10 **" the stately Pantheon " :** a large concert hall and theatre in Oxford Street, near Poland Street. It was burned down in 1792, twice rebuilt, and in 1834 turned into a bazaar. Wordsworth's reference is in the opening stanza of *Power of Music*.

52 11 **apocalypse :** a revelation or disclosure.

52 16 **panacea :** a universal remedy.

52 16 **φάρμακον νηπενθές :** "drug-banishing sorrow," *Odyssey*, IV. 220.

52 25-26 **" tempt the spirit to rebel " :** Wordsworth, Dedication to *The White Doe of Rylestone.* The paragraph following is a good example of De Quincey's " impassioned prose."

53 4 **Phidias** (*c.* 500 B.C.) : famous Athenian sculptor ; responsible for several of the marble sculptures on the Parthenon and other buildings for his friend Pericles.

53 4 **Praxiteles** (*c.* 360-340 B.C.) : Athenian sculptor, famous for his *Aphrodite of Cnidos.*

53 5 **Babylon :** the Hanging Gardens of the palace of Nebuchadnezzar, King of Babylon (604-561 B.C.), were reckoned among the Seven Wonders of the World.

53 5 **Hekatómpylos :** the hundred-gated ; an epithet applied to the town of Thebes in Egypt to distinguish it from the *heptapylos,* or seven-gated, which designated the Grecian Thebes, near Athens. Thebes (modern Luxor) is the site of many splendours of Egyptian civilisation.

53 5-6 **"from the anarchy of dreaming sleep "**: Wordsworth, *Excursion,* IV. 87.

THE MALAY

53 23 **lustrum**: space of five years among the ancient Romans.

54 11 **"That moveth altogether . . ."**: Wordsworth, *Resolution and Independence,* Stanza xi.

54 16 **Kant**: German philosopher (1724-1807) ; well known for the difficulty of his works.

56 13 **"Anastasius"**: a novel by Thos. Hope (1819) ; it takes the form of the autobiography of a disreputable and unscrupulous Greek, and has a Glossary of oriental words at the end.

56 15 **Adelung's " Mithridates"**: a dictionary of oriental languages by J. C. Adelung (1732-1806), a German philologist.

56 25-26 **inter alia**: among other things.

OPIUM-DREAMS

58 1-2 **Roman centurion**: see *Luke* vii. 8.

58 8 **Œdipus**: in Greek legend, the King of Thebes, who solved the riddle of the Sphinx. His tragic story is the subject of several plays by Sophocles.

58 8 **Priam**: King of Troy; father of Paris, who abducted Helen and caused the Greek-Trojan War.

58 8 **Tyre**: city of ancient Phœnicia, one of the most famous trading towns of the East in the time of King Solomon.

58 8 **Memphis**: formerly the capital of Egypt ; on the Nile, 10 miles from modern Cairo.

58 21 **Midas**: King of Phrygia, to whom Bacchus granted the request that everything he touched should become gold. When he found that even his food became gold, and that he was in danger of starving, he prayed to have the power removed.

58 28 **sympathetic ink**: ink which remains invisible until heat or acid is applied.

59 28-29 **a near relative of mine**: Dr Garnett states that De Quincey's mother is meant.

60 5-6 **dread book of account**: cf. *Rev.* xx. 12.

60 27 **Livy**: (59 B.C.-A.D. 17) Roman historian ; author of *History of Rome*.

60 32 **Consul Romanus**: one of the two supreme magistrates.

61 20 **a certain day in August 1642**: De Quincey, in a note, relates that this refers to the setting-up of the royal standard of Charles at Nottingham. It was blown down during the night, and this was considered an evil omen.

61 22 **Marston Moor**: the defeat of Rupert and the Royalists, 2nd July 1644.

61 22 **Newbury**: there were two indecisive battles at Newbury in 1643 and 1644.

61 22 **Naseby**: the crushing defeat of Rupert and Charles in 1645, which practically decided the issue of the war.

61 25-26 **the court of George IV.**: the reigning king when the *Confessions* were written.

61 31 **paludament**: a military cloak worn by the staff of the Roman Imperator.

61 31 **Paullus**: Lucius Æmilius Paullus (*c.* 229-160 B.C.), the Roman general who defeated Perseus and destroyed the great kingdom of Macedonia in 168 B.C.

61 31 **Marius**: Gaius Marius (157-85 B.C.) ; Roman general and statesman who saved Rome from the invasions of the German tribes at the end of the second century B.C. He was reckoned the greatest Roman general before Julius Cæsar.

61 32-33 **crimson tunic**: signal announcing the day of battle ; cf. *Julius Cæsar*, V. i. 14.

61 33 **alalagmos**: the battle-cry of the Roman army.

62 1 **Piranesi**: (1711-1778) Italian engraver and architect; he reproduced in engravings much of the ruined architecture of Rome, but many of his drawings are visionary in character.

62 32-33 **a great modern poet**: Wordsworth, *Excursion*, II. 834-51.

63 33 **the last Lord Orford**: Horace Walpole (1717-97), famous wit and letter-writer ; author of the novel, *The Castle of Otranto*.

65 13 **castes**: the hereditary social classes of India, which are kept strictly apart.

65 19-20 **officina gentium**: " workshop of the nations," *i.e.* where nations are manufactured.

66 11 **the wrath of Brahma . . .**: the divine Triad of the

Hindu religion : Brahma the Creator of the universe, Vishnu its Maintainer, and Siva the Destroyer.

66 13 **Isis and Osiris :** Isis was the principal goddess of ancient Egypt ; she was identified with the moon, and was the sister and wife of Osiris, the sun-god and ruler of the kingdom of the dead.

66 14 **ibis :** a bird of the stork order ; the ibis and the crocodile were sacred in Egyptian worship.

67 25 **cæteris paribus :** other things being equal.

67 29 **solecism :** inaccuracy of language.

68 24 **Easter Sunday :** cannot be as late as May.

69 3 **the grave of a child :** the reference is to Catherine Wordsworth.

69 9 **the first-fruits of Resurrection :** cf. I *Cor.* xv. 20.

69 27 **Ann :** a poor girl who befriended De Quincey during the period in London. When he returned to the city after a brief absence she had disappeared, and he never saw her again.

70 13 **Then suddenly would come . . . :** one of the best examples of De Quincey's prose-poetry.

70 18 **Coronation Anthem :** composed by Handel.

71 3-4. **" Deeper than ever plummet sounded " :** *Tempest*, V. i. 56.

71 15 **with a sigh . . . :** see *Paradise Lost*, II. 746. The incestuous mother is Sin, the mother of Death, and the two figures guard the gates of Hell.

LEVANA AND OUR LADIES OF SORROW

This remarkable piece is one of an incompleted series which appeared in *Blackwood's Magazine* in March 1845, and which was apparently intended to be a further series of *Opium Confessions*, under the title of *Suspiria De Profundis*, or *Sighs from the Depths*. Only five pieces appeared in 1845, including *The Affliction of Childhood*, *Levana*, and *Savannah-la-mar*, but Dr Japp has recently shown that De Quincey planned to publish at least 32 articles, including the *English Mail-Coach*, which was later extended and issued separately.

The series is intended to illustrate the power of suffering to develop the intellect and spirit, to illustrate the mind, and to open up a conception of the infinite. Each of the pieces has its origin in dreams. *The Affliction of Childhood* records the sensitive visions of his early days in Manchester, and the later papers present " dreams and noon-day visions " that arose " under the latter stages of opium influence."

The literary character of these pieces is in advance of the *Confessions*: the Opium-Eater himself obtrudes less, and we are concerned solely with the unearthly pictures of the visions themselves. De Quincey ranked the *Suspiria* as his finest specimens of imaginative and eloquent prose, describing them as " modes of impassioned prose ranging under no precedents in literature."

71 22 **Levana**: goddess in Roman mythology, the protectress of children ; Lat. *levare*, to raise, also signifies, in a derived sense, to lighten, relieve, and so to alleviate.

72 34 **the mighty wheel of day and night**: De Quincey notes that the " fine image of the revolving wheel " is taken from Wordsworth's *Miscellaneous Sonnets*, II. xxxvii.

73 6 **grief such as mine**: referring to the death of his sister Elizabeth. *See* Introduction, pp. x and xxiv.

73 14 **rules of Eton**: apparently there was no such rule, the statute providing that boys should be eligible from 8 to 12 years of age.

73 14 **on the Foundation**: *i.e.* holding free scholarships.

73 27-34 **the Graces . . .**: goddesses in classical mythology. The Graces, or daughters of Venus, were symbols of youth and beauty ; the Parcæ, the three Fates or Destinies, controlled the lot of mortals ; the Furies were three sister goddesses who tormented the souls of sinners ; the Muses (usually represented as nine) presided over poetry and the fine arts.

73 29 **arras**: tapestry, from Arras in France, where it was made.

74 4 **one of whom I know**: Mater Lachrymarum. For the effect of the deaths of his father and two sisters on De Quincey, *see* Introduction, pp. xxiv, xxv.

74 33 **dulcimer**: a musical instrument resembling a flat box with wires stretched across the top. It was played by striking the wires with two small hammers.

75 4 **hieroglyphics**: picture-writing ; the sacred characters of the ancient Egyptian language.

75 18 **in Rama**: cf. *Jer.* xxxi. 15.

75 21 **Herod's sword**: *Matt.* ii. 16.

75 33 **keys more than papal**: the Pope's emblem, the crossed keys, refers to his claim to be the direct descendant of St Peter, who was given, symbolically, the keys of heaven. See *Matt*. xvi. 19.

76 15 **the Czar:** the Czar Nicholas, whose third daughter, Princess Alexandra, died in August 1844, at the age of 19.

76 24 **Madonna:** Lat. *mea domina*, my lady.

77 12 **Mediterranean galleys:** until 1854 French criminals were often condemned to labour in the galleys.

77 13 **Norfolk Island:** in the South Pacific, east of Australia ; used by the English as a penal settlement until 1856.

77 18 **oblations:** acts of offering.

77 20 **Every slave that at noonday . . . :** probably a reference to slavery in North America (not strictly in the tropics), which was not abolished until 1865.

77 31 **sepulchral lamps:** lamps used to illuminate the family tombs when they were visited by the Romans to make offerings to the dead.

77 31-32 **every nun defrauded . . . :** *i.e.* who has been forced to enter a convent to save the cost of her maintenance.

78 4 **tents of Shem:** see *Gen*. ix. 27. The Shemites were wanderers and gypsies.

78 15 **Cybele:** the mother of the gods, worshipped in Phrygia. She is represented in a chariot drawn by lions, and wearing a turret on her head.

79 4 **Semnai Theai:** the name given to the Eumenides at Athens.

79 5 **Eumenides:** the '' well-disposed '' ; the Greek name (given in the hope of propitiation) for the Furies.

SAVANNAH-LA-MAR

Savannah-la-mar is a small coast town in Jamaica, which was visited by De Quincey's brother. The name (*la mar*, the sea) itself suggests the city sunk, with all its towers standing, beneath the ocean, through which it is still visible in fair weather.

De Quincey expresses the meaning of the piece in the text, that '' the future is the present of God,'' and for this He sacrifices the human present, working by earthquakes and grief.

80 8 **Pompeii:** an ancient city of Italy at the foot of Vesuvius. It was used as a pleasure resort by the Romans, but was destroyed by a volcanic eruption in A.D. 79.

80 24 **Fata-Morgana revelation**: a vision supposed to be caused by the fairy (fata) Morgana, a sister of King Arthur, in the medieval legends.

80 27 **cerulean**: sky-coloured, azure.

81 5 **jubilate**: exultation ; the opening word of the 66th and 100th Psalms.

81 6 **requiem**: hymn or mass sung for the rest of the souls of the dead.

81 15 **clepsydra**: an instrument used by the Greeks and Romans for measuring time by the trickling of water through a small aperture.

82 22 **sanctus**: the ascription " Holy, holy, holy, Lord God of Hosts," from *Isa*. vi. ; a musical setting of the same.

THE ENGLISH MAIL-COACH

This work was intended to form one of the papers in *Suspiria De Profundis* (see p. 222), but apparently it grew beyond the limits of that series, and was published in *Blackwood's Magazine* in Oct. and Dec. 1849. The articles were carefully revised by De Quincey and brought together under one head for the collected edition in 1854.

Scheme : It is essential to grasp the relationship between the various parts. In De Quincey's introduction to the 1849 edition he describes the scheme as follows :—

Part I. (*a*) The general characteristics of the Mail-Coach, one of the most important being the publishing of national news, as an example of which he gives

(*b*) A vivid narrative of a journey first announcing a victory of Wellington in the Peninsular War.

These characteristics are suggested by

,, II. An accident, which is circumstantially described, and which threatened sudden death to a woman concerned in it. The accident was seen by De Quincey himself from the top of a Mail-Coach, and the memory resolves itself into

,, III. A series of troubled dreams, in which the details of the accident occur in various forms.

THE GLORY OF MOTION

"The permanent features of distinction investing the mail itself lie," De Quincey states, "1st, in velocity unprecedented, 2ndly, in the power and beauty of the horses, 3rdly, in the official connection with the government of a great nation, and 4thly, in the function, almost a consecrated function, of publishing and diffusing through the land, the great political events, and especially the great battles, during a conflict of unparalleled grandeur."

83 2 **Mr Palmer**: a native of Bath who inaugurated a scheme for superseding slow private conveyance, by official Post Office coaches, to carry both mails and passengers. Commencing on 8th August 1784, the new system was a great success and Mr Palmer became Comptroller-General of the Post Office.

83 7 **Galileo**: (1564-1642) Italian astronomer; he improved the telescope and discovered the satellites of Jupiter.

84 12-13 **apocalyptic vials**: see *Rev.* xvi.; the wrath of God is described as in vials or bowls, from which the angels pour it out.

84 13-14 **Trafalgar . . . Waterloo**: victories over the French in the Napoleonic Wars.

84 23 **Te Deum**: an old Latin hymn sung at services of public thanksgiving; its opening words are "Te Deum laudamus"—"We praise thee, O Lord."

85 26 **posting-houses**: roadside inns where relays of horses could be obtained.

86 2 **quaternion**: a body of four persons.

86 5 **delf-ware outsides**: Delf (from Delft in Holland) is ordinary earthenware as distinguished from the fine porcelain earthenware originally made in China.

86 6 **attaint**: disgrace; Lat. *tinctus*, dyed, stained.

86 11 **Pariah**: an outcast; originally a member of a low caste in Hindu society.

87 6 **objects not appearing . . .**: a Roman legal phrase, "The same law applies to things that do not appear as to things that do not exist."

87 16 **snobs**: the term originally meant a shoemaker; it was afterwards applied in university towns to those not belonging to the university, and finally to any low, common people.

87 19 **penumbra :** partial shadow, bordering the total shadow of an eclipse.

87 23 **boxes :** corresponded to the modern Dress Circle as well as to the side boxes.

88 9 **metaphysical :** according to the rules of metaphysics, the science of thought.

88 18 **wits jump :** *i.e.* think alike. Prof. Masson notes that this paragraph is a caricature of a story told in Staunton's account of the Earl of Macartney's Embassy to China in 1792.

88 31 **hammer-cloth :** covering for the box-seat.

89 23 **check-strings :** string connections for communication between the passenger and driver, to signal stops, etc.

89 24 **jury-reins :** " jury " is a nautical term applied to anything erected temporarily.

90 8 **turnpike gates :** gates set across the road to stop travellers until the toll is paid.

90 16-17 **crane-neck :** an iron bar, bent like the neck of a crane, which joins the back and front timbers of a vehicle ; here used for the carriage itself.

90 17 **quarterings :** from Fr. *cartoyer*, to drive to one side, to avoid a rut or an obstacle.

90 23 **benefit of clergy :** the right of clerics, under old English law, to plead exemption from trial in secular courts.

90 25 **systole and diastole :** the alternate contraction and dilation of the heart.

91 19 **false echoes of Marengo :** the Austrians were defeated by Napoleon in 1800 ; the " false echoes " were the words supposed to have been used by Napoleon to the memory of Gen. Desaix, who was killed in the battle.

91 29 **a fortiori :** with stronger reason.

92 14 **Brummagem :** a slang expression for Birmingham.

92 16 **Luxor :** the site of the tombs of the kings at Thebes ; *see* note to 53.5.

92 19 **jacobinical :** revolutionary ; from the Jacobins, the extreme party in the French Revolution.

92 30 **hunting-leopards :** leopards trained for hunting deer in India.

93 1-2 **" which they upon the adverse faction . . ." :** Shakespeare, *Richard III.*, V. iii.

93 24 **one of our elder dramatists :** Thos. Heywood (died *c.* 1650), *The Royal King and Loyal Subject*.

93 27 **omrah :** itself the plural of Ar. *amir*, a nobleman.

94 18 **Edward Longshanks :** Edward I. ; there is, of course, no such law.

95 4-5 **not magna loquimur, . . . but vivimus :** not " we speak great things," but " we live them."

95 18 **Salamanca :** victory of Wellington in the Peninsular War against France in 1812.

96 8 **pot-wallopings :** " wallop " means to boil with much bubbling and noise ; the " pot " is the boiler : an onomatopœic word.

GOING DOWN WITH VICTORY

" The fourth and grandest distinction of the mail "—to publish and diffuse news of national events—De Quincey's note states, " belonged exclusively to the war with Napoleon." The journey with the news of a victory is therefore used to illustrate all the characteristics of the mail : velocity, the power and beauty of the horses, and the connection with the government.

96 27 **Titans :** in Greek legend, the children of Uranus (heaven) and Ge (earth) ; hence synonymous with physical greatness.

96 27 **inappreciable :** *i.e.* too great to be estimated.

97 2 **baubling :** contemptible.

97 16 **prelibation :** a foretaste.

97 20-21 **Lombard Street :** *see* note to 39.19.

97 24 **attelage :** coach and team of horses.

99 16 **Badajoz :** Wellington captured this important frontier fortress after several severe sieges in 1812.

100 19 **Barnet :** village in Hertfordshire, 11 miles N. of London.

102 12 **the gazette :** originally one of the official papers of the kingdom ; afterwards an official announcement taken from the *London Gazette*.

102 31 **fey :** not Celtic, but Anglo-Saxon *faege*—doomed. Applied to a person of strange behaviour or excitement, which was thought to presage approaching death.

102 33 **wake :** fair ; originally held to celebrate the wake, or watching, at the dedication of a church.

103 22 **Talavera :** victory of Wellington in July, 1809, though the weakness of his Spanish ally Cuesta caused heavy losses and made it impossible to follow up the victory.

104 20 aceldama : lit. field of blood ; originally the field near Jerusalem purchased by Judas Iscariot with the bribe taken for betraying his master.

THE VISION OF SUDDEN DEATH

De Quincey describes the incident on which this passage is based as follows : " Thirty-seven years ago, or rather more, accident made me, in the dead of night, and of a night memorably solemn, the solitary witness of an appalling scene, which threatened instant death in a shape the most terrific to two young people whom I had no means of assisting, except in so far as I was able to give them a most hurried warning of their danger ; but even *that* not until they stood within the very shadow of the catastrophe, being divided from the most frightful of deaths by scarcely more, if more at all, than seventy seconds." *See* Introduction, p. xxxv.

The intellectual reverie (actually several pages longer than the extract given here), which precedes the dramatic narration of the accident, should be noted as an example of effective contrast.

105 31 Cæsar the Dictator : Suetonius, Plutarch, and Appian, all confirm this remark of Julius Cæsar's, which was uttered at dinner in the house of Marcus Lepidus, the day before the assassination.

107 32 jus dominii : the right of ownership.

108 9 jus gentium : the law of nations.

108 16 laudanum : fluid extract of opium.

108 25-26 Virgil, " Monstrum horrendum . . . " : the description of the Cyclops Polyphemus in *Æneid*, III. 658.

108 30 Calendars : Order of Dervishes in Turkey and Persia, who preach in market-places and live on alms. The reference is to the story of the three one-eyed princes in the *Arabian Nights* who disguise themselves as Calendars.

109 7 Al Sirat : in Mohammedan teaching, the bridge over Hades across which souls must pass to Paradise. It is only as wide as a sword's edge, so that none cumbered with sin can hope to cross it.

109 11 cognominated : named.

109 13 **diphrelatic:** a coinage of De Quincey's.

111 6 **aurigation:** the art of driving horses attached to carriages.

111 7 **Apollo:** the god of the sun, who thus drove the chariot of the sun across the sky.

111 7 **Aurora:** goddess of the dawn; she traversed the heavens in a chariot drawn by two horses.

111 12 **Pantheon:** a temple dedicated to all the gods; hence Pagan Pantheon = all the heathen gods put together.

112 16 **Lilliputian Lancaster:** Lancaster, though the County town, is dwarfed by the more modern cities of Manchester and Liverpool. Lilliputian—from the island of dwarfs in Swift's *Gulliver's Travels*.

113 33 **halcyon repose:** the days of calm when the fabulous birds, the halcyons, are supposed to breed.

115 6 **radix:** the fundamental number, or base of a system.

115 34 **quartering:** *see* note to 90.17. De Quincey's use of the term, to drive to the side, is etymologically correct.

116 28 **taxed cart:** a little spring-cart; formerly vehicles not over the value of £21 were exempt from tax.

116 29 **gig:** a light carriage with one pair of wheels.

118 6-7 **the shout of Achilles:** see *Iliad*, XVIII. 217, where Achilles is roused from mourning for his friend Patroclus by the messenger of Pallas Athene (or Minerva), the goddess of war. He issues forth unarmed, and his shout, swelled by the voice of Pallas, strikes fear into the Trojans. Achilles was the son of Peleus and the sea-goddess Thetis.

121 9 **Faster than ever millrace:** note the short, vivid simile.

121 14 **swingle-bar:** the cross-bar by which the horses are yoked to the carriage, and to which the traces are fastened.

DREAM-FUGUE

The connection between the last section and this is described by De Quincey thus: "A movement of horror, and of spontaneous recoil from this dreadful scene, naturally carried the whole of that scene, raised and idealised, into my dreams, and very soon into a rolling succession of dreams. The actual scene, as looked down upon from the box of the mail, was transformed into a dream as tumultuous and changing as a musical fugue.

This troubled dream is circumstantially narrated in Section the Third, entitled ' Dream-Fugue on the theme of Sudden Death.' What I had beheld from my seat upon the mail, the scenical strife of action and passion, of anguish and fear, as I had there witnessed them moving in ghostly silence, this duel between life and death narrowing itself to a point of such exquisite evanescence as the collision neared : all these elements of the scene blended, under the law of association, with the previous and permanent features of distinction investing the mail itself.''

123 — Fugue: *see* Introduction, p. xxxiv. A fugue is a polyphonic composition constructed on one or more short subjects, which are announced by all the parts in turn and introduced from time to time, monotony being avoided by the occasional use of episodes, or passages open to free treatment. The theme thus appears and disappears at intervals, connecting and interweaving the melodies into one complex whole.

The arrangement of De Quincey's variations is as follows :—

Introduction : The vision of sudden death, under the symbol of a dead woman waiting for Resurrection, which over-rides his dreams.

Exposition, or relation of the theme by the various instruments :

   (i) Vision of the woman in a fairy pinnace viewed from a lofty three-decker ; the sudden change in the appearance of the pinnace ; the wreck.

  (ii) The woman, now on a frigate, passes on the sea and disappears into the storm.

 (iii) The woman, seen by the dreamer from a small boat, runs in panic over the shore and is engulfed in the quicksands.

 (iv) The dreamer in a triumphal car journeys through a strange land, carrying news of grandeur and joy ; they enter a mighty minster containing the tombs of the dead ; a female child is seen on the last tomb ; a Trumpet heralds the Judgment on the woman, who is defended and saved by her good angel.

Conclusion : The final harmony of all the parts : the general Chorus of Thanksgiving for the salvation of the girl.

All the parts of the fugue are thus bound together by the common theme—the despair of the woman in the gig, the inability of the dreamer to help her, and her sudden vision of Judgment. In

addition, the reminiscences of actual details of the accident
should be noted : the reverie on sudden death and judgment ;
the peaceful prelude—the summer eve, the ocean " tranquil and
verdant as a savannah "—; the approach of the vehicles ; the
moment of panic ; the inevitability of the woman's fate ; the
memory of the triumphal journey connected with Waterloo—
the headlong pace ; the vista of arches and long cathedral
aisles ; the efforts to save the woman ; the Trumpet, recalling the
horn of the Guard ; the sudden transition from the scene of the
tragedy.

123 — **Tumultuosissimamente** : most tumultuously. *Cf.* the
indication of tempo in a musical score.

123 8 **averted signs** : although he saw the agony of the lady's
gestures, he caught sight of her only from the rear, never seeing
her full-face.

123 11 **Ionic form** : referring to the gracefulness of Ionic
architecture as distinct from the severity of the Doric or the
floridity of the Corinthian. The idea may have been suggested
by the fact that pillars were often shaped in the form of women,
these being called *caryatides*. Good examples can be seen on
St Pancras Church, London.

124 3 **savannah** : a tract of level land ; a treeless plain.

124 5 **pinnace** : a small vessel with oars and sails.

124 18 **corymbi** : clusters of fruit or flowers.

125 14 **quarrel** : the square-headed arrow of a cross-bow.

125 18 **vortex** : whirlpool ; eddy.

126 8 **Sweet funeral bells** . . . : this third movement is especially full of musical effects.

128 33 **traceries** : the stone ornamentation with which the
arches of Gothic windows are filled, and which support the glass.

128 34 **white-robed choristers** . . . : a reminiscence of the
Vision in *Revelation*. Throughout this passage the language
recalls that of St John.

129 10 **Campo Santo** : the cemetery at Pisa ; here used for
the gravestones which in many cathedrals form a flat pavement
over which carriages and horses *might* run. (D. Q.)

129 11-12 **necropolis** : a cemetery.

129 21 **sarcophagi** : stone tombs.

129 25 **bas-relief** : designs in which the figures are slightly
raised from the groundwork.

130 32 **aboriginal** : first, primitive.

131 5 **Then a third time . . .:** another reminiscence of *Revelation*. Cf. *Rev.* viii. 10; xii. 5, etc.

132 14 **sanctus:** *see* note to **82**.22.

133 7 **A thousand times . . .:** the fugue closes with a magnificent sentence of rhythmic character, which falls at times into regular poetry.

BIOGRAPHY

JOAN OF ARC

Issued as two articles in *Tait's Magazine* for March and August, 1847, and reprinted by De Quincey in the collected edition in 1854.

The biography was a spontaneous effusion, inspired by a perusal of Michelet's history, and it is considered to be one of De Quincey's best-sustained efforts. It was the first sane and true picture of the Maid in imaginative writing, and it went far in counterbalancing the unworthy treatment of her in Southey's *Joan of Arc*, Schiller's *Jungfrau von Orleans*, and Voltaire's *La Pucelle*.

History. De Quincey's article is rather an appreciation than a narration of facts. The main events of Joan's life are as follows : She was born at Domrémy in 1412, the daughter of a peasant, and passed her childhood in rural seclusion. The English held all France north of the Loire, and Henry VI. aspired to the French throne by over-riding the claims of the Dauphin. Joan suddenly appeared before the court, claiming the inspiration of heavenly voices, and persuaded the Dauphin to give her the command of an army. She raised the siege of Orleans on April 29th, 1429, conquered the English at Patay on June 18th, and enabled Charles to reach Rheims and be crowned on July 17th. In May 1430 she was captured by the Duke of Burgundy and sold to the English. On the ground that her successes were due to witchcraft, she was condemned and burnt as a heretic at Rouen on May 30th, 1431.

For a stimulating essay on Joan the Preface to Bernard Shaw's *St Joan* should be read. Other accounts are Andrew Lang's *Story of Joan of Arc* and Mark Twain's *Saint Joan of Arc*.

134 3 **the Hebrew shepherd boy :** David in his first fight with Goliath.

134 9 **an act:** see 1 *Sam.* xvii.

134 10 **Lorraine :** Joan was born at Domrémy, Lorraine.

134 27 **Vaucouleurs :** a town near Domrémy. Joan first made known her mission to the captain of Vaucouleurs, and begged him to send her to court. *See* Shaw's *St Joan,* i.

135 13 **apparitors :** legal officers ; the summoners of the ecclesiastical courts.

135 15 **en contumace :** contempt of court ; legal term for failure to appear.

135 16 **as even yet may happen :** the sentence on Joan was revoked by the Pope in 1456 and her inspirations accepted as genuine. She has since been beatified by the Roman Catholic Church, and is accepted by France as a national heroine.

135 33 **Rouen :** Joan was burnt in the market-place of Rouen, Normandy.

136 11 **the lilies of France :** the *fleur-de-lis,* the royal emblem of France until the Revolution.

136 13 **in another century :** that of the Revolution.

136 24 **Roman martyrology :** the official list and account of the martyrs of the Church.

136 25 **Miserere :** the penitential 51st Psalm, which begins with '' Miserere ''—have. mercy ; hence any prayer beseeching the pity of God.

137 16 **" Abbeys there were . . ." :** a free rendering of Wordsworth's *Peter Bell,* Part II.

137 19 **German Diets :** assemblies of princes and delegates in the old German Empire ; hence any parliaments.

138 5 **Carlovingian princes :** the line of kings founded by Charlemagne.

138 10 **those mysterious fawns :** in medieval legends there are stories of knights being lured by fawns and other animals into the land of the fairies.

138 12-13 **that ancient stag :** a similar legend is related in connection with several famous characters. *See* Hardwicke, *Traditions, Superstitions, and Folk Lore* (1872), p. 154.

138 19 **marches :** borderlands. The title marquis is properly derived from march.

138 28-29 **Sir Roger de Coverley :** this judgment of Sir Roger was given in a dispute between two fishermen. *See* Addison's *Spectator,* No. 122.

139 26 **La Pucelle :** The Maid ; the common French designation of Joan.

140 9 **Patay**, near Orleans ; the French, inspired by Joan, were victorious here on June 18th. Troyes, the capital of Champagne, was besieged and captured by Joan on July 8th.

140 10 **coup-de-main** : stroke of the hand ; a military term for a rapid and sudden attack.

141 15 **Michelet** : (1798-1874) author of the monumental *History of France*, from which the *Joan of Arc* section was reprinted separately.

142 3-4 **" Nolebat uti ense . . . "** : she would not use her sword or kill anyone.

143 2 **Compiègne** : 50 miles N.E. of Paris ; regarded as the important gate of the road between Isle-de-France and Picardy. Joan fought her last fight here on May 23rd, 1430.

143 7 **her trial** : she was captured by Count John in May, 1430, sold to the English in November, and in June placed in the hands of Pierre Cauchon, Bishop of Beauvais. The trial lasted from Jan. 9th to May 24th, 1431, during which time she was treated with ignominy. A complete account of the proceedings was kept in official notes which were afterwards edited in Latin by Pierre Cauchon, and these form the basis of subsequent accounts of Joan's judgment and death. For a vivid account of the trial, *see* Kitchin, *History of France*, iii. 125, and, for a dramatic treatment, Bernard Shaw's play.

143 9 **Beauvais** : in Normandy. The Bishop, Pierre Cauchon, was a supporter of the English party, having been promised the archbishopric of Rouen.

143 15 **triple crown** : the official head-dress of the Pope—a tiara encircled by three crowns.

144 1 **judges examining the prisoner** : the practice still exists in France, though condemned by other countries, of a judge questioning a prisoner minutely when he is first taken, and before trial.

144 8-9 **jurisprudence** : the science of law.

144 20 **casuistical divinity** : relating to cases on conscience ; casuistry is the reasoning enabling a man to decide in a particular case between apparently conflicting duties.

144 24 **Dominican** : one of the order of Preaching Friars founded by St Dominic in 1216. They had considerable influence until the rise of the Jesuits. The Grand Inquisitor at Joan's trial was a Dominican.

144 25 **an objection** : probably Joan's insistence on a personal relationship with God instead of through the mediation of the Church.

144 32 **Her answer:** " I know not ; I leave it to God."

145 19 **a less cause than martyrdom:** *i.e.* marriage. See *Gen.* ii. 24.

147 2 **Mozart:** (1756-91) German musician.

147 3 **Phidias:** *see* note to 53.4.

147 3 **Michael Angelo:** (1475-1564) Florentine painter and sculptor.

147 8-9 **dead men's bones:** cf. *Ezek.* xxxvii. 1-10.

147 20 **Tellurians:** inhabitants of *tellus*, the earth.

147 23 **St Peter's:** *see* note to 21.11.

147 24 **Luxor:** *see* note to 92.16.

148 7-8 **Marie Antoinette:** (1755-93) wife of Louis XVI.; executed in the French Revolution.

148 10 **daughter of Cæsars:** Marie Antoinette was the daughter of Francis I., head of the Holy Roman Empire, who thus continued the line of the ancient Roman emperors.

148 13 **Charlotte Corday:** (1768-93) the young girl of Caen who came to Paris during the Revolution and murdered the extremist Marat for the good of France. She was guillotined.

148 29 **catacombs:** subterranean burial-places.

150 10 **mirage:** optical illusion—the fancied appearance of pleasant scenery in the desert.

150 34 **the English Prince, Regent of France:** the Duke of Bedford, uncle of Henry VI. and Regent of France.

151 1 **Lord of Winchester:** Henry Beaufort, half-brother of Henry IV. ; the most important prelate of his time. He was the only Englishman in the Court to condemn Joan. For De Quincey's reference to his death *see* Shakespeare's 2 *Henry VI.*, iii. 3.

151 22 **Who is this . . . :** cf. *Isa.* lxiii. 1.

151 23-24 **bloody coronation robes:** Joan is reported as appearing at the coronation of the Dauphin in her armour, which might reasonably be imagined as " bloody."

151 28-29 **shall take my lord's brief:** *i.e.* shall act as his counsel.

10

HISTORY

REVOLT OF THE TARTARS

First issued in *Blackwood's Magazine*, 1837, and reprinted with but few verbal changes in the collected edition of 1854.

De Quincey's version of the revolt is based solely on the account given in *Nomadische Streifereien unter den Kalmuken in den Jahren* 1802 *und* 1808, by Bergmann, a German traveller, who, De Quincey states, had resided a long time among the Kalmucks.

De Quincey himself divided history into three classes—(i) pure narrative, *i.e.* a bare record of facts, (ii) scenical history, and (iii) philosophical history—and while most of his historical writings belong to the third class, it should be realised that *Revolt of the Tartars* belongs to the second. The vivid pictures of great empires, vast distances, unspeakable horror and misery, appealed to De Quincey's imagination, and these, rather than accurate historical research, form the basis of his work, which is esentially imaginative and poetic history. A brief summary of the discrepancies of De Quincey's version as compared with the authoritative account in the Chinese document purported to be written by the Emperor Kien Long himself, is appended to the notes on this section. A French translation of this Chinese account was published by the missionaries of Pekin in 1776 in *Mémoires concernant les Chinois*.

History. *The Kalmucks* were descendants of the Mongol-Tartar races which, in the thirteenth century, dominated China and Russia, and menaced Europe. A great Tartar Empire was built up by Genghis Khan (1162-1227), but it was disintegrated by the nomadic tendencies of the tribes, who rapidly scattered. The Kalmucks, with whom De Quincey deals, belonged to the tribe called Torguts (or Torgouths), who in 1616 (according to Bergmann—probably at the beginning of the eighteenth century) migrated from their country of Sungaria in Thibet, and, exchanging their allegiance to the Emperor of China for the Czar of Russia, settled in the lands between the Volga and the Ural. However, they never lost touch with China, and in 1770-71 the increasing tyranny of the Russian government—their demands for levies of soldiers and heavy taxes—combined with the danger of religious isolation, led to a decision for the whole tribe

to revolt from Russia and return across the Kirghiz steppes to
the frontiers of China, where the benevolent and sagacious
Emperor Kien Long was reigning.   De Quincey, following Bergmann, attributes the flight to a sinister plot for revenge by
Zebek-Dorchi, Oubacha's relative and rival.   The tribe, numbering several hundred thousand, with their wives and children and
all their baggage, journeyed for eight months across the steppes,
through the snow and ice of winter, and, later, the cruel heat of
summer.   The revolt happened just after the great plague of
Moscow, when there was much popular unrest in the Russian
Empire, and Catherine II., feeling that her supremacy over the
nomad tribes was at stake, and stung by the transfer to a
hereditary enemy of a tribe which furnished some of her best
cavalry, made bitter efforts to intercept the flight.   After the
miseries detailed by De Quincey, the remnants of the tribe arrived
in China, and were hospitably received by the Emperor.

152 — Kalmuck : *see* introductory note above.   The term
Kalmuck is used by De Quincey interchangeably with "Tartar,"
though the Kalmucks were more probably a branch of the
Mongolian family.   They were divided into four tribes dwelling
in China, western Siberia, and south-east Russia.

152 — Khan : sovereign prince.

152 5 Tartar : originally applied in China and medieval
Europe to the central Asian nomad tribes, who, in the fifth
century, occupied Mongolia and Chinese Tartary.   De Quincey
uses the term generally for Mongolian.

152 5 steppes : level tracts or plains, characterised in Europe
and Asiatic Russia by grassy vegetation, lakes, and rolling hills.

152 6 latter half of the last century : 1770-71.

152 6-7 terminus a quo : starting-point.

152 7 terminus ad quem : goal ; terminating point.

152 19 lemming : a rat tribe, remarkable for its periodic and
destructive migrations to the sea.

152 20 locust : when a cloud of locusts settles on a tract of
land they destroy all tender vegetation.

152 23 Miltonic images : Milton's *Paradise Lost* is famous for
the sublimity of its images, *e.g.*, II. 24-30; II. 77; II. 172;
VI. 834.

152 24 the solitary hand : see *Paradise Lost*, VI. 139.

154 33-34 a rival . . . almost a competitor : "rival" is
derived from Lat. *rivales*, those with equal rights in the use of a

brook (Lat. *rivus*), hence "rival" implied common rights or privileges. A competitor is one who strives for the same prize as another.

155 15-16 **Machiavellian**: Machiavelli (1469-1527), the Florentine statesman and author of *The Prince*, was a famous expositor of unscrupulous statecraft and political cunning.

156 3 **behemoth**: Heb. "great beast"; the word occurs in *Job* xl. 15, and probably referred to the hippopotamus.

156 3 **Muscovy**: old name for Russia, derived from Moscow.

156 5 **"lion ramp"**: ramp=spring, or leap; the phrase is from Milton, *Samson Agonistes*, 139.

156 6 **"baptised and infidel"**: *i.e.* Christian and Mohammedan; cf. *Paradise Lost*, I. 582.

156 8 **"barbaric East"**: an inaccurate rendering of *Paradise Lost*, II. 3-4.

156 14 **tragic fable**: here used for "plot"; *i.e.* the revolt was as carefully and compactly planned as a good classical tragedy.

156 27 **Czarina**: Catherine II., Empress of Russia, 1762-96; she was one of the most able and influential sovereigns of her day, and her reign greatly enlarged and strengthened the power of Russia, chiefly at the expense of Turkey.

157 15 **in that view**: *i.e.* with regard only to distance.

157 19 **Kien Long**: Emperor of China, 1735-96; the fourth Chinese emperor of the Mantchoo-Tartar dynasty, and a man of great ability.

157 21-22 **head of their religion**: the religion of the Kalmucks is Lamaism, a degraded form of Buddhism. There are two chiefs, or Lamas, of whom the Dalai-Lama at Lhasa in Tibet is the superior, occupying a position similar to that of the Pope in Roman Catholic Christendom. The elaborate respect for the Dalai-Lama is explained by their doctrine of reincarnation, according to which each Dalai-Lama is the reincarnated Buddha.

157 23 **Chinese Wall**: an extensive fortification running along the boundary between China and Mongolia. It was built for defence against the northern Mongols in the third century, and is about 1400 miles long, in some places 30 feet high, and 25 feet broad.

157 31 **Russian captive Weseloff**: a Russian gentleman of some rank at the court of the Khan, whom, for political reasons, it was thought necessary to take with them as a captive. After rendering an important personal service to the Khan on the journey, he was allowed to escape, and on his return to Russia he prepared an account of the occurrence.

158 10 **sanctions:** here means things ordained; sacred, and hence obligatory.

159 29 **Sargatchi:** Zebek-Dorchi had persuaded the Russian Government to re-organise the Kalmuck State Council, or Sarga. This consisted of eight members, called Sargatchi, who had hitherto been entirely subordinate to the Khan. They were now placed on a footing of perfect independence, and, as regards responsibility, on a footing of equality with the Khan.

160 14 **Wolga:** pronounced and usually written in English "Volga." The Kalmucks occupied the region near the southern course of the Volga.

160 18-19 **Year of the Tiger:** "The Kalmuck custom is to distinguish their years by attaching to each a denomination taken from one of twelve animals, the exact order of succession being absolutely fixed, so that the cycle revolves of course through a period of a dozen years" (De Quincey).

160 34 **Kirghises:** barbarous tribes of mixed Mongol, Tartar, and Turkish stock, living in the steppes east of the Caspian Sea.

160 34 **Bashkirs:** a tribe partly Mongol (*i.e.* of the same race as the Kalmucks) and partly Finnish. They were Mohammedans of inferior intellect, and during the recent war they had revolted from Russia and supported the Sultan of Turkey.

161 23 **Sarepta:** a Moravian colony near the great bend of the Volga. Baldwin notes that the point of the reference is that Sarepta was founded in 1764 by a colony of industrious Germans.

162 31 **Temba:** the Jemba, or Emba, one of the rivers flowing into the north-east of the Caspian Sea.

166 26 **Huns:** a Mongol people who crossed the Volga in 375 and, under their king, Attila, overran a great part of Europe in the first half of the fifth century. Their progress was eventually arrested by the Roman general Aëtius at the battle of Châlons, A.D. 451, and they were ultimately subdued by Charlemagne.

166 26 **Avars:** a Turanian people who invaded Europe in the sixth century, settling between the Elbe and the Black Sea. Charlemagne brought them within his empire, and after his time they disappear, as a nation, from history.

166 27 **Mongol-Tartars:** *see* introductory note. It was under

Genghis Khan (1160-1227) that the Mongol-Tartars penetrated into Europe as far as the Danube. They also subdued the empire of the Chinese and overthrew the Caliph of Baghdad.

166 32 **French retreat from Moscow:** Napoleon invaded Russia in 1812 with 600,000 men. In his retreat from Moscow he lost 90,000 men, and in two months the army dwindled to 20,000.

167 4 **vials of wrath:** *see* note to 84.12; cf. *Rev.* xv. 7; xvi. 1.

167 19-20 **Children of Israel:** see *Exodus* i.-xvii.; *Joshua* i.-xii.

167 30-31 **pestilence . . . which visited Athens:** Thucydides describes the great plague which came to Athens from Egypt in 430 B.C., during the Peloponnesian War between Athens and Sparta, and carried off one-fourth of the people (*Thuc.*, II. xlvii.).

167 31-32 **London . . . Charles I.:** The Great Plague of 1664-66. Defoe, in his *Journal of the Plague Year*, relates that at times over 7000 a week perished.

168 5 **The siege of Jerusalem:** after two unsuccessful sieges in the reign of Nero, Titus, the son of the Roman emperor Vespasian, captured Jerusalem in A.D. 70. Josephus describes the siege in his *Jewish War*, v. and vi.: it lasted over a year, more than a million people perishing in the siege itself, and many more from internal factions. In the famine, mothers were known to kill and devour their children.

168 18 **River Jaik:** now called the Ural.

169 31 **acharnement:** ferocity, bloodthirstiness.

170 13 **by wholesale:** to sell " by wholesale " originally meant to sell only a whole piece, and subsequently any large quantity.

170 16 **Cossacks:** an independent people of Russian stock, dwelling mainly in the Ukraine. They have always been noted as fierce fighters, and for centuries provided the cavalry of the Russian army.

170 24-25 **Koulagina:** one of the forts of the Ural, about 50 miles from its mouth; probably the modern Kologinskaia.

171 3 **Bactrian camels:** there are two species of camel—the dromedary, or single-humped variety, which is a native of Arabia, and the Bactrian, or double-humped type, which belongs to Central Asia. Bactria is the ancient name of a district in Afghanistan.

171 13 **ouloss:** a large tribal company.

172 24 **champaign savannahs**: grassy plains.

172 29 **Torgau**: or Torgai, now Turgai—a tributary of the Irgiz-Koom.

173 28 **trashed**: retarded by incumbrances too valuable to be left behind.

173 33-34 **summa rerum**: the chief of things; the critical thing.

175 19 **in reversion**: a legal phrase—for the remainder.

176 1 **Ouchim**: Ichim, a pass in the Ural mountains.

176 2 **Mougaldchares**: the southern spurs of the Ural mountains.

176 28 **Polish dragoons**: the epithet refers not to the nationality, but to the equipment; it was a military term for "heavy-armed."

176 29 **cuirassiers**: mounted soldiers; equipped with a cuirass, or breastplate.

177 4 **Irgitch**: the Irgiz-Koom, which flows into Lake Chalkar.

177 16 **served under the Sultan**: there were continual wars between Catherine II. and Turkey.

178 13 **howling wilderness**: a biblical phrase, cf. *Deut.* xxxii. 10.

179 23 **adust**: Lat. *adustus*—burned; *i.e.* looking scorched.

179 33 **tears of Xerxes**: Herodotus records that when Xerxes (King of Persia, 485-465 B.C.) reviewed his forces crossing the Hellespont to invade Greece in 480 B.C., he was moved to tears by the thought of the brevity of life, that " of all here collected, no one will be alive a hundred years hence " (*Her.*, VII. xlv., xlvi.).

180 9 **scapegoat**: one made to bear the blame of others; derived from the Jewish ritual (see *Levit.* xvi. 21), in which, once a year, a goat is brought to the door of the tabernacle, the sins of the people symbolically laid upon it by the high priest, and the animal sent into the wilderness, bearing the iniquities of the whole people.

181 10-11 **land of promise . . . house of bondage**: as Canaan and Egypt respectively were to the Israelites (cf. *Deut.* viii. 14, ix. 28; *Exod.* xx. 2).

181 20 **Orsk**: on the river Or, near its junction with the Ural.

181 22 **Oriembourg**: not the large modern town of the same name, west of Orsk, but a fort (mod. Oremburg) on the Turgai.

183 29 " more fell than anguish . . . " : Shakespeare, *Othello*, V. ii. 361 ; fell—cruel, deadly.

184 20 " fierce varieties " : a reminiscence of *Paradise Lost*, II. 599 ; VII. 272.

184 22 post equitem . . . : " Behind the rider sits black care " —Horace, *Odes*, III. 40.

184 23 undying worm : cf. *Isa.* lxvi. 24.

184 32 " from morn to dewy eve " : *Paradise Lost*, I. 742-43.

185 20 countermarches : returns on the previous route.

186 1 On a fine morning . . . : there is no historical basis for the details of this final scene in De Quincey's account. The presence of the emperor at the hunting lodge, his view of the arrival of the Kalmucks, and the final massacre at the lake, are all imaginary and unlikely.

186 26 yagers : Ger. *jäger*, a huntsman ; hence a rifleman.

187 2 fetching a compass : making a circuit.

187 20 indorsed : carrying on their backs ; cf. *Paradise Regained*, III. 329.

189 17-31 fresh-water lake . . . Tengis : Lake Balkash is obviously the one meant. It is one of the largest lakes of the steppes (about 350 miles long and 50 broad), but its water is actually salt.

189 31 Kobi : the Gobi desert ; a wide region to the west of Lake Balkash, now part of Mongolia and Chinese Turkestan.

192 24 " globes " and " turms " : bands and squadrons ; probably reminiscences of the Latin military terms *globi* and *turmae* ; cf. *Paradise Lost*, II. 512 and *Paradise Regained*, IV. 66.

193 21 River Ily : the Ili, which flows into Lake Balkash.

193 24-25 household lares : household gods ; in Roman mythology the spirits of departed ancestors, who presided over the house.

193 30 Arcadia : *see* note **20.26**.

194 1 half a million : Bergmann apparently exaggerates, both as to the total number and the losses on the way. The Chinese account claims that about 300,000 Kalmucks arrived in China.

194 4 at Athens : after the plague ; *see* note **167.30-31**.

194 30 columns of granite and brass : another invention of De Quincey's.

195 13 Grecian : *i.e.* belonging to the Grecian Church.

The main discrepancies between De Quincey's account and the official version are:

1. The date of the original migration to Russia—De Quincey follows Bergmann in putting this at 1616; it was probably at least seventy years later.

2. The imaginative expansion of the scenes of the flight for pictorial and dramatic effect.

3. The cavalier handling of facts: the attribution of the revolt to the machinations of Zebek-Dorchi; the final burning of the villages (for which there would be no need, the Kalmucks being a nomad people dwelling mainly in tents); the elaboration of the persecutions of the Kirghises and Bashkirs, etc.

4. The culmination at Lake Tengis (Balkash) to provide a dramatic climax. Actually the journey and the skirmishes of the Kalmucks extended considerably past this point.

5. The struggle in the lake between the Kalmucks and their enemies.

6. The presence of the Chinese emperor at Lake Balkash, and the connection of the Chinese with the approaching combatants.

7. The monuments and the inscriptions, of which there is no mention in historical sources.

LITERARY CRITICISM

THE MEANING OF LITERATURE

From the Essay on Alexander Pope, which first appeared in the *North British Review*, August 1848, as a review of Roscoe's edition of Pope's works, and was reprinted in 1858 in the collected edition. It is best known for the passage given here, the criticism of the poet himself reflecting the lukewarm attitude of the early nineteenth century to Pope and his school.

196 21 Attic: Athens was the principal city of Attica, Greece.

197 5 forensic: (Lat. *forensis*, from *forum*, a court) belonging to public discussion or debate.

197 26 dry light: *see* Bacon's essay *Of Friendship*: " Heraclitus saith well, in one of his Ænigmaes, *Dry Light is ever the best*. And certaine it is that the Light that a man receiveth by

Counsell from Another is Drier and purer than that which commeth from his owne Understanding and Iudgement; which is ever infused and drenched in his Affections and Customes." The correct version of the " ænigma " is " the dry soul is the wisest and best " (Stobæi, *Florilegium*, v. 120).

197 26 proximately: immediately; by immediate relation to.

197 29 iris: the rainbow.

199 4 Jacob's ladder: see *Gen.* xxviii.

199 31 epopee: an epic poem; epic poetry.

200 25 quamdiu bene se gesserit: during good behaviour.

200 30-31 " Principia " of Sir Isaac Newton: Newton (1642-1727), the mathematician and discoverer of the theory of gravitation, which was set out in the *Philosophiæ Naturalis Principia Mathematica* in 1687.

201 2 La Place: (1749-1827) the greatest French mathematician and theoretical astronomer; he corrected several details in the work of Newton.

201 7 nominis umbra: the shadow of a name.

201 9 Aeschylus: (525-456 B.C.) the first of the Greek tragic poets.

201 19 Praxiteles . . . Michael Angelo: *see* notes on 53.4.

202 11 κτήματα ἐς ἀεί: possessions for ever, cf. *Thuc.* i. 22.

202 15 Chaucer: (1340-1400) the greatest medieval English poet; author of *The Canterbury Tales*.

202 19 Dryden: (1631-1700) Restoration poet and playwright; wrote lyrics, satires, and translations of the classics.

202 19 Pope: (1688-1744) poet and satirist; author of *Essay on Man*; *Satires and Epistles*.

202 19 Wordsworth: (1770-1850) founder of the Romantic school of poetry. He modernised three of Chaucer's tales.

202 21 Pagan tales of Ovid: Ovid (43 B.C.–A.D. 17), the Roman poet, wrote a large collection of stories involving changes of form, called the *Metamorphoses*. In the Epilogue to this work (ll. 1-9) he prophesies that his name and poetry will live " through all centuries."

203 8 phylacteries: in Jewish antiquities, strips of parchment inscribed with texts from the Bible, fastened on the forehead and left arm.

203 9 κατ' ἐξοχήν: in its essentials; *i.e.* in its highest form.

ON THE KNOCKING AT THE GATE IN *MACBETH*

Originally written for the *London Magazine*, October 1823. De Quincey expressed his intention of enlarging the paper for the collected edition, but he died before reaching the last volume, in which it was to appear. Thus it remains as first written. For the scene, see *Macbeth*, Act II., Scene ii.

205 12 **quoad**: with respect to; for the time being.

205 22-23 **Mr Williams . . . Ratcliffe Highway**: De Quincey early showed an intense interest in crime. A full account of the Williams murders was added in the collected edition as an appendix to *Murder considered as one of the Fine Arts*.

205 22 **début**: first appearance.

206 7 **dilettante**: an amateur; one who pursues an art desultorily, or for amusement.

206 23 **"the poor beetle . . ."**: Shakespeare, *Measure for Measure*, III. i. 78.

206 34 **"with its petrific mace"**: cf. *Paradise Lost*, X. 293-96.

207 17-18 **the gracious Duncan**: Macbeth's description of his sovereign in Act I. i. 65. Duncan had given many honours to Macbeth after his victory over the Norwegians.

207 18-19 **the deep damnation . . .**: Macbeth's soliloquy, Act I. vii. 20, where he thus describes the projected murder of Duncan.

208 22 **"unsexed"**: cf. *Macbeth*, Act I. v. 38-41, where Lady Macbeth calls on the spirits to "unsex" her, that she may be steeled to the murder of Duncan.

QUESTIONS AND ESSAY SUBJECTS

(a) DETAILED

1. Give an account of De Quincey's experiences at Manchester Grammar School, and criticise the educational methods pursued there in his time.

2. How far do the *Confessions* seem to you to be a genuine record of personal experiences ? What light do they throw upon the writer's knowledge of life and literature?

3. Trace carefully the adventures of De Quincey between his departure from Manchester and his admission to Oxford.

4. Narrate the incident of the Malay, and show how it influences De Quincey's later dreams.

5. Describe the physical effects of opium according to De Quincey, and illustrate these by examples from the opium-visions.

6. Illustrate from the visions De Quincey's skill in the delineation of (*a*) the sublime, and (*b*) the pathetic.

7. Describe fully any one of the opium-visions, and analyse its characteristics.

8. Explain the following allusions: '' the Athenian captives . . . winning noble mercy for themselves''; '' the great Emathian conqueror . . . relented at the thought of literature''; '' plagosus Orbilius''; John o' Groat's house ; *Grammar* School; the prayer against the perils of darkness; the Bore; Euripides; Deucalion and Pyrrha; Indian Summer; court of pié poudré; '' Ut puto, Deus fio ''; camera obscura; Bluebeard room; Hekatómpylos; Consul Romanus; the great *officina gentium*; Brahma, Vishnu, Seeva.

9. What is an allegory? Illustrate your answer by reference to *Levana and Our Ladies of Sorrow* and *Savannah-la-mar*.

10. Describe carefully the persons and functions of the Three Ladies of Sorrow.

11. Write a description of a coach ride through the country in 1815, before railways had come into use for passenger traffic.

12. Narrate fully the journey of the mail-coach carrying the news of Talavera.

13.   " Romance ! " the season-tickets mourn,
       " *He* never ran to catch his train,
       But passed away with coach, and guard, and horn."

14. Describe in detail the events of the accident which De Quincey calls *The Vision of Sudden Death.*

15. Justify the title of the piece *Dream-Fugue.*

16. Trace carefully the relation between the details of the accident and the incidents of the visions in *Dream-Fugue.*

17. De Quincey's conception of the character and work of Joan of Arc.

18. Compare De Quincey's account of Joan of Arc with that contained in Shakespeare's *Henry VI.*

19. "*Joan of Arc* probes to the bottom all the tragedy of suffering that can overwhelm the individual soul." Discuss.

20. " The *Revolt of the Tartars* and *The English Mail-Coach* both start from fact, both move in dreamland." Discuss, with special reference to De Quincey's use of his historical material.

21. Who were the Kalmucks ? Trace the history of the tribe before their departure from Russia.

22. Trace carefully the incidents of the flight of the Kalmucks from the departure from Russia to the battle at Lake Balkash.

23. Describe the various difficulties with which the Kalmucks had to contend during the flight.

24. Give an account of the arrival of the Kalmucks in China, and the battle at Lake Balkash.

25. Justify the term " scenical history " as applied to the *Revolt of the Tartars.*

26. Explain the allusions : Sargatchi ; Muscovy ; Tartars ; Dalai-Lama ; Year of the Tiger ; Bashkirs ; the Huns ; the Avars ; the pestilence of Athens ; the siege of Jerusalem ; Cossacks ; Bactrian camels ; ouloss ; the tears of Xerxes ; the Great Wall of China ; Arcadian beauty.

27. Explain carefully the distinction drawn by De Quincey between the literature of *Knowledge* and the literature of *Power.* Give examples from your general reading.

(b) GENERAL

28. Illustrate by examples from the text De Quincey's classical learning.

29. Discuss the range and accuracy of De Quincey's historical knowledge.

30. De Quincey's humour has been described as " scholar's humour; scholarly not in treatment, but in subject." Discuss De Quincey's humour; give examples; and compare him in this respect with Addison, Lamb, and Carlyle.

31. " De Quincey digresses on the slightest provocation from the subject in hand." Give examples; show how they are introduced; and indicate their effect on the style of the passages in question.

32. Illustrate from De Quincey's writings the meaning of his distinction between the literatures of *Knowledge* and *Power*.

33. What impression do you get from his writings of the character and personality of De Quincey?

34. " From my birth I was made an intellectual creature, and intellectual in the highest sense my pursuits and pleasures have been." Discuss and illustrate.

35. Give examples of De Quincey's power of graphic description, and indicate the elements of pictorial effect in the passages chosen.

36. What is the meaning of Wordsworth's dictum that Style should be the *incarnation* of thought, and not its *dress*? Illustrate by reference to De Quincey's style.

37. What are the special excellences of De Quincey's style? Give examples.

38. " The style of sustained splendour, of prolonged wheeling and soaring, as distinct from the style of crackle and brief glitter" (Minto). Discuss this judgment of De Quincey's style.

39. " His works are still the crowning delicacy for lovers of formal, punctilious exactness " (Minto). Give examples of De Quincey's range of vocabulary; of his precise use of words; and of his special liking for certain adjectives, *e.g.* " tumultuous."

40. What is meant by " impassioned prose "? Is it a legitimate form of literature? Illustrate by reference to De Quincey.

41. Give five examples of De Quincey's effective use of figures of speech, and explain each.

42. Illustrate De Quincey's skill in the analysis of emotion.

43. Explain the part played by contrast in *On the Knocking at the Gate in "Macbeth."* Illustrate the use of contrast as a stylistic feature in De Quincey's works.

44. De Quincey's excellence as a writer of narrative. How far is his style adapted to historical writing?

45. " He takes rank with Milton as one of our greatest writers of stately cadence " (Minto). Quote examples of sonorous and stately rhythms from De Quincey, and point out the features which contribute to the excellence of each.

46. Discuss and illustrate from De Quincey (*a*) his paragraph construction, and (*b*) the variety in the length of his sentences.

47. " His skill in narration, his rare pathos, his wide sympathies, the pomp of his dream descriptions, the exquisite playfulness of his lighter dissertations, and his abounding, though delicate and subtle humour " (Findlay). How far does this seem to you a just and adequate summary of the excellences of De Quincey ?

SUGGESTIONS FOR READING

Collected Works, 14 vols., edited by Prof. MASSON.
De Quincey's Literary Criticism.   H. DARBISHIRE.

De Quincey.   MASSON (English Men of Letters).
De Quincey article in *Encyclopædia Britannica.*   FINDLAY.
De Quincey in *Dictionary of National Biography.*   LESLIE
     STEPHEN.
Personal Recollections of Thomas De Quincey.   FINDLAY.
De Quincey Memorials.   JAPP.
De Quincey and his Friends.   JAMES HOGG.
Hours in a Library (1st Series).   LESLIE STEPHEN.
English Prose Selections (H. CRAIK).   Article by R. BRIMLEY
     JOHNSON.
Landmarks of English Literature.   NICOLL.
Essays Biographical and Critical.   MASSON.
Essays about Men, Women, and Books.   A. BIRRELL.
Masters of English Literature (*De Quincey*).   Introduction by
     SIDNEY LOW.

History of Nineteenth-Century Literature.   SAINTSBURY (Chap.
     IV. for style).
Manual of English Prose Literature.   MINTO (elaborate analysis
     of style).
How De Quincey Worked.   DOWDEN.
The Prose Poetry of Thomas De Quincey.   COOPER.
Biographic Clinics (*De Quincey*).   GOULD.
A Study of English Prose Writers.   SCOTT CLARK.